Sir Terry Wogan KBE was born in Limerick, Ireland. After leaving college he went into banking and five years later joined RTE as a newsreader/announcer. In 1969 Terry stood in for BBC Radio's Jimmy Young and later that year was given his own daily shows on BBC Radio 1 and 2. In 1972 he took over the prestigious morning show slot and it's been downhill since then.

Terry's extensive television credits include his live chat show series *Wogan*, The Eurovision Song Contest, *Come Dancing, Blankety Blank* and *Children in Need*, to name but a few. In 1993 Terry rejoined Radio 2 to present *Wake up to Wogan*, the most listened to breakfast show in the UK with over 8 million people tuning in every morning. In a moment of weakness the Queen honoured him with a knighthood in 2005.

He is married to the sainted Lady Helen, the present Mrs Wogan, and has two sons and a daughter.

WHERE WAS I?!

WHERE WAS I?!
The World According to Wogan

Terry Wogan

First published in Great Britain in 2009 by
Orion Books
an imprint of the Orion Publishing Group Ltd
Orion House, 5 Upper St Martin's Lane,
London WC2H 9EA
An Hachette UK Company

3 5 7 9 10 8 6 4

A CIP catalogue record for this book
is available from the British Library.

ISBN 13: 978 0 75288 844 6

Printed in Great Britain by Clays Ltd, St Ives plc

The Orion Publishing Group's policy is to use papers that
are natural, renewable and recyclable and made from wood
grown in sustainable forests. The logging and manufacturing
processes are expected to conform to the environmental
regulations of the country of origin.

www.orionbooks.co.uk

Like everything I've written, this is for the people who matter most to me: Helen, Alan, Mark, Katherine, Susan, Henry, Kate, Freddie, Harry, Iris, and the next little one. Then, there are my friends, my listeners, my wonderful TOGs. None of them will ever know how much I need them . . .

Frequently asked questions

Why do you need my debit or credit card details?
We need your details in order to cover any charges for which
you might become liable during your treatment at the hospital.

**I'm insured, do I still have to give you my debit or credit card
details?**
Your details may be used to pay for items which are not
covered by your insurance company, for example
take-home drugs, telephone calls, visitors' meals, crutches,
certain treatments and insurance excesses or shortfalls.

**I've paid up front, do I still need to give you my debit or credit
card details?**
It is possible that you may incur further charges during your
stay, for example take-home drugs, further tests, telephone
calls, visitors' meals, items not included in a package etc.

I don't intend to incur any extra costs.
If you do not incur any extra costs, your stored card details
will not be used.

**How will I know if BMI intend to use my debit or credit card
details?**
We will send you a detailed invoice showing any outstanding
charges before taking payment using your stored card
details. You will have a minimum of 14 days to query
your bill and/or make payment yourself either online at
www.bmihealthcare.co.uk/onlinepayments, over the phone on
0161 216 2500 or by sending a cheque in the post. If you do
not pay your bill upon presentation, we may use your stored
card details to take payment as a last resort. Should we take
a payment using your stored card details, we will send you
confirmation in the post.

How do I know that my debit or credit card details are safe?
The way in which your card details will be stored adheres to
the Payment Card Industry Data Security Standard (PCI DSS)
which was developed by Visa, Mastercard and other credit
card providers to protect cardholder data from fraud.

Your card details will be recorded and stored securely.

If you incur any charges that are not covered by an insurer or company, we may use these details to take payment.

Please turn over for some frequently asked questions.

You will be required to bring a valid debit or credit card with you each time you attend our hospital as a patient.

Important changes to your registration procedure

Acknowledgements

For the inspirational Amanda, the beaming Bonomi, son Mark who doesn't like to see me just sitting there, and the great *Woman's Weekly*, from whose pages these deathless words are culled.

Some of this stuff was written almost a decade ago, but it could have been written yesterday.

Scary, or what?

INTRODUCTION

You know me: never listen to myself on the radio, never watch myself on television. It's embarrassing. Who is that pie-faced, overweight eejit bursting out of his suit? God, does that goddam gobdaw ever shut up? Oh, it's me. The shame of it. I shouldn't be doing this job at all, I should have stayed in the bank. It's pathetic, all this showing-off. The nuns and priests who educated me well beyond my intelligence must be very disappointed in me. I was taught modesty, duty, self-control and a strong sense of sin. Vanity, self-aggrandisement, attention-seeking were beyond the Pale, the marks of an outsider, someone who would never be a Child of Mary, an altar boy or amount to anything much. Be nice to everybody, don't be rude, don't talk back, conform, do what you're told. What am I doing here? My mother and father were pleased and proud of my success, but surprised and bemused by it. An old pal of mine in Dublin, obviously as surprised as everyone else, once said to me, 'People are always saying to me that you must have been very ambitious and determined to get where you are.' I said I'd never noticed it. 'You weren't, were you?' No, I wasn't, no, I'm not. I've never knocked on a door and cried 'Gissa job!' in my life. I hate the limelight. I'm totally and utterly wrong for the game I'm in. Don't ask me how I got into this – I woke up one morning, and there I was, on the radio. And I love it, and I've always loved it. It's what I do. I'm not nervous doing it, I've no idea what I'm going to say until I open the microphone, and when I'm done, I go home. My mother said when I was a little boy, I'd play with my friends, but always close the garden gate behind me when I came home.

Because that's what I've always liked best: home, comfort and the love of my family. Everything else, ambition, fame, success are as the idle wind . . .

Even as you flick through this book, deciding whether to buy it now, or wait for the inevitable car-boot sale, you may detect a certain *deja-vu*, particularly as an avid reader of a certain women's magazine in the naughty nineties. If so, Heaven bless your memory, because when I read these fragrant nosegays again, I didn't remember a single word. And, if you don't mind me saying so, they might well have been written yesterday. 'Plus ça change, plus c'est la même chose', as Carla Bruni/Sarkozy puts it so well, and I'm sure she didn't mean her 'bon mots' to be translated as 'It's the same old thing.' That's a slur you could just as easily hurl at my daily morning effusions on BBC Radio 2. Same person, same voice, saying the same old things. Except that eight-and-a-half-million people choose to listen, every morning. That's more than listen to any other broadcaster in Britain or Europe, more than watch *Eastenders*, *Big Brother* or Ant and Dec. 'In Heaven's name, why?' I hear you cry. As the song says, 'Who can explain it, who can tell you why – fools give you reasons, wise men never try . . .'

Put it down to fellow-feeling, a shamed sense of life's essential foolishness, predictability, if you like, mutual regard – no, make that love. We're the 'Folks Who Live on the Hill', my listeners and me – Darby and Joan who used to be Jack and Jill. They know every word I've ever said, and can anticipate everything I'm about to say, before I've said it. I'll swear that they can sense when I cock an eyebrow or scratch an ear. I've always said that the reason for my success as commentator on the Eurovision Song Contest was that I got my shot in a split-second before the viewer. I hope that's the way you'll feel about this book: you could have written it yourself . . .

'Do I Come Here Often?'
(Wogan's Life)

The Home for the Bewildered

As that 'rara avis', the regular listener to *Wake up to Wogan* on BBC Radio 2 will know all too well, if it wasn't for my listeners, I would sit in front of the microphone mumchance, without a word. I'll admit that there's a strong body of opinion that feels the programme would be all the better for that, but like a good politician, I'm going to pretend I didn't hear that point of view, otherwise we'll be here all week. The point I'm trying to make, Jeremy, if you'll let me, is that without the hundreds of e-mails, faxes and letters and postcards I receive every day from the deranged, demented and blatantly bewildered folk who gather around the wireless to listen to my foolishness every morning, there'd be a lot more pauses in between the music. More than pauses, actually. Hiatuses, more like lacunae. A deathly hush.

These good, if wildly misguided people are what keep me going. Without them, the BBC would have rumbled me years ago. Dammit, I owe everything to my listeners; they've put my children through college, kept the present Mrs Wogan in the extravagant comfort to which she has become accustomed. I rarely meet my benefactors, except when they come to my television shows, masquerading as ordinary people. They soon give themselves away, of course, by putting on funny hats, opening their cardigans to reveal Terry's Old Geezer sweatshirts (bearing the proud legend, 'Do I Come Here Often?') and hurling smarties and ancient tins of rhubarb at me. (Don't ask me to explain the rhubarb and the sweets – it'll end in tears.) They come to my book signings, and inflame the crowd with their whispering: 'Ooh, he's much fatter/older/

smaller/uglier than he looks on the television, isn't he?'. . . They bring me my book for an autograph, and when I enquire 'Who's it for?', they say, brightly, 'It's for me!' They demand photographs, with cameras that don't work: 'Did the flash go off?' 'Oh, hang on, I've forgotten to wind it on . . . ' They have their own Conventions, to which they forget to invite me, and every year 40,000 of them turn up in Hyde Park for *Proms in the Park*, and drown out my every word with community singing. You see, they know that I need them more than they need me. My recurrent nightmare is that one day in the not-too-distant, they'll ignore me altogether, and write to each other. What am I saying? They do that already; they've got their own website on the internet (www.togs.org) where they chatter away merrily without ever mentioning me . . .

I'll miss 'em, when they go; the little kindnesses: 'Terry, here's a tip to save money. Old telephone directories make ideal personal address books; simply cross out the names and addresses of people you don't know.' 'Wogan, me old mucker, don't fret. Age is only important if you're a cheese . . .'

And blindingly original ideas: 'How's this for a brilliant new TV show? A huge production team scour the country looking for people who have no talent, but huge egos and an all devouring wish for money and fame. Most of them will have no skills nor qualifications. After lots of heartbreaking live auditions the worst of the lot are taken away and locked up in a secret mansion, to be groomed for their release on the public. Yes, they are going to be asked to join the next government and run the country for four years! Anyway, they are locked away in this secret hideaway, watched only by the whole world over the internet and via TV cameras, and one by one the most hideous are voted off to form a cabinet. After four weeks the lone survivor is Prime Minister . . . Good eh?'

You see, it's mad, but only slightly. The lines between reality and the image, between fact and the message, become more blurred every day. I well remember a website inviting contributors to pay tribute to Alma Baldwin, who died so tragically in *Coronation Street*. She was a character in a soap opera, for Heaven's sake! The actress who played her is walking the streets, in rude good health! Hey-ho, at least we know we're loonies, my listeners and me.

Looking for Something in Beige?

Loonies? Fools for good, more like. Over the past few years, TOGs have transformed themselves from a happy-go-lucky crowd of ne'er-do-wells, whose greatest delight was to make me look like an eejit, into an extraordinary force for raising money for the BBC's Children in Need Appeal. Inspired by the creative genius and indomitable spirit of Hellen Bach (she wouldn't want me to use her real name – no true TOG ever does; they'd rather embarrass me with double-meaning pseudonyms – Tess Tickle, Rudolph Hucker, Drew Peacock and the like . . .) TOGs have raised well over three million pounds over the last three years. Starting with the TOGs Calendar, they moved on to the million-selling *Janet and John* CDs, then last year's triumphant *Bandaged* CD, and a host of T-shirts, sweaters, mugs, car-stickers and even jewellery. All of it done on the internet, the world-wide web. If you're interested, and would like to help, it's www.charitygoods.com. If you'd like to join in the grand lunacy of TOGdom, it's www.togs.org. Trust me, you'll never be the same . . .

Bandaged is a shining example of the single-minded, imaginative force of nature that is our Hellen Bach. When she first mooted a compilation CD of the musical talents of Radio 2, I'll confess that myself and Barrowlands Boyd, producer to the quality, were sceptical. I wouldn't say that we scoffed, but we did pat the little woman's hand quite a lot, smiling sympathetically . . . Hah! *Bandaged*, with little or no promotion other than the website, sold, and continues to sell, in its thousands. When last I looked, it had netted one hundred and fifty thousand pounds for the charity. All of Radio 2 rallied round, fearless of their musical limitations: Ken Bruce with 'Donald, Where's Your Trousers?', Alex Lester's 'My Bruvver', Mark Radcliffe's 'Right Said Fred', matched only by my own pathetic effort at the 'Hippopotamus Song'. Aled Jones and I combined for 'Little Drummer Boy', which for a couple of glorious weeks, looked as if it might make the Christmas Number One in the pop charts. We were thwarted in the end by the Pop Idol winner, but the single made more than fifty thousand pounds for Children in Need.

Another magnificent idea that gave us all a good laugh was Hellen and her husband Norm's brainwave of a 'TOGs Cruise'. It was only when three hundred and fifty TOGs, The Voice of the Balls, Janet and John Marsh, Barrowlands Boyd, Charles Nove, Lynn Bowles the Totty from Splott, and me found ourselves having the time of our lives aboard Cunard's *Queen Victoria*, that we realised what a blinding idea it really was. We did two live morning shows from the good ship, a concept which involved the loose cannon himself, Rev. Roger Royle, and Barrowlands coming up through a hole in the stage playing the old Joanna, and an episode of *Janet and John*. What the Japanese and Americans in the audience made of it, we, mercifully, will never know. But I saw the sun come up over the Straits of Messina, and thanked the Lord for TOGs . . .

A Taste of Sin

When I was a lad, said the tiresome old geezer, everything was a sin. And sin came in a variety of packages, like breakfast cereal these days. Incidentally, I didn't have any breakfast cereal until I was eight years of age, and I only got that because my father was a grocer; and he came by an American treat called 'Grape-Nuts'. He poured them into a bowl for his little son, then a dash of milk and sugar, put the spoon in my hot little hand, and stood back to watch and enjoy my childish delight. I couldn't eat them. They were foreign to a little fellow brought up in the War Years on porridge.

Of course, saying that you never tasted this or that in the thirties and forties makes you sound like a second-hand Monty Python sketch. My radio producer, Paul Walters, claimed that he 'never saw a banana' until he was twelve. Others will shout the odds about 'never tasting chocolate' until they were fifteen. Do you remember your first taste of the exotic? Mine was a Coca-Cola. There was an American Air Force base not far from where we lived, and the Yanks came to town with all manner of forbidden fruit: Hershey bars, chewing-gum (Got any gum, chum? Not a lick, chick) and this strange-looking black drink, in an even stranger bottle. I'll never forget my first taste of it. So different from lemonade, orange squash and the other soft drinks of my previous childish experience. I've been lucky enough to have eaten at some of the world's best restaurants, and drunk of the finest wines, but my first Coca-Cola I will never forget. I think I can taste it yet . . .

Hang on a minute. How did you side-track me into flavours, when I wanted to talk about sin? Not so fast . . . Sin was a cottage industry where I came from. You could hardly open your mouth, or go outside your front door, without committing one. There were grievous ones, Deadly ones, Mortal ones and Venials. The first three categories were Biggies, and if you did a Mortal, you were toast, condemned to the eternal flames of Hell – unless, of course, somebody threw you a life-line by way of Confession, or an Indulgence. Venial sins were like walking on egg-shells, trip-wires at every turn: Lies, Disobedience, Bad Language, Impure Thoughts – you couldn't get through five minutes of a normal day without a handful of Venials to your name. In the fullness of time, these would guarantee you a light frying for several aeons, in Purgatory. And you were getting off lightly at that . . .

The Big One was Sex. You couldn't even think about it. And in the Ireland of my youth, thinking about it was all you could do. There wasn't a lot of it going. The next Worst Thing was Vanity (Murder came way down the list). You could get into trouble looking in the mirror. You grew up learning not to boast, push yourself forward, preen or show off. And you know, as I look around me, that wasn't such a bad thing. Today, all is Vanity: if you've got it, flaunt it. The Wannabes are everywhere: wannabe rich, wannabe noticed, wannabe famous. And they're prepared to do anything, no matter how degrading, to strut their stuff in front of the cheap seats. The sound of this millennium is a shriek for attention, Me, Me, Me. And if that's not a sin, it's a shame . . .

School Days Are the Happiest . . .

Funny, the things that stay in your memory . . . More years ago than I, or you, would care to remember, I was a young father. With a young wife and mother to go with it, and two little boys. Well, one little boy and a baby. The elder was five, and we deemed it proper that he assume his station in life as a man, beginning with school. He'd been to nursery school, of course, but this was the big stuff, preparatory. Off he went, school cap, uniform, school bag. We hated it, his mother and I. One day I went to collect him from school and spied him walking in the school yard with a friend. Two little old men, heads bent in serious talk, with matching blazers, trousers, ties and caps. It was quaint and funny, and yet oddly saddening, and I've never forgotten it. It wasn't the end of innocence, but I felt I was losing a child, that my dear son's childhood had slipped away. Abba have an affecting song, that starts 'Schoolbag in hand, she leaves home in the early morning . . .' That catches the heart-scald, the poignancy, of watching your child leave home for the first time. You walk them into the classroom, and they stand there bemused, as a kindly teacher takes over from you, and introduces them to the other children, and the strange room with its funny smell. You don't want to go, but your child has already left you, engrossed in the new surroundings, the new people. There's a dull ache in your heart as you leave, and it stays with you all day, even when you pick the child up after school. It never really goes away, because in your heart, you know that it's only the first of many separations, all of which bring that sinking pain that only a father and mother know.

I got used to it, by the time his younger brother, and then sister, in turn got into their school uniforms, but I never got over it . . . It wasn't as if the school was miles away, it was only down the road. How can anybody send children *away* to prep school? Surely not without permanent damage to the heart . . .

Bad enough having to get them togged out in their uniforms; not that they mind, of course. Little children are conformist. All of their little lives they've been told what to do and how, when and where to do it, no argument. And *don't* do that! . . . They're

conventional little creatures that we've created and they don't like to
be different. They want to be the same as everyone else, a member
of the club, a part of the pack. I know, I was one myself, and I've got
to the age when all my childhood memories are beginning to seep
back. I have only the faintest grasp of what happened the day before yesterday, but I can remember my own first day at school as if
it *were* the day before yesterday. Short trousered, pullovered, tied
and fine-featured, my mother led me by the hand the half mile or
so to the good nuns of the local convent school. It seemed to go well
enough, but by the time we had our first break and were allowed
out to play in the school yard, I felt that I'd seen, heard and experi-
enced more or less everything that education had to offer. More-
over, I was missing my mother, and if it came to that, lunch (or
dinner, as I called it then. I'll bet you did, too. Oh, sorry, you're
twenty years younger than me). Well, anyway, I can't quite remember my mother's face, but I can picture it, when she opens the front
door and finds, standing there fresh-faced, the same infant she has
just deposited at school . . . They came for me, of course, the nuns
– I had to go back.

The following twelve years were all uniforms: first, pullovers and
short trousers (regulation prison grey), then caps and blazers, then
blazers, long trousers and school tie. My children have always been
tremendously clothes- and fashion- conscious; I, in common with
the rest of my generation, couldn't have cared less. Even haircuts
didn't matter much in the fifties. At least, not until Elvis. Not that
mothers, and particularly mine, weren't meticulous. Fashion, my
mother could take or leave alone; cleanliness and the well-pressed
short pant was something else. Another memory that this time
sticks unpleasantly in my craw is a nasty piece of work of a Jesuit
pointing out to the rest of the class: . . . 'And then there's Wogan.
He's got a crease in his short trousers . . . ' You know, I can still
remember the little fink's name, and picture his little rat face . . .

I wouldn't mind, but my hero was William Brown of Richmal

Crompton's 'Just William' books. Mrs Brown, William's mother, would send him out spick and span, and within five minutes his socks would be about his ankles, his knees scuffed, his trousers torn, his blazer in shreds and his cap over his left ear. Heavens, how I envied him! He'd never have tried that on with my mother . . . Mind you, she didn't have all the advantages of modern science and technology. If the television ads are anything to go by the country is full to bursting of glamorous young mothers who, when not filling their children's faces with all manner of 'convenience' foods, are positively glorying in their muck and dirt, dispersed in a trice by some wonder washing powder that leaves the entire house looking and smelling like a field of buttercups. 'Oh darling! Your school clothes are filthy again! Never mind! Tra-la-la!' It's my own personal conviction that the decline in children's discipline and obedience is in direct relation to the disappearance of the washboard and the mangle . . .

All of my children reacted differently to their first day at school (nurture? Forget it, nature wins every time . . .) One took it placidly, accepting the change, though not with any noticeable enthusiasm. Another flung themselves into the fray with all guns blazing and took over the classroom within minutes. The third of our children cried and cried . . . They've been like that all their lives.

We never sent our children away to boarding school at all. Call it selfish, if you like, but we wanted them around. I'm not one of those who criticises parents who send their children away to school, it can be very beneficial, both academically and socially, for some children; but I have sometimes observed a barrier that boarding school builds, between parents and children, particularly between father and son – a lack of intimacy, an inability to make contact at a deeper emotional level. My wife went away to boarding school, and loved it. I didn't go. I would have hated it. I did hate the boarding schools I visited, while playing rugby. They seemed cold, they all smelt, and the food was rubbish. I've always said that my dear mother couldn't cook to save her life, but after a day at a boarding school, I was very glad of rashers and egg.

I hated my children going off to university, particularly the one who went off to a foreign country. We went to visit for a weekend, and when it was over a face waving goodbye from a taxi window nearly broke my heart; I hate it when my children, big grown up adults as they are now, have to leave after a weekend at home. You see, I never left home. I lived with my parents until I got married, and I've lived with my wife and family ever since.

That little fella who walked all the way home alone from school on his first day, was father to the man. A very lucky man.

I'm A Father, Get Me Out Of Here . . .

Ah Spring! A livelier iris gleams upon the burnished dove, whatever that may mean, and a young man's fancy lightly turns to what he has been thinking about all year anyway. Everywhere, buds are bursting forth, bunnies are bounding about and birds are kicking up an unholy racket that disturbs the gentle doze. Rebirth and renewal are putting themselves about like nobody's business, and all nature is indulging in wholesale slap and tickle. And here it comes: no bigger than a speck on the horizon, but burgeoning and blooming, as it hurtles towards us, scattering rice and confetti in every direction. The Wedding Season . . .

Don't talk to *me* about weddings. After a blameless life, during which I have harmed no man, struck no woman, and spread sweetness and light in all directions, one might be pardoned for expecting a gentle slippage into the land of Nod, a fair passage into peaceful decay. Am I not entitled to a decent living, after all these years promoting walk-in baths, stair-lifts and insurance policies to cover funeral expenses? I know the lines off by heart: 'No salesman will call' . . . 'This attractive carriage clock can be yours' . . . And what is my lot, in the twilight of my years? Weddings. Not one, but *two*! If I'd known this was going to happen, I would have started saving when I was three! Have you any idea what a wedding costs these days? Take the number you first thought of, and multiply it by ten. Oh, and by the way, you've forgotten the cost of the flowers, and of the bridesmaid dresses . . .

I'm steeped in the lore of weddings; up to my shoulder pads. There's nothing you can tell me about marquees, catering and mobile loos. I could write a small book on all of them. To the untutored, table plans and invitations may seem like a piece of cake. Let me disabuse you. It's at least as complicated as DNA, and as nerve shredding as your first time on television. And we haven't even got to the point yet where things start to go wrong; usually the week before the Happy Day itself. Battle-hardened friends, who had been forged in the white heat of family nuptials, warned of the fear and loathing that lay ahead. God help me, I scoffed at their weasel words, much as you are doing, even now, at mine.

Let me fill you in on a few minor details that may soften your cough. You want to pitch a tent in your back garden for your daughter's Big Day? Forget your days in the Girl Guides or the Scouts. That little ol' tent is going to run into five figures, most of them zeros. You need a floor, heaters, tables, chairs, lights. And you've still forgotten the flowers. And a stage for the *band*! Forgotten them, as well, hadn't you? Did you know you've got to pay for the waiters' outfits? And that the chef will cost £35 an hour? I could go on, but I've no wish to cause parents with unmarried daughters to rush, screaming, from the room. It could cause people to abandon weddings; thereby extending the life span of husbands and fathers far beyond their natural limit, and creating panic and early retirement among bank managers and loan sharks.

What's happened to weddings? My own, a scant thirty-eight years ago this year, had a free bar, a five-course meal, hundreds of guests (most of them friends of my wife's father, I hardly knew anybody there . . .), skin and hair flying in all directions, but I don't remember any great fuss. There was no palaver, no voices raised in anger, little rending of garments. My wife's mother and father were the very acme of calm and self-possession, and the present Mrs Wogan herself only fainted twice. I don't recall the slightest hiccup of stress in the run up to the Great Day. A certain frisson at the dinner itself, when the wife's father interrupted my own in the middle of his finely honed encomium, but the contretemps was settled without recourse to fisticuffs.

Now that I think of it, most weddings I've attended have been joyful, relaxed occasions. There has been little sign of temperament, frazzled nerves, or barely suppressed hysteria. Now that I'm involved myself, I know all that surface calm to have been but a hollow sham. There are months to go yet, and I'm up to ninety already.

And I've just had a horrible thought. Did anyone remember to book a photographer . . . ?

Missed Again

Is there something missing in your life? There's so much missing in mine: I miss my parents, I miss my first daughter, who only lived for such a short, sad time. I miss my granny, I miss my maiden aunts. I miss the corncrake singing on the banks of the river Maigue, near Limerick; I miss seeing the mayfly rise and die in a day. I miss the kindness of my people, and their love of laughter.

I miss the friends I made at school, perpetually young and carefree in my memory.

I miss the things that aren't around anymore, like my bicycle, my trusty velocipede, that took me back and forward to school, and bequeathed me the manly thews that still make maidens gasp and look away, blushing. I wouldn't chance it now, not with *my* knees. I miss the thud and blunder of the rugby field, although it was that that *gave* me the gammy knees. And it's not just my bicycle that's not around anymore: I haven't tasted really fresh sea-bass since my father last caught one off Portmarnock Strand near Dublin in the late fifties. When did you last taste a new potato you remember from before the war? Okay, the Korean War . . .

These aren't the bleatings of a sad old curmudgeon. Although it's true that 'they don't know they're born, these days.' My great-aunt Mag called a chemist an 'apothecary'; now they want to put a pharmacy in every supermarket, so that, having strangled the life out of every family butcher and small grocer, they can put paid to the High Street altogether, and see off the little town and village communities for good and all . . . There are lots of things missing – and before you say my marbles, where have all the marbles *gone*? You never see children playing marbles anymore. And conkers? When did you last observe a couple of grimy urchins trying to knock seven bells out of each other's conker? Then there are boils. Or, at least, there were. In my youth, it was commonplace for every classroom to boast at least one unfortunate holding his head at an angle of 45 degrees, to avoid a pulsating boil rubbing against his collar. You'd go a long way before you'd see a decent boil these days. Anyone seen a policeman on a bicycle? Anyone seen a policeman? The only time I ever see the boys in blue is sitting in their car, waiting to catch somebody speeding on the motorway . . .

There's a deal of high-sounding talk these days of people suffering from their 'nerves'. There were no 'nerves' in my young days. You had a fit, and got over it. If you were actually climbing the walls, there was always 'Nerve Tonic'. I know plenty of people, particularly on television, who could do with a good dose of *that* nowadays. I miss Carter's Little Liver Pills – nobody cares about livers anymore (except the French; every illness there is put down to a 'crise de folie'). Dr Collis Brown's Chlorodyne was a boon that ought to be sorely missed, if people had any sense. I miss that for *everything*. Talk about a cure-all; you took it for toothache, face ache, backache, gout, neuralgia, pneumonia. Some people rubbed it into their scalps to avoid baldness. Others praised it as a sovereign remedy for sinusitis and earwax. Dr Collis Brown's Chlorodyne had a peculiar and not unpleasing effect while working its magical curative powers: it caused you to walk about six inches off the ground, and see the world from a rosier if somewhat blurred, perspective! Eventually some interfering busy body had the stuff analysed, and found that it contained a copious dose of morphine. Nobody has seen a bottle of the good Doctor's snake oil since . . .

I miss *Dallas*. Don't try to tell me that Phil Mitchell is worthy of polishing JR Ewing's cowboy boots. How could Peggy ever compare with Miss Ellie, or Tracey with the Poison Dwarf? I miss Ena Sharples and Albert Tatlock. Where's Amy Turtle? I miss Benny with his bobble-hat. Went out to get a screwdriver in the old Cross-roads Motel, and never came back . . .

So many things I miss. And you know, I wouldn't have missed them for anything . . .

I'll Be Alright in a Minute . . .

As I write, the Wogan household is in a state of flux. Or 'a state of chassis' as Brendan Behan put it. The mistress of the house, a kindly but firm woman, has decided to 'change the look of the place'. They always say that next to birth, death and marriage, the most traumatic event in anybody's life is moving house. I've done it four times, and I'm not arguing. Moving things about, without actually moving yourself, is not in the same league but it can be pretty unsettling. Particularly in the cheque-book area . . . I'm not saying I wake in the middle of the night in a cold sweat, but when you've seen a picture hung, and taken down, four times in the one morning, it's not unreasonable to seek a dark corner, and a nice cuppa tea. I've moved carpets. Ever tried that? On the face of it, it seems a clean job, light and undemanding. Unlike furniture, carpets appear pliable, easily manoeuvrable. I can just hear a kindly parent, advising their son on a career: 'Go into carpets son. You won't get your hands dirty, you'll never put your back out, and you'll live a long and stress-free life.' I might have been that poor deluded fool of a parent, if I'd never lifted a carpet – they bend in the middle. And you've got to lift all the furniture anyway, to lay the carpet. I've never been called to the undertaking profession, but I'm sure carrying a carpet around can't be a million miles away from doing ditto with a dead body. And I'm talking a 20-stone dead body here . . . If you treasure your loved ones, don't ask them to move the carpets. Bring in a pit pony, or a team of oxen . . .

We got the walls of the with-drawing room done while we were away. And the settees and the chairs recovered and the curtains done. I thought the old stuff was okay, but Herself felt the wind of change. And the fire at Christmas gave her the excuse she was looking for. A word of advice here, before we proceed further: Never light a candle in a dried flower arrangement . . . One minute we're all standing around on Christmas Eve, glugging away good-oh, and the next, a conflagration sprung up that would do credit to *London's Burning*. One of the neighbours ran to the kitchen, soaked a cloth, and threw it towards the flames, missing completely. The fire roared merrily on, burning walls and ceiling, and dropping hot wax on all who approached. Eventually a better man than I picked the whole flaming caboodle up, instructed me to open the doors, and charged outside, where he hurled the blazing bundle into the snow . . . Friends and neighbours have been asking ever since if there's any chance of a similar firework display next Christmas? None. A makeover such as I'm going through should only be endured once in a millennium. Now Herself is eyeing the dining-room . . .

It's not just the carpets, the furniture, the re-positioning, the re-decorating. It's the new stuff. We apparently desperately needed new furniture, new chairs, new paintings. And I don't mean new. I mean old. And everybody knows what that means . . . Lots of it . . . I saw a painting in a gallery the other day that looked perfect for one of the newly-painted walls that are suddenly empty. Beautifully painted, impressionistic, right size, right colours! I asked the civil, beautifully dressed young man in the gallery about it. 'Couldn't agree with you more, Sir. A wonderful piece of work. And a bargain at £200,000' . . . Surely it flies in the face of all that our proud, capitalistic way of life stands for, that the older a thing is, the more valuable it becomes? Isn't this a consumer society, where we throw things away as soon as they become out of date, and replace them with the new? Why didn't I get more selling my old Morris Minor than I paid for it? If I was to take Herself down to the nearest White Slave Trade Market now, do you think I'd get more for her than I would have thirty years ago? . . .

Sorry, I got carried away . . . Don't tell her I said that . . . I'm just a bit overwrought . . . She wants the big mirror moved. Again . . .

Is There a Doctor in the House?

Recently, the University of my old home town in Ireland, Limerick, honoured me, by conferring on my untutored seven-and-five-eighths head, a Doctorate of Literature. There can be few things more flattering, and at the same time more embarrassing, than having your questionable virtues extolled in front of an audience of distinguished academics, and a couple of hundred interested spectators. Most of my family were there too, but decently enough, they refrained from hooting with derisive laughter as the good Professor heaped praise upon my undeserving head. A head which, at the time, was covered by a capacious velvet beret, while the rest of me was draped in robes of white, gold and red. I looked like nothing so much as some unfortunate prelate who was about to get it in the neck from Henry VIII. This attractive outfit had earlier provoked such laughter from my daughter that she had to be led away. Takes after her mother, I'm afraid – no sense of dignity . . .

Neither had my supposedly loyal listeners on Radio 2. They were immediately to the fore, with cheap jibes and gratuitous insults. Several wished me to come around and look at their bunions. Others wanted to know if I could drop by to slip a poultice on their varicose veins. These were the least distasteful of their requests; I will not trouble you with the more offensive ones, suffice it to say that not many were above the belt . . . Then there were those who congratulated me on my Doctorate, and wondered how I had kept so quiet about my seven or eight years of hard studying, and working like a dog in hospitals. Many sympathised with my lot as a graduate, and wondered kindly how I was proposing to pay off my debt to the Government? People in the public eye are supposed to have no feelings, of course . . .

The Irish newspapers were kind in their reporting of this earth-shattering event, although there was the inevitable 'I don't wish to appear to be begrudging' piece, which, of course, went on to begrudge like billy-oh, along the lines of whether those in the public eye, 'celebrities' forsooth, are worthy of such accolades. Well, that's something you can kick around from here 'til doomsday, like the British Honours System. And I've got one of those as well. I won't be sending that back, either, no matter how many people think a mere radio and television presenter unworthy, and no matter how much I may agree with them . . .

I won't insist on being called Doctor, if that's all the same to you. Not that you were going to, anyway. In Britain, mercifully, Honorary Doctorates are just that, Honorary. Only Ph.Ds, and the medical profession, are called 'Doctor'. For Ireland, it's different. You can't throw a stone in a country road without hitting someone calling himself 'Doctor'. In Europe, it's the same: every dog and divil with a degree in anything at all is a 'Doctor'. It does remind you of that immortal Tony Hancock sketch, where, after he has declaimed pompously on some medical matter, someone asks Hancock, 'Oh, are you a Doctor then?' To which he replies, 'Nah! I never really bothered!'

The added bonus to the honour done me by the University was returning to the town where I was born and lived for fifteen of my formative years. I've hardly been back at all in the fifty years since I left. We moved to Dublin all those years ago, and I left all my boyhood friends behind. And it's only in later life that I've realised how much I missed them, and the old town. As I drove into Limerick from the airport, the memories came crowding back. We passed the avenue where I'd lived for fifteen years. When I was little, it had seemed like a wide boulevard, at least a mile long. And there it was, hardly a hundred yards in length, with barely enough room for the cars parked on either side. We drove along the road, and over the bridge across the Shannon where I, and my trusty velocipede, had cycled four times a day, back and forward to school. There were about 20,000 people in Limerick when I was growing up; there are 120,000 there now. There are one-way streets, and new buildings, and a magnificent University, but the façade of my father's old grocery shop is still there. And the cement factory past which my father would cycle every Sunday, with me perched on the cross-bar, going fishing.

It's mundane, but the older I get, the more I realise I left my home-town fifty years ago. But it's never left me.

Foreign Parts

It was reported recently in one of the tabloid newspapers (so it must be true) that a British holiday maker in Kuala Lumpur bitterly complained to the hotel staff: 'I can't tune into Terry Wogan on my bedside radio.' Their response is not recorded, but it was freely pointed out to me by my loyal, ever-offensive listeners, there's many a tortured soul in dear old Blighty who'd give a King's Ransom to be able to say the same. I'm supposed to have no feelings, of course . . . These are the same gratuitously hurtful folk who declare that I'm very popular in hospitals, because the listeners abed there are too weak to reach out and switch me off. Talking of switching things off and on, a tourist at the Information Centre in Reykjavik, Iceland, was heard to ask: 'When do they turn the Northern Lights on?' People get confused, once they're out of their element. Away from home and hearth, things are apt to get a little blurred. And it doesn't help if you've lost your way in Ireland, for example. 'I wouldn't start from here in the first place' is no-one's idea of a road-map, and there is the salutary tale of the traveller who inquired of the barman in a Cork pub: 'What's the quickest way to Dublin?' 'How are you travelling?' asked the barman, 'by foot or by car?' 'Oh by car,' said the traveller. 'That's the quickest way,' came the reply . . .

If you do find yourself hanging around the Emerald Isle, whether lost or not (and there's no finer place to get misplaced) there's one feature of the landscape that must not be missed. And no, it's not the Black Stuff, the Hard Stuff, the smoked salmon, the oysters, the soda bread, nor even the Ulster Fry (heart attack on a plate). It's Irish local radio. Everything's up for discussion, from mastitis in cattle to the Bishop's mating habits. A listener to Radio Kilkenny the other day heard the presenter play a record by Willie Nelson, and afterwards say 'That was for Bridget of Thomastown, who is a great willy fan' . . . The high-spot of the day, however, on all Irish local radio stations, is the reading of the obituaries and death notices. Trust me when I tell you that, without exception, the Bereavement Shows are Irish local radio's top-rated attraction. I suppose it's something to do with that joke about the old geezer who always went straight to the obituaries, the moment his daily paper arrived. 'If I'm not included in there,' he said, 'I get out of bed.' The Irish, of course, take as much pleasure out of funerals as they do out of births and marriages . . . Anyway, another of my spies in Ireland swears that on another little local station there, he heard the presenter read out the death notices, and then cheerily announce 'And here's the Hollies, with "I'm Alive"' . . . I myself am not guilt-less in this regard, once having played 'Isn't it Grand Boys' on the 'Hospital Requests' programme on Irish National Radio. I hadn't realised that after 'Isn't it Grand Boys', the next line was '. . . to be bloody well dead' . . .

And I'm not exactly Mr Know It-All when it comes to getting it all wrong in Foreign Parts, either. Some years ago, the Plucky

Little Woman and myself drove the highway from Phoenix, Arizona, to Las Vegas, Nevada. As we crossed the Boulder Dam, the sign warned us to adjust our time-pieces as we were entering the Pacific Coast time-zone. As ever, suiting the action to the word, I put my watch back one hour. The restaurant in which we had dinner that night seemed surprisingly empty, in view of the fact that it was eight in the evening. We slept well, ignoring the mirror over the bed, and left the hotel at ten, to drink in the sights of Las Vegas. The boulevard was pleasingly free of sightseers, although none of the attractions seemed to be ready to start on time. 'Pirates of the Caribbean', in which two full-sized men-o-war blow each other to pieces in a lake in the middle of the street every couple of hours, was obviously postponed. After a pleasant day's sightseeing, we turned up at a recommended Chinese restaurant, which I had booked for 8 pm. It was empty, except for a couple of waiters playing mah-jong. One of them came over. 'A table in the name of Wogan,' I said, 'booked for 8 o'clock.' He looked at me, slightly foxed. 'It's only 6 o'clock,' he said . . . I'd put my watch back instead of forward at Boulder Dam, and we'd spent twenty-four hours in Las Vegas, two hours early. We'd walked the boulevards at 8 o'clock in the morning. You see, there are no clocks in Las Vegas.

Well, that's my excuse . . .

You'll Never Know

If the present Mrs Wogan has a fault, and I must tread carefully here; if she has a fault, this gem in the diadem of womanhood is a hoarder. She never throws anything out. Which may explain the longevity of our marriage . . . We've got drawers, shelves, dressers, wardrobes, cases full of stuff that's of no earthly use to God nor man. I've just opened a drawer that's bursting with sunglasses. There's a shelf-full of old drinking glasses so cloudy with use that Herself wouldn't be seen dead with them on the table. There's another drawer full of half-used rolls of sellotape, broken spectacles, blunt kitchen knives and rusty secateurs. I won't even go into the wardrobes, heaving with clothes, shoes, socks and hankies. At least I gave away my old shirts, ties, trousers and suits to the needy. I can throw anything away but a shoe. Don't get me wrong, I'm no Imelda Marcos – although someone else I could mention in the family comes close – but I have a couple of shelves of tired brogues, slip-ons and moccasins that ought to be given a peaceful death. It's just that shoes are more personal than trousers, somehow, and then again, very few apart from the odd geisha have my dainty feet. The plain, but honest offer: 'Hello, Mick. Would you like a pair of shoes?' could easily lose you your teeth where I come from. The implication being that the poor sod hasn't a brass farthing. Only the very wealthiest of the British gentry admit happily to penury. I would have no more hesitation in offering a pair of old shoes to the Duke of Devonshire than he would have in accepting them . . . Do you think he'd take a boxfull?

Then there are magazines. Does anybody in your house ever get rid of a magazine? Every bedroom, bathroom and loo in our place is up to its rafters in magazines. Some go back at least ten years, like the *Field and Streams* and *Country Lifes* you see in dentists' waiting-rooms. Friends who come to stay in our house, or who are even passing through to use the loo, have been reading the same magazines for as long as they have known us. I suppose it's the fam-iliar-ity of long-standing friendship, like putting on an old shoe; but let's not get into that again.

What is it that makes us hold on to things that have long since outlived their usefulness? Nostalgia? Memories? There are not many memories in a drawer-full of sunglasses, and I'm sure you've noticed that when you really look for something that had significance in your past, you can never find it. Chez Wogan, only stuff that's important gets thrown out ... What happens when people decide to sell the old homestead, and move to smaller, more manageable accommodation? All over the country, in storage, there must be thousands of chests of drawers, dressers, wardrobes and tea-chests full of antimacassars, cushions, tablecloths, place-mats, sugar-bowls; all the flotsam and jetsam of our ordinary lives that we cannot bear to throw away. That may just 'come in handy' again. That's it, isn't it. The 'you never know' syndrome. You just might need that old tea towel again, some day.

Early to Bed – Early to Rise

Gainfully employed as I am, desperately trying to keep the non-viewing public awake by the dawn's early light, I rarely get an opportunity to see the morning goings-on, on the television. Only when Mother BBC sees fit to grant me a brief respite from the coal-face, do I get the chance to drink in the delights of Dermot and Natasha, Moira, Eamonn, Bill and the other bright morning faces of Breakfast TV. I lie there on my day-bed, idly toying with a cup of Earl Grey and the remains of my Ulster Fry, and I'm humbled. Have you any idea what time these people have to get up in the morning? I'm forever beating off admirers, who seem astounded that I get up at half-five every weekday morning, in order to welcome my listeners with cheery bonhomie at half-past seven. 'How do you do it?' is the astonished cry. Implicit in the query is the more hurtful: 'Why do you do it?', but the answer is the same: It's what I do. It's how I make my living. And I'm damned lucky to be doing it.

It's easy to be cheerful, when you're doing something that you love. As I drive through the waking streets of London, I see hundreds of people already about their business – butchers, bakers, newsagents, café owners, street cleaners, taxi and bus drivers – people up at all hours, many of them doing jobs that they hate. People like me should never forget how lucky we are.

Sometimes, I wonder what else I could have done in life. If my father had been a doctor or a vet, an architect or an accountant, my education and upbringing would have dictated that I follow in his profession. I would have conformed, because that was the way it was when I was growing up, and I've always taken the easy way out. Luckily for me, my father was in the victualling trade, and never gave me the slightest encouragement to join him in the dispensing of fine wines and comestibles. So, rather than have a path picked out for me, I was allowed to drift; nobody insisted that I go to university, when I couldn't see any point in further study, nobody minded when I joined a bank, and everybody seemed quite pleased for me when I got a job in Irish Radio, although it probably was not as 'steady' as a bank job. And there it was. Something I could do, and be happy doing, for the rest of my working life. It didn't happen through single-minded ambition, nor ruthless determination. I've never stuck my foot in anybody's door, and pleaded for a job, in my life. Life happens, and not always for the best. But if we can recognise the breaks, and take them, we've a fighting chance of getting through. Not unscathed; nobody gets it for free. 'Into each life, some rain must fall.' Particularly in July . . .

Getting up at half-five in the morning to work at something you like, with people you like, is no hardship. But getting up at half-past three, into your best suit or frock, and full make-up, before presenting yourself in front of a bank of glaring television lights, and being required to smile warmly at an audience that is barely awake, or even human, that's what I call tough. I get into the radio studio, devoid of eye-shadow, mascara or powder, dressed as I please, open the microphone, and begin to speak, without a thought in my head. Dermot and Natasha, Eamonn and the rest, have to run the gauntlet of researchers and producers, newspapers and tabloids, journalists, and all the other hobbledehoys that insist on getting their names on the credits at the end of the programme. Breakfast television is about News, and that's something you have to be careful with – it takes time to get it right, it takes careful preparation, particularly since the Gilligan Affair, and the Hutton Report. That's why, apart from the make-up and the frock, the early-morning boys and girls have to rise well before cock-crow. I don't know how they do it: what time do they go to bed – half-eight in the evening? What sort of a life is it, that you have to go to bed as soon as *Eastenders* is over? They've probably forgotten what Sir Trevor Macdonald looks like. And what of their loved ones, husbands, wives, partners? Are they all off to the Land of Nod at half-eight, and up at three-thirty with a cup of tea? Meanwhile, there's Jeremy Paxman, slipping between the sheets, as Dermot and Eamonn are getting up, rising gently at midday, lunching expansively at his Club, before strolling in to work at nine in the evening. Then a glass or two of champagne, and on to Stringfellows. Probably never even heard of Natasha . . .

Easy Does It

I have been accused of decrying, disparaging and otherwise deprecating the worthy exercise bike. Guilty, M'Lud. I have boldly stated that in every simple home in this great land, can be found several items that have been used just once, if at all, and then put aside in some corner, there to gather dust. A juicer, an ice-cream maker, a set of allen keys, a mangy koala bear and an exercise bicycle, usually with five kilometres on the clock. I have only lately myself disposed of a ski-walking machine, tonight, in the heat of the moment, after a bracing week in the Swiss Alps. I nearly broke my neck every time I tried to use this damned thing, and it took up most of the attic (or, as the present Mrs Wogan calls it, the Penthouse Suite). It took three men to get it down the stairs and out of the house, and all of them sustained contusions, minor cuts and bruising. The exercise bike is still there, a mocking commentary on the foolishness and vanity of a once fine athlete going to flesh.

The listener who took me to task over my harsh words on the bike, declared that she was living proof that not all such equipment lies cobweb-covered in some forgotten space under the stairs. 'I use,' she trumpeted, 'my exercise bike with unwavering persistence – three times a week, twenty minutes a time!' I hang my head chastised, not for the first time, by a superior being. Or, as we men know them, a woman. Now read on: 'That is, three times a week, for a week in January (in a desperate attempt to repair the ravages of Christmas excess), three times a week for a week in May (in preparation for the bingeing of a summer holiday in June, and the remote chance that I might, in a moment of drunken weakness, attempt to struggle into a bathing suit). Three times a week for up to two weeks in December (in a hopeless effort to be able to squeeze into my party frock for another Christmas, in which I can eat and drink like a savage, knowing that I'll soon repair any damage with my January work-out on the bike). So remember, next time you're tempted to malign the blessed exercise bike, not all of us are as self-indulgent as you!'

And that's it, isn't it? That's what exercising, dieting and de-toxing is all about. Sticking plaster. Like government policies; something needs fixing, stick a plaster on it. Do something, any-thing, temporary, to cover up the problem. It'll solve it for a while; of course the problem will come back, but for the moment it's okay – the frock fits. Diets never last, the metabolism adjusts to the smaller amount of food, and the weight loss gets less and less. And then, inexorably the ounces slowly creep back on. You simply can't diet and detox forever. But hey, do you really want to look like those stick insects in the pages of the glossy magazines? Have you seen their legs? As a friend of mine put it: 'The last time I saw a pair of legs like those, they were standing in a nest . . .'

What of exercise, I hear you cry; they say that the answer to good health and a long life, not to mention a racing-snake figure, is regular exercise. All about us people are running, walking briskly, lifting weights, stretching lycra to the limit with aerobics, boxing, skipping, rowing – anything to keep the heart ticking over, and the old flab on the move. I've always sturdily maintained that you can have too much of a good thing, and indeed, can be heard muttering, 'You'll kill yourself!' at distressed looking joggers of an early murky morning. And have you ever seen a happy-looking jogger? Have you ever seen anybody chuckle, or even smile, while they're exercising? Ha!

So it was no surprise to find my simple philosophy of just lying there, while the rest of the world exhausts itself, entirely vindicated recently by two German doctors, who said that all exercise was good for, was wearing the body out. Stay in bed, they said. Relax, be a couch potato. Don't stress yourself, animals that move slowly, live longer. Take it easy, life's short enough as it is, without rushing it . . . I knew it all along. Peel me a grape, will you?

Forward Planning

I'm sure you're familiar with the old joke: Plan ahead . . . I hate it (the planning, not the joke) but you've got to, these days. Nothing fills me with greater trepidation than to flick through my diary and see appointments for June, August, even October. As a matter of fact, I know what I'll be doing for Christmas; but then that's the same thing every year: spend, spend, spend, family, food, drink, warmth, love – and I never want it to change. I know exactly when my holidays are this year, and where I'll be. I know what I'll be doing on the radio, and television, until the turn of the year, unless some higher power at the BBC decides that it's time to wipe the slate clean and have all of television and radio presented by screaming adolescents – as distinct from the present 80% . . . Strange isn't it, that someone of my age can't make a comment like that without feeling that I'm turning into Norman Tebbit? . . .

You can do nothing these days without preparation: Try turning up to have a trip on the London Eye without a pre-booked ticket . . . Try walking on to an aeroplane without weeks of meticulous planning . . . And, of course, they're still entitled to throw you off, if they've overbooked . . . Try getting a table at a smart London restaurant if you haven't reserved one three months in advance . . . Unless you're with Tara Palmer–I-need-a-Good-Slap-Tomkinson, or Michael-Ditto-Winner . . . Try walking up to the Headmaster of Eton College and saying – 'This is my Egbert, I want him to start next term . . .' You need generations of planning (or money) for that.

It's stressful, particularly for somebody like myself, who hates preparation: those who can be bothered to scrape up an acquaintance with me will be the first to tell you, after they've listed my shortcomings, foibles, and other drawbacks, that I'm not a great one for taking pains. 'If you want a job doing well, Terry's not your man,' is the watchword. If it's meticulous planning, and an eye for every little detail you're after, get an accountant, a lawyer. Go to Yellow Pages, if you're that desperate, but leave me out of the loop. I've never been one for the small print. 'The devil's in the detail', they say, but I've never understood what that means. I'm a Big Picture man. 'Show me the money!' as Cuba Gooding Junior shouted so memorably in *Jerry Maguire*. It's why, despite the present Mrs Wogan's pleading, I will never participate in a rubber of bridge. I haven't got the brains for it, and I know it. Perhaps it would be more accurate (and indeed kinder to myself) if I qualified that: I haven't got the right *kind* of brain for bridge. The very idea of having to remember who played what, when and where, brings a flop-sweat to my upper lip. And the post-mortems! I've never seen the point of dissecting what's done and dusted. Let the chips fall where they may, let's move it on out. I cannot bear discussing the pros and cons of a radio or television programme after it's done; which, I suppose, is why I love doing 'live' shows. Get on your toes, keep your wits about you, say goodnight politely when it's over, go home and enjoy your dinner . . . Wogan's Golden Rule of broadcasting.

And there's the nub of it. It's because of what I do for a living, that the bit of my brain that could be used for analysis, nit picking, and sifting the wheat from the chaff, has atrophied. If it was ever there in the first place . . . Years ago, when I was a boy broadcaster in Ireland, and a slave to learning scripts off by heart, endless rehearsal, and remembering where to put my feet, so that I wasn't addressing the nation in the dark, I heard tell of the great Dean Martin, who would walk in off Sunset Boulevard, on to the TV studio floor, and without fuss, preamble or rehearsal, would start his 'live' and highly successful television show. 'That's the bag for me!' I resolved, and after centuries of hammering down the prejudices, procedures and needless spit and polish of television and radio production, that's the way it is, now. Rehearsal knocks my edge off, and endless research ought to be superfluous, unless you never pick up a newspaper, nor book. And how much practice do you need, if all the words are written for you, and are running in front of your very eyes, on the autocue? Or your questions are inscribed on an idiot-board just before the camera, or a clip-board on your knee?

When all of your professional life is spent making it up as you go along, walking a verbal tightrope, preparation goes out the window. I hate rehearsals, I hate sitting round in dressing rooms while they get the lighting right. I've never gone in for production, because I know all the little fiddly things that can go wrong would drive me up the wall. I've no capacity for getting it right. I just want to get it done. I'm sure my family would tell you it's impatience; but I think they'd also tell you that I'm only impatient when people don't get the plot. If you're not quick on the up-take, I'm outta here . . . My dear departed Mum and Dad would tell you it's laziness, intellectual *and* physical. And for the most part, they'd be right. They watched me through my boyhood, doing just enough to get by, in the classroom and on the playing field. If it took too much time and trouble I let it go. To this day, I abhor tying my shoelaces. I actively dislike time wasted in the shower, the bath, shaving and cleaning my teeth. I never even got to the ski-slopes. Trying to get those clod-hopping ski boots on, put me off for life. I enjoy a game of golf, but putting all the stuff in the back of the car, and assembling the trolley when I get to the course, gives me the willies. I'm impatient with inanimate objects. They don't respond to persuasion, or the kindly word, and when you drop them, they deliberately roll into the most inaccessible place. I'm hopeless on the phone – just gimme the facts, and never mind the small talk. It's beyond me how my wife can spend a day with her friends, and then talk to them for hours on the phone when she gets home. Do you think that's anything to do with the fact that I talk for a living . . . ?

Everybody needs a diary these days – in the good old days of yore, only Samuel Pepys had one . . . Nowadays, most days you need to be in two places at once, and as I slip effortlessly into my declining years, I find that I'm usually in the wrong place, 50% of the time . . . Down in the South-West of France, where I spend some time every year, people live longer than anywhere else in the world. Statisticians put it down to the diet, the fresh air; but they're wrong: it's the lack of stress. The good farmers of Gers live and work by the seasons. They sow, they reap, they plant, they harvest. They too, know exactly where they're going to be, this time next year – this time, five years . . . They don't have to plan ahead – they know the plot, and for generations to come. I'll bet that they don't even have a word for 'diary' . . .

Plan ahead, because you have to, these days. But don't forget to Enjoy the Day . . .

I'll Be Off Then . . . But Not Yet . . .

Some time ago I made the mistake of offering a rash generalisation to a journalist, who, as always, was pretending to conduct an interview, while in fact looking for a cheap headline and the opportunity to show what a smart-alec he was. I should have known better, but sometimes the tongue outspeeds the brain and you grow weary of answering the same old questions with the same old tired clichés. 'Any plans to retire?' 'Oh, you know – it comes to all of us, except Joan Collins. You've got to get off the beach before the tide comes in . . .' Or some such well-worn old codswallop. 'Wogan To Retire!' said the headline. And you can't argue with that. It's inevitable that one day, and not a hundred years from now either, I'll be down the Post Office collecting the dues of decades of National Insurance contributions. I'll be riding the buses for nothing, zooming down the deserted bus-lanes that drive me to apoplectic fury today as a motorist. But not yet. When that headline hit the fan, I was inundated by this letter: 'You're not going to retire are you? Say it isn't so! Who will I have to shout abuse at in the morning?' Bless him, but I'm not going. Not yet . . .

Isn't that what everybody says, once the Grim Reaper starts hoisting the Storm Cones? 'Oh of course I'm going to retire but I don't feel that I'm quite ready to go just yet. Many a tune played on an old fiddle you know . . . And anyway, there's no one to take over . . .' Everybody wants to go to Heaven, but nobody wants to die. Not that you're going to. Die that is. Well, not yet. And that's the problem about retirement for most people, particularly men, they think that it's going to be a slow, living death. No more the daily camaraderie of the office, nor the factory floor. No more the satisfaction of a job well done, a deal closed, a promotion well deserved, a colleague fired, a boss disgraced. No more decisions, no more responsibilities, no more relying on you . . . No more the tedium of the daily commute, forty years of the same old car, train, bus or underground journey. But what are you going to get out of bed for? What are you going to do all day? How often can you play bowls, golf, bridge or tiddlywinks every week? How many movies can you take in? Is the high spot of every afternoon to be tea, toast and *Countdown*?

Most women fear retirement, even more than men. Not because they'll feel useless, nor redundant. Because of 'him'. He'll be under their feet all day; complaining about the government, the neighbours, and bringing dirt into the kitchen from the garden. I wish you could read the heartbroken letters I get from women with newly retired husbands who have taken to following them round the supermarket. 'He questions everything I buy . . . He's forever checking the bill . . . He loses his temper trying to open the little plastic bags . . .' I digress, but why is it only women can open those damned things?! Marriages that have been rocks of certainty, nay, contentment, are falling apart in the aisles of supermarkets, all because your man wants to prove that he's still useful, and needed. The old hunter-gatherer is fresh out of things to hunt or gather . . . It's back to the tepee to fall asleep in front of the fire . . . And that's the fear, that's what brings on the 'not yet . . .' factor when you talk to a man about retirement. Women handle these things much better than men do; they come to terms much more easily with life's changing pace, the body's slow decline. Well, most women . . . There are the slaves of the plastic surgeon, the laser and line-erasing Botox, the creams, the unguents, the bras that lift, the knickers that do ditto. It's the female version of: 'I know I'm getting older . . . but not yet . . . '

And yet . . . And yet . . . I love friends who glory in their retirement; my friend the doctor: 'It's such a relief to know that I might not kill anybody today . . . ' The stockbroker: 'I should have done this years ago . . . ' Those who love the free time, the load off their shoulders. Those who stay out of the kitchen and the supermarket. People who don't think of retirement as an ending, but a new beginning. Anyway, it's coming – to all of us, and as my accountant said to me lately: 'You'd better think of taking your pension soon – otherwise it won't be worth your while . . . ' Still, mustn't grumble, eh . . . ?

Red Letter Days

January

It's January, and as black as your hat. Never mind that the shortest day was supposed to be in December, and the days lengthening since then, that's just another spurious statistic. I know, I get up at all hours. I go to work in the dark, and when I walk out of the BBC of a morn, it's still dark. It brightens up for about ten minutes, and then gets gloomy again. If it wasn't for the Christmas lights still on in Regent Street, you couldn't see your hand in front of your face. Alright, it's not quite that bad. In fact it's not bad at all if you compare it with Oslo. I was there, in the capital of Norway, in November. Rising from a breakfast of reindeer, I took to the streets at about ten in the morning. A sort of murky, oyster light could be seen. I walked about a bit, drinking in the sights (there's nothing else to drink, their licensing laws were formulated by Luther) and waiting for the gloaming to disperse. It never did. At three o'clock in the afternoon darkness fell, and that was it. That was November – Thor knows what it's like there now! You think you've got it dark? Try Scandinavia.

A friend of mine once said, 'I like the winter. I get to see more of my friends.' I know the immediate response of the cynics among you . . . 'And that's a good thing?' No, come on now, be sociable! We all do huddle together for warmth more in the winter. We're not off gadding about in the Cote D'Azur or in the Bahamas. Yes, I know half of you are in Barbados, and the rest soaking up the rays on Bondi Beach, but indulge an old fool. I like to stay at home in January, and February if it comes to that. In March, like an old hedgehog, I stick my nose outside the barrow (do hedgehogs have barrows? Don't be so picky), sniff the air and begin to make plans for the year ahead. But January, sad old January, is when I like to stick close to the fire and the warmth of loved ones and friends, too. Red wine tastes better in January, and armagnac and a Havana cigar. Lots of things are better in the dark, particularly when you get to my age. I look better in the dark, particularly in the dark with the light behind me. I could do with a bit more dark lighting on the television, bright lights make you look like the wrath of God. On a sunny day last October, Gaby Roslin and I did a promotional film for Children in Need. It was bright, very bright, and the director insisted on Gaby and me squinting into the sun. I don't know if you saw it, but it was enough to frighten the horses. I looked like the Phantom of the Rue Morgue, and Gaby was so drained of colour, she looked like she'd just spent the night with Christopher Lee.

Bright is not always the bees knees, and anyway, you can't let yourself fall to pieces just because it's gone a bit overcast. Think of the dangers of too much sunlight – ageing, wrinkling. Remember the smooth, baby-faced complexions of nuns, who never go outside the cloister. Give yourself a face lift, sit in the dark. And while you're there, count your blessings. Go on, you'll find 'em if you really try. It's too dark and cold to play golf; the weather's too awful to visit your mother-in-law; the roads are too bad for the children to come home with their washing; you can't be expected to go to the supermarket on a day like today; he can't go to the pub. Wait a minute! This means you're going to have to talk . . . Never mind, there's always the television, you never know, they might have something on home decoration, cooking, or gardening that you can watch . . .

Have A Heart

Nobody ever sent me a Valentine's Day card when I was a lad; and I never sent one. And before you start with the crocodile tears, and the sympathetic 'oohs' and 'aahs', spare me that pillow that you cry on. Nobody else I knew ever got a Valentine either – they were after my time. I spent my formative and early teenage years in a dampish town on the River Shannon, in the South-West of Ireland. Nobody had ever heard of *teenagers* nor to mind St Valentine. There were literally thousands of other saints, a church on every corner, plenty of religion, and even more religiosity, but no sign of a patron saint of love and romance. There was St Jude for hopeless cases, St Anthony if you lost anything, St Christopher if you were lost yourself, St Patrick for Snakes and Shamrock, St Francis for the Birds and Bees, and Litanies of the Blessed for everything from corns to the advent of the Grim Reaper. A saint for every day of the week, and a saint for everything that ailed you. We used to say that the patron saint of campers was St Pius the Tenth, but for that joke to work you have to be Irish, and drop your 'th's' . . . On a recent visit to India, I learned that the great Hindu religion has 300 gods, one for every three inhabitants of the sub-continent. We weren't *that* far behind with the saints of Holy Ireland.

Divil a sign of a saint for the sundered heart, though. I don't remember a great deal of romance; if it comes to that, I don't remember any. I left Limerick for Dublin at the age of fifteen – and I'd never been kissed. Neither had anybody else I knew. There were, doubtless, a few precocious Don Juans around but I'd never met them. And my friends would have told me if they had scored,

43

believe me. They'd have shouted it from the rooftops. As I write this, I realise that 'scored' would mean something entirely different in sexual terms to a teenager of today; a far cry from a kiss . . . Before you start, this is not some cry from the heart from a crotchety old misanthrope who wants to stop the world, get off and go back to the supposed innocence of his simple boyhood. Although I can do that act whenever called upon; I have found it invaluable over the years for winding up the younger Wogans. I don't begrudge the young their share of sex and romance, although the two don't necessarily go together. Just because I got nothing as a boy or a young man in the way of even the most rudimentary sexual contact, doesn't mean that I resent the sexual free-for-all of today's youth. Not much . . .

Still, let's not get distracted. St Valentine is not about sex. He, or is it she?, is about love. Love unknown and unrequited. Love divided, love unreciprocated. A hidden love, a forbidden love. A secret passion, yearnings that, sometimes, even your best friend knows nothing about. A St Valentine's Day card should be unexpected, a mysterious whisper to lift the heart. My wife and I send Valentines cards to each other, as do married couples, partners and lovers all over the world, but that's not really what the good old saint is about. St Valentine wants to start something: 'Is it him?' 'Is it her?' 'I'll bet it's from . . . I never knew he/she cared . . .' What a lift to the spirit for those who think themselves unloved. Those girls who think themselves too plain to ever find romance, all those young men struck dumb in the presence of female beauty. All those people with so much love to give, and afraid to reach out for it. St Valentine's Day is for them, a metaphorical kiss for the lonely, and the sad at heart.

So, don't be one of those soreheads, always complaining about the 'commerciality' of it all. So, it's another bonanza for the greeting-card industry. So what? If a Valentines card brings a tear and a smile to a heart that thinks itself rejected and alone, can you put a price on it? My wife used to send an anonymous Valentine to my

daughter when she was in her early teens; I think my daughter sus-
pected the truth, but there was always the suspicion of an unknown
admirer, that made her smile and blush. Don't brush St Val aside,
he/she's important, very important. Send a card. Send it anony-
mously, with love, to someone who needs it. Who doesn't . . . !

The Winds of March

There's a line in that lovely song, 'These Foolish Things': '. . . The
winds of March that made my heart a dancer . . .' Talk about poetic
licence! All the winds of March ever did for me were to blow me
sideways off my little bike as I toiled up and down the roads of
Limerick, as a lad. There's an old Irish blessing: 'May the road rise
with you – may the wind be ever at your back – and may you
be half an hour in Heaven before the Divil knows you're dead . . .'
Admirable sentiments; but let me assure you that if it's March we're
talking about, the wind will be ever in your face . . . Indeed, I remember doing a 'live' outside broadcast from Cheltenham in March
where the wind started somewhere round the ankles, and blew
snow straight up my nose . . .

There's not much of the favouring zephyr about March, but it
has a couple of things going for it: it's not January, nor February.
The mornings are brighter by the day, the earth is stirring, the trees
are coming back to life. Now's the time of the year when my more
romantic Radio 2 listeners begin to detect the rising of the sap, the
harbinger of spring. They've been hearing the cuckoo for some
weeks now, and some claim to have spotted the first caravans head-
ing for the Dawlish Sea-Wall . . . Mind you, the seasons are less well
marked than in the golden days of youth: nowadays, just turn on

the television and it's sunshine somewhere in the world. There are no seasons for fruit and vegetables any more, and again thanks to the almighty goggle-box, gardening has become 365 days of frantic planting, weeding and mulching. Oh, for those stately days of Radio 4's *Gardeners' Question Time*, when old Percy Thrower or Bill Sowerbutts would intone . . . 'Now's the time to be thinking about your purple-sprouting broccoli . . .' A far cry from the ever-present bonhomie of Alan Titchmarsh, and the earthy charms of the ubiquitous Charlie. Gardening is big television nowadays, and even bigger business. For Heaven's sake, a recent poll of apparently sane women had old Titchmarsh up there with Sean Connery as the man they would most like to split a pea with . . . Thirty years ago who could have predicted that gardening would become the new opium of the people? And the garden centre the social hub of the community? Never mind Alan, Charlie and Tommy, who could have envisaged letting Diarmuid Gavin loose in their garden? Last time I was brave enough to look, he had turned some unfortunate's little patch into a bog and covered it with wire cages. Just try to sell that, when the time comes.

Mind you, those who know me best will be quick to point out that I'm scarcely in a position to jibe or cavil where gardening is concerned. Sorry, but I don't like dirt under my fingernails. Call me a dandy, an effete urbanite if you will, call a spade a shovel, as long as you don't call on me to lift one. Spare me the honest fork, let me forget the wheelbarrow. Don't even mention compost, not to mind manure. Yes, somebody has to do it, and I'm happy to pay them, because there's nothing I like better than enjoying the delights of a well-tended garden. My own is a credit to the present Mrs Wogan, and her band of horny-handed helpers. I have no objection to people working in my garden – I will often sit and watch them in the unlikely event of a sunny day, and indeed, offer the occasional word of encouragement or mild criticism: . . . 'Look – you've missed that bit there . . .', or '. . . Is that a flower or a weed?' . . . The Lady wife doesn't take it all that well, but I'm a bit of a perfectionist about those things . . . As the man in the Chinese restaurant said to me: 'If you would be happy for a week, take a wife; if you would be happy for a month, kill your pig; but if you would be happy all your life, plant a garden.'

And if you can persuade the BBC to do it all for you for nothing, you've got a real result, my son . . .

Good Ole Summertime

Don't forget now: Spring forward, Fall back! That's one watchword at this time of year, otherwise we wouldn't know where we were. And don't ask me whether that means an extra hour in bed, or one less. Working that out has always made my head spin, rather like algebra in school, or those terrible questions you got asked in arithmetic, like 'If a hen and a half lays an egg and a half in a day and a half, how much will she lay in a week and a half?' The hours of blood, sweat and tears that kind of thing caused me as a little lad, and for what? Anybody seen a hen and a half lately? Don't ask, either, why clocks go forward and back every year – something to do with Scottish farmers, I understand. And good luck to them; in no time at all they'll be able to see their hands in front of their faces! Personally, I've been lumbering about in the gloom for what feels like five years, but I'm persuaded it is only the statutory six months of winter. It's been black as your grandfather's hat when I go to bed, get out of bed, go to work and finish work. The shortest day is the 21st December, but I'm here to tell you that there's no perceptible light in the early morning sky over my neck of the woods until sometime in March! My loony listeners on Radio 2, of course, claim to see a great stretch in the evenings from Christmas onwards, but then, they're hearing cuckoos from January, and spotting gambolling lambs in early February. I'm an optimist myself, but wearing rose-tinted spectacles in the winter only makes things darker . . . And while I'm at it, for the benefit of those who have been known to pick holes in my usual sartorial impeccability when a black polo neck may shriek at a navy-blue trouser: The answer is 'Yes, you gobdaws. I did get dressed in the dark! . . .'

The Irish have the best attitude to Times Winged Chariot: 'When God made time, He made plenty of it . . .' There's a story of a man in a motor-car, on an Irish country road, passing a farmer driving a pig before him, on the way to market. Pigs aren't easy to keep in a straight line; up and down the ditches it ran, side to side, backwards and forwards, prodded ever onwards by the patient farmer and his stick. The motorist passed by, arrived at the little market town, finished his business there, and in the manner of all Irish gentlefolk, repaired to the local pub for a pint of the black stuff. As he supped away to himself, he noticed the farmer who had been driving the pig along the windy, dusty road to town. The motorist brought his pint over to where the man was sitting. 'How're ya?' He greeted him, in the time-honoured Irish fashion. 'I saw you', he continued, 'back the road a few miles, driving that pig into market.' 'Right enough,' answered the farmer. 'That was me.' 'It just struck me,' said the motorist, 'that it might help if you had put the pig in the back of a truck, or a van, and driven it into market that way.' The farmer looked at his pint reflectively. After a long pause, he said, 'And why would I do that?' 'Well,' said the other, 'to save time.' An even longer pause. Then the farmer looked away from his pint, and at the motorist. 'And what does a pig know of time?' he asked, gently.

Remember that, when they try to tell you that 'time and tide wait for no man . . .' Time is what you make it, no, what you make of it. And always remember the ancient motto of the Wogans: 'Time flies like an arrow – but fruit flies like a banana . . .'

National Days

On the first of March, St David's Day, I opened my radio show with 'Help Me Rhonda' by the Beach Boys. As the record played, my producer, the aged but beautifully marked Pauly Walters, sprang to wakefulness. 'Rhonda!' he shouted triumphantly. 'Rhonda, on St David's Day! Rhonda Valley! D'you geddit?' 'I'd think a lot more of it, if I thought for one nano-second it was done deliberately,' I replied tartly. 'A happy accident,' he muttered, before slipping back into the arms of Morpheus. That's his excuse for everything, and indeed, probably sums up the programme, as any regular listener will readily agree. However, I made the most of it, and kicked up a bit of a fuss about St David, Wales, and how the Wogans originally came from there. (They left for Ireland in a marked manner, when the Normans stole their castles. Much good it did them; a few hundred years later the English stole their Irish castles.) The reaction from Wales to my mention of the day was gratifying. Emails flooded in from the Principality 'Bore da!' 'There's lovely!' Aled Jones promised to send me some laverbread, and carried away, somebody else sent me a crumpled, unsigned photo of Catherine Zeta Jones. Later in the morning a great box arrived, full to bursting of Welsh good things: leeks, daffodils, traditional cakes, orange juice (I know – not indigenous to Wales – don't be picky) and Welsh whisky. And don't knock that, either, it's as good as anything you'll get north of the border, Jimmy . . . I woke the producer up, and we ate well that morning.

Actually, we're pretty indiscriminate in our eating habits of an early morning. Well, we've been up since all hours and by eight o'clock, it's lunchtime, as far as our grumbling stomachs are concerned. The untutored and weak of digestion fall back aghast at what myself and my minions (yes, 'minions' – 'underlings' is too harsh) can put away before most of the nation is even conscious. I mind well a turkey dinner that some kindly bird-farmer sent us last Christmas: I'll be honest, we didn't eat it all. The brussels sprouts were cold . . . We've put ourselves outside a hearty fish and chip supper, shortly after dawn has broken, and there can be few things tastier than a chicken tikka massala during the eight o'clock news. The great British Breakfast Week brings the Full English, right down to the fried bread, and on St Patrick's Day the even heartier Ulster Fry. Of course, with the Irish Breakfast, there comes the obligatory half-dozen bottles of stout. These we leave for the broadcasters who come in later in the day, as we do with the haggis we inevitably receive on St Andrew's Day. The whisky we keep for ourselves for medicinal purposes, or an outbreak of nerves.

Chinese New Year produced a particularly splendid array of good things to eat, starting with prawn crackers, and going right through the card, to the crispy duck with plum sauce. 'Rubbery', as the old Chinese joke has it. We received this Heaven-sent bounty because I happened to mention that for the Chinese, this was the year of the Rooster. It is truly said that you can never open your mouth on the radio without offending someone. Indeed, in my experience there is a hard-core of people out there, crouched over their wireless, waiting to be offended. Anyway, my passing reference to the New Year produced this tirade:

'What's up with you? Cock new year, cockerel new year, rooster new year – whatever. It's complete and utter rubbish. How can there be a year of a bird? What has a chicken got to do with the way the year pans out? It might as well be the year of the stag-beetle, the crombie overcoat, the cucumber or some other such uninteresting or inanimate object. The thought that a bird would have any bearing on how I behave, is beyond me. I'm a geezer, and nothing and no one makes my decisions for me. Must go now, the wife's calling . . . '

National days have become nothing more nor less than marketing ploys, another opportunity to sell something to the un-suspecting consumer, like Mother's Day. (Did I see cards from cats, dogs and other pets to Mother on the shelves, or were my little old eyes playing me tricks?) When I was a short-trousered little twerp in Ireland, all St Patrick's Day was good for was a day off school, and an opportunity to eat sweets in the middle of Lent. I'm sure that my Welsh and Scots peers will tell you the same story of Saints David and Andrew. So there's no need for the English to get worked up, as some do, over the by-passing of St George. If the marketing boys could figure out some way to sell dragons, good old George would be all over the shop . . .

Foolish April

Call me an old curmudgeon – not that you've ever needed an invi-tation – but if there's one thing about this showery month of April that gives me the galloping heeby-jeebies, it's the first day of the blessed month: April Fool's Day. If you've got a friend who's a prac-tical joker, I hope you've come through the ordeal unscathed, and restrained the pardonable urge to disembowel the eejit. I've always ranked the practical joke, along with the pun, as the last refuge of the witless.

Puns and practical joking must go together, like mathematics and music. Sorry to digress, but did you know that? Not many people do . . . It wasn't Michael Caine but a preparatory school headmaster, who told me that in his observation of pupils over many years, those who were good at maths, also did well at music.

And, in many cases, sport as well. And not so hot at languages, literature and the classics . . . There! Who says that I don't add to the gaiety of the Nation?

Where were we? Ah; the practical joke. April Fool's Day, the Practical Jokers' Paradise. Be honest with me – am I the only one who doesn't think they're fuuny? As Terry's Old Geezers put it, all too frequently, on Radio 2 – Is It Me? When people were falling about laughing at the laboured contrivances every first of April on BBC TV's *Panorama* – all right, it was many years ago, in black and white, with Richard Dimbleby, but don't try to pretend you don't remember – merry japes, like spaghetti growing on trees! How we laughed. Talk about tedium. But the journalists thought it was funny; a welcome break from the deep seriousness of their calling. They're still at it: most of the newspapers on April the First tried a heavy-handed piece of tongue-in-cheek. Nobody paid any attention – but there will always be a few, a very few believers. I suspect that they're the kind of people the *Daily Mail* seems to cater inordinately for: The Crop-Circle addicts; the 'I saw Lord Lucan behind the Bacon Counter at Asda last week' crowd . . .

I suppose the real reason I'm not big on practical jokes, if it matters, is that they seem to epitomise the 'sneering' element that is a regrettable part of British humour. A practical joke is an attempt to score off people, make them look foolish. It has the cruelty of schoolboy humour; it picks on the weakest. It's being smart at other people's expense. It has its finest flowering in the TV show *Have I Got News For You*. That show has its moments of wit and humour, but the sneer is its least attractive quality.

I find the same to be true of the series *Louis Theroux Meets . . .* This is just one long sneer from beginning to end, in which lovable Louis pretends to be a gauche, friendly, gently inquiring journalist, who then cuts his victims to pieces off-camera on the commentary, and in the editing room. Of course, people only have themselves to blame for agreeing to appear, but why is such a programme necessary?

Do some people actually enjoy the discomfiture of others? Of course they do, while thanking the Lord it's not them.

Let's admit it, we all do, watching from behind the settee. That doesn't mean that we have to applaud. I'm for a kinder, gentler humour – where the practical joke is on the perpetrator . . . Nothing dates like humour, and nothing, or no one, dates even more than the old geezer who complains about the bitter taste of modern humour. Still, we can't blame *Have I Got News For You* for April Fool's Day. Let's just be grateful that it's eleven months to the next practical joke.

Easter Eggs

'The hounds of spring are on winter's traces', as someone once put it so well. And if it wasn't Emily Dickinson, I'd be amazed. She had a marked predilection for the simpler sentiment, and probably believed in fairies. Not that that's as outrageous as it sounds, there seem to be growing numbers of apparently sane people who'll believe anything. The cult of the guardian angel for instance. It's probably due to a movie called *City of Angels* starring Nicholas Cage and that cute Meg Ryan, which had guardian angels all over Los Angeles, spending their evenings in the library, and their mornings on the beach. There appeared to be less than a hundred of them, which in a city of several million souls, somewhat discredits the idea that we've all got an angel of our own. It's a nice idea, that there's a bloke with wings keeping an eye on you from just off stage, and a friend of mine firmly believes it, and says that you always know when an angel has been, they leave a white feather behind! Honest . . . whatever gets you through the day, as Wittgenstein used to say.

Whatever about the hounds, the harbingers of spring are everywhere. Never mind the first cuckoo, strictly for the birds and the kind of people who think that letters to *The Times* are funny. The first squashed hedgehog is more to my Radio 2 listeners' liking, but for me, the first encouraging sign of the rising sap, is the appearance of Easter Eggs in the shops, and in the television commercial breaks. Since this harbinger makes its appearance in early January, I'm well into spring before most people have recovered from Christmas, but it probably accounts for my cheery good humour on dark and dreary mornings. My doctor tends to put it down to a mild form of insanity, but what does he know?

I know that it's because of my upbringing and education in Holy Roman Catholic Ireland, but I have got qualms about Easter. It's a joyful Christian festival, and you're encouraged to eat, drink and be merry, but only because you've starved and deprived yourself for the previous forty days and forty nights during the Holy season of penance, Lent. And while I'm at it – what did you give up? I thought so. And you still think that you're entitled to stuff yourself? At the beginning of Lent, the priest would get up in the pulpit and tell us what we were entitled to in the next six weeks. It wasn't much, featuring fish pretty heavily, no dripping on your bread, and a lot of what were described as cold collations. This was arcane church language for dry bread and tea without milk or sugar. Hard to believe nowadays but people kept religiously to the rules. Except on Sundays and St Patrick's Day, when apparently the Patron Saint of Ireland had negotiated a truce. So, as you may well imagine, by the time Easter came around, and the church blew the whistle on self denial, people were ready to eat a baby's bum through a wicker work chair. You felt entitled to eat and drink yourself senseless. And there's the rub: I don't feel justified in putting myself outside even one of those disgusting creme eggs, not to mind those huge chocolate numbers with little bunnies or chickens on the top. Bunnies and chickens; they're the modern motifs for Easter. Don't ask why it's fur and feathers with the duck thrown in for lunch on Easter Sunday. And where does the chocolate egg come in? The painted hard-boiled egg was good enough for your granny. I'll chew a chocolate with the best of them, but my personal preference at Easter is for the duck. I like it to hail from Aylesbury, with its skin nice and crisp. And hold the orange sauce; whose idea was that for Heaven sake?

Years ago a demented listener wrote in to tell me that a man's best friend was his duck, and futhermore the gifted little birds repaid observation in the matter of weather forecasting:

'If your duck do bite you twice
It's certain that there will be ice
If your duck stump on your toe
You can expect a fall of snow
If your duck do kick your nethers
You probably won't care what the weather's . . .'

Bank Holiday Blues

It's about this time of the year when you, gentle reader, begin to think once more of the great outdoors. Winter, with its frost and snow, conspicuous lack of gritters, and driving rain, is but a fading memory. Now spring is sprung, the grass is riz, and the little boidie is everywhere – and I'm not just talking about Kylie Minogue. Incidentally, I have a problem with Kylie. Everybody else in the known world professes to find her the sexiest creature on the planet since Brigitte Bardot. I can only see her as an Australian person of severely restricted growth. Don't get me wrong; don't start reporting me to the size police. Small is okay. It's as good as tall, any day. I just don't find it sexy, that's all. Look at the Krankies. Ronnie Corbett is a good friend of mine, but is he as sexy as Gisele Bündchen? I rest my case . . .

But I digress, and not for the first time. Smart operator that you are, you'll already have booked your summer holiday – the Big One. Where to this year . . . ? That reminds me of an ad that used to feature heavily on television in the early seventies. It starred a chap who was obviously very successful, in a highly desirable job. He is directing a film or television show. He leaps to his feet. 'That's a wrap!' he shouts, dramatically. His acolytes swarm about him, full of enthusiastic congratulations. 'Where to this year?' one of them adoringly enquires of this godlike man. 'Butlins again!', he smiles; a man at the top of the tree, who knows exactly where he's going . . . And before you start reporting me to some other politically correct quango, I've nothing against holiday camps either. I loved *Hi-Di-Hi* . . .

It's the little ones I'm thinking about. No, not Kylie Minogue again. The *little holidays*: the Bank Holidays. The three-day weekend, the day trip. Time to dust off the camper van and the old tent. Is there anything better than a couple of nights under canvas, an evening meal cooked under the stars, followed by a hearty singsong around the old campfire? Or everybody snug and cosy in the trusty little camper van, going wherever the road takes us? Well, *anything* actually, since you didn't ask. If a tent is my idea of hell then a caravan must be purgatory. I never joined the Scouts, and I don't feel that I missed anything. Look, it's not the tent itself – I'm sure there are some very nice ones – it's just that I know that I could never *erect* one. It's the kind of thing that's beyond me. I never wanted a sailing ship either. The very idea of taking up and down the sail makes me want to lie down. My dear Auntie May once gave me a present of a Meccano set for my birthday. It was the worst present I've ever had in my life. You see, I'm not interested in 'how things work'. Inanimate objects fight me. They are not susceptible to persuasion nor cajolery. You can't unscrew them, and when you do, they roll under some cupboard where you'll never see them again. I know that many of you swear by camper vans and caravans, but I know that I would fall at the first hurdle: hitching the damned thing on to the bumper of my car. And then, having to unhitch it. It would take me hours, put years on my life.

It's not much of a boast, but you see before you a man who has never, in his adult life, gone anywhere on a Bank Holiday. I have an excuse for not joining the merry throng of the soaked, the steaming, and the stationary. I work on Bank Holidays. Okay, it's not a proper job, it's not real work, but I sit in front of a microphone or a camera, and speak. Heavens, now that I see it in print, how ridiculous it sounds. Why am I telling you? You know that already – you're the ones that sit there and suffer. Bless you. As my Granny used to say, we were put here to suffer . . . Now that I think of it, my Granny never went anywhere on a Bank Holiday, either. Indeed, I don't remember her going outside the front door, any day of the year. She didn't have a bike, not to mind a car, and I don't think she could be bothered walking all the way up the road just to catch a bus. But then, she belonged to a generation who stayed more or less where they were, all their lives. You never travelled anywhere, unless you had to. People were born, lived and died without ever moving outside of their parish. Mind you, it's only a matter of time before the same thing happens to people who use the M25 . . .

Honestly, are we any the better for our endless toing and froing, these days? Has the accessibility of far-flung foreign parts made us more enlightened, more understanding, more tolerant of our fellow man? Has travel helped the notoriously jingoistic Anglo-Saxon to view the foreigner in a different, more kindly, light? Has it enabled us to develop culturally, to imbibe and enjoy the arts and traditions of other lands, other peoples? Give over. Ask the inhabitants of anywhere that has played host to England's football team. Ask the people of Ibiza, Majorca, Tenerife. We bring our prejudices with us wherever we go, and return home with all of them untouched . . .

It's pretty obvious that travel, and our ability and resources to go more or less wherever in the world our restless feet take us, have not made us better, more fulfilled people. I'm not even sure that holidays make us any happier. Next time you're at an airport, look at your fellow-travellers' faces. All you'll see is stress, strain and worry. You can count on the fingers of one hand the smiles at an airport terminal. When the children are young, family holidays can be a nightmare – when they're teenagers, and out all night God knows where, it's worse. Now that air-travel has become so popular, and the skies above us so congested, it's almost a matter of course that flights, and particularly cheaper charters, will be delayed, not just for hours, but for days.

Where's everybody going? And why? We see a brochure of a sun-kissed beach, an exotic island, and we must be off, with never a thought of the travail: the packing, the carrying, the endless waiting in terminals and traffic-jams, the scorching, the peeling, the dickie-tummies, the disgusting showers, the all-night discos, the noisy drunks in the apartment next door. Is it worth it? Wouldn't you be better off staying in the comfort and security of your own home, and spending the holiday money on the best of food and drink; romantic meals in the best restaurant in town; toys and treats for the family; the little luxuries you think you can't afford?

Maybe I've got it all wrong. Maybe people like spending hours in traffic-jams, and struggling for a spot on a crowded beach, or being trapped in a caravan park in the rain. I've never wanted to go anywhere on holiday where I'm going to be less comfortable, less happy than I am at home. Roughing it is something I've never wanted to do. And don't tell me that a 'change is as good as a rest'. If I'm going to have a 'change' I want it to be for the better. For Heaven's sake, give yourself a break this Bank Holiday – relax, enjoy yourself. Stay home.

The Madness of May

'The wisdom of winter is madness in May' – who was it said that?
Sounds like Noël Coward, or the Bad Lord Byron. I heard it from
my bank manager, who came into the safe as I was wrapping up
lodgement dockets. He'd say things like that for no reason at all,
and follow it with: 'There's no business like show business Wogan.
And there's no people like show people. They laugh when other
people cry . . .' As I've said elsewhere, I shall carry that picture of
flint-hearted show people with me to the grave . . . I don't know why
he said stuff like that, it had nothing to do with the day to day business of banking. He'd say it, and then walk off in his open-toed sandals and hopsack shirt, leaving me bemused over the unwrapped
lodgement dockets. He'd say it at any time of the year as well, leading to further confusion among lowly bank-clerks.

The trouble about May is that it's a flibbertygibbet. It may, or
may not. It's like a bimbo that can't make up her mind . . . May is
unpredictable, yet full of possibilities and promise, with the hint of
warmer, better days to come. The fact that May has been a liar for
at least the last four years, the false dawn of a hundred rain-soaked
summer days, should not blind us to her virtues, nor to besmirch
her honour. And anyway, May, of whom I've written before, was my
favourite maiden aunt, and I won't hear a word against her . . .

May – it's a lovely sound, isn't it? It sounds like a flower, you feel
it should have a scent. It's soft, innocent and yielding. May flowers,
May blossom, even the Mayfly. Find a darkened corner, and recite
the months of the year to yourself. Only 'May' lifts the corners of
the mouth into the suggestion of a smile. Next time they take your

photograph, don't say 'Cheese' – say 'May'. You'll look younger, softer. It's as good as a vanishing cream . . .

May is everywhere, in a thousand different guises: Mayday means much more than leaping around that foolish totem pole. It's the international call for help. Mayfair – still the smartest address in London, even if I'm not very sure where it is – off Park Lane? Or Berkeley Square? It speaks of the soigné, and suavity; elegance with just a hint of the raffish. Sloane Street is Tara P-T, Victoria Hervey; dresses cut a little too low, slashed a little high; McQueen, Galliano, Choo; youth, bull-at-the-gate experience. Mayfair is Barbara Goalen, the cat-walk, Hardy Amies, timeless; the West End where once was held a fair, in May . . . *Mayflower*, the ship that brought the Plymouth Brethren and stern Christianity to America, but also the flower of the hawthorn, that became a Christian symbol, but long before that was a pagan one. What about May-dew – the very dew of May, especially that of the early morning of the first day of the month, to be gathered up to whiten linen, and beautify the face? The earliest vanishing cream . . . May is youth and beauty: 'For it's a long long time, from May to December, and the days grow short, when you reach September . . .' 'May/December' is how my granny would describe a romance or marriage between a young woman and a much older man . . .

Yet, and yet . . . there is an element of the unpredictable about sweet little May. She may, and maybe she won't. She's a bit of a tease, leading us on to the promise of summer. Watch her; she'll do it again this year, and we'll lug out the garden furniture, and scrape the rust off the barbeque. Ever hopeful, buoyed up by the seductive smiling May, we anticipate the warm summer days, and the still velvet nights. But the little baggage gives no guarantees, just promises with her eyes. I've known a few like her in my time . . . I can't believe she'd deceive us again this summer, but you and me pal, we've always been a sucker for a pretty face . . .

Midsummer Madness

'Where are the snows of yester year?' cried Proust, or if he didn't, I'll bet he felt like it. In the same vein – where are the summers of my long-lost youth? Only the other day, an otherwise sensible person said to me, 'I don't know what's happened to the summer; when I was a boy, I remember endless days of sunshine, sandy beaches, warm rock-pools, ice-creams to cool you down in the heat . . .' Who doesn't? All the summers of our youth had endless sun and clear blue skies. I remember picnics in the sand hills of Quilty, on Ireland's Atlantic West Coast, the sea warmed by the Gulf Stream, the flawless sand sifting through my toes. Games of beach rugby on huge Brittas Bay, south of Dublin, on the much colder Irish Sea, not that that stopped us from flinging ourselves into it, when we needed to cool off. Endless, lazy, crazy days, bright with sunlight. On the crossbar of the Da's bike, as we went fishing for flounders on the little River Maigue, just outside Limerick. We usually caught eels, and threw them back – my mother had the greatest of difficulty with mashed potatoes; cooking an eel, or even looking at one, would have been completely beyond her. Picnics in the sand hills of the beaches of County Clare; ham and corned beef from the Da's grocery store, tea, lemonade and sand in your mouth, your ears, your hair – days later, you'd still leave a ring of sand every time you took a bath. And the sun, softened by Atlantic breezes, shone all day and every day . . .

Of course, if you'd care to peruse the records of the Irish Meteorological Office for Limerick in the forties and fifties, you'll find that it was raining. It rained a lot in Limerick – it's probably chucking it down even as we speak. People who saw the film *Angela's Ashes*, set in the Limerick of my childhood, saw virtually every scene depicted through the lashing rain. People couldn't believe that with so much drought in the world, so much water could fall on one little spot. 'Believe it,' I assured them, but only because it's true. I don't remember it myself. Do you think, just as the body has no memory of pain, so it is with rain? And if I can't remember rain, how come I can remember sunshine? Or am I just imagining it? Did I cycle the dusty little roads of Ireland, bedewed with boyish sweat, or drenched with rain? Where did the endless warm days of our youth go? Nowhere. They have remained in our memory, like all the happy days of our lives, made brighter by the glow of reminiscence. We just don't remember the dull days, the lonely ones, the unhappy ones. We don't want to remember. Our minds block our rain and tears alike. The body has no memory of pain. Otherwise, no woman would ever have more than one child.

It's different now. The years have taken their curmudgeonly toll. I remember how it rained last summer, and the one before that – and the one before that. People come to me with phrases like 'but we had a lovely May last year . . . ' at their peril. 'In your dreams!' I snarl. And as for the 21st June! Of all the things that never crossed my mind when I was young, the Longest Day stands pre-eminent. Now I begin to fret, as soon as the mornings begin to brighten up, in April. 'A grand stretch in the evenings,' a neighbour will cheerily remark. 'Yes,' I will grumpily reply. 'Soon it will be the Longest Day, and it's all downhill to Christmas' . . .

Don't think I don't know what you younger limbs are saying, 'the ould eejit has gone gaga. Give the Home for the Bewildered a buzz, and see if there's a vacancy.' For the young –and as far as I'm concerned, that's anybody under forty – summer stretches away endlessly into a lazy blue horizon. For people of my mature years, one blink, and hello! Is that the snow? Why is it that times winged chariot turns turbo-charged when we turn fifty? Why does time speed up as we slow down? Sorry, I know that's not germane, but I thought it might cheer you up, if like me, you're taking the Victor Meldrew view of midsummer. I haven't even mentioned the grass growing at a foot a week, and the weeds at six inches an hour, so don't say I'm not trying to look on the bright side. And I see that I've given the game away again, with 'foot' and 'inches'. I know, I know – centimetres and metres! I can't help it; I'm one of the lost generation that translates centimetres into feet, and vice versa. Bring back rods, poles and perches is what I say, give the kids something to really think about in maths class. Don't know they're born . . .

As we drift towards Autumn, it's easy for an ageing geezer like myself to identify with the passing season. Life's like summer – you wonder where it went; why you didn't pay more attention to it while it was flashing by. All of a sudden, it's the autumn of your years, and you're hoping things will slow down a bit, rather than pick up speed down the slippery slope to the winter of your discontent. Now's the time of my life to make a conscious effort not to turn into Victor Meldrew; a curmudgeonly old begrudger who resents all change, hates youth, and can't find anything worth watching on the television. Time to remind myself that you can't hold back time's winged chariot, any more than you can prolong the summer. But you can still stop to smell the flowers . . . and wasn't it a great year for the roses? . . .

'Tis the Season

As keen observers of the social merry-go-round, you will not need the likes of me, a mere hobbledehoy, to signal the start of The Season. No, for Heaven's sake, not the chaffinch sings on the orchard bough' one, nor even 'summer is icumen in'. It's the Holy Season, the only one that really counts, my dear. It's the Holy Season of Hats and Frocks, Buttonholes and Toppers, Pink Blazers and Club Ties, Strawberries and Cream, Pie and Mash and Jellied Eels. That will have given a clue to those of you still muttering, 'what's the old geezer on about now?' The Derby, for those of you still thrashing about in the fog. Yer working-class end of The Season. Jolly Pearly Kings and Queens, and their salt-of-the-earth subjects, all together on the Epsom Downs, for a right old knees-up, and the premier thoroughbred horse race of the year. Her Majesty, who loves nothing better than a well-turned fetlock, is usually there, at the better end of the course. Who can blame her? Least of all those of us unlucky enough to have tried Pie and Mash and Jellied Eels. And don't think I'm scoffing from a position well above the masses. I've been to the Derby. On a double-decker bus with Frank Bruno. It was an open-top bus, Frank stood up to wave to a passing pedestrian, and only by the merest centimetre escaped decapitation by a low bridge. The Derby itself? Didn't see it, miles from the action, surrounded by drunken Jellied Eel eaters. It took me about three days to get home.

I watch the Derby on the box now. Which is more than I do for the Henley Royal Regatta, another gem in the diadem that is The Season. There are a few things more terminally boring than watching boats race. And it's even worse when you're actually there. Even copious injections of Pimms fail to dull the nagging, awful tedium. The Braying of the Hooray is heard from every marquee, nobody pays the slightest attention to the races, you get a terrible headache from drinking so much so early in the day, your good shoes are ruined, and it takes you two days to get home; only because you live closer to Henley than you do to Epsom . . .

I can get home in less than a day from Wimbledon, another seasonal treat. Mind you, you have to set out a couple of days early, if you want to get there on time. It's best to park your velocipede or horseless carriage in Hyde Park, and walk from there. One year, I shamelessly curried favour with a friend who had not only tickets for the Centre Court, but a Car Park Pass! Determined not to miss a precious, bejewelled moment, we took a picnic, and sat in the driving rain and bitterly cold wind, before taking our seats on the Centre Court, where you watch those highly trained groundsmen pulling on the covers with their legendary precision and timing. I loved every minute of it, even if Cliff Richard could not be persuaded to sing that day. Every cloud, as they say ...

And then there's Ascot, Royal Ascot; the fairest of them all. It's upon us even as we speak – have you got your hat? Who's got the passes to the Royal Enclosure? We don't want to be turned away, like Joan Collins! On the other hand, they don't seem to mind letting Rod Stewart in. Perhaps they think he'll sing a couple of songs if it rains ... I loved Royal Ascot. Great friends of ours had a house not far from the course, and we would repair there, for a grand lunch before racing. Champagne and strawberries, poached salmon and Chablis. All too soon, the host would blow the whistle, and we'd all have to be off, so as not to miss the first race. I never wanted to go. 'Leave me with the port and cheese,' I would plead. 'I'll help with the washing-up.' I never did get to finish lunch, and I don't think Her Majesty would have particularly missed me.

Cecil Beaton's wonderful staging of the 'Ascot Gavotte', in the film *My Fair Lady* is how those who haven't been there imagine Royal Ascot to be, particularly on Ladies' Day. A far cry from the reality of heaving humanity, and some drunken old biddy trying to conduct the band. Elegance is in short supply, diminishing as the day wears on, and the empty bottles pile up. There are fewer sadder sights than watching the crowd leave Ascot: hats askew, dresses awry, shirts open, finery now dishevelled, teetering, staggering on its high heels ...

Take the advice of an old Ascot hand: stay, and finish your poached salmon. Her Majesty won't even notice.

Under the Volcano
(A funny thing happened on the way to . . .)

In the early part of this glorious summer (where's the Green House
Effect when we need it? Where's all that global warming we were
promised?) the present Mrs Wogan and your humble servant were
privileged to join our friends, Sirs Don and Ron, on a cruise that
took us to Sorrento, Sicily, Dubrovnik, Venice and Corfu. Helen
and I are not big on cruises; for a start, like so many people born on
an island, She can't swim. It's not for want of trying, nor swimming
lessons; we put it down to a little-known condition: negative buoy-
ancy. It's a condition shared with my good woman by stones, and
people wearing concrete overcoats who have offended the Mafia.
This cruise, however, was different. We were among a host of good
friends and the Band of the Royal Marines. And Roger Royle, a
loose canon not unknown in this parish . . .

Sorrento was delightful, but up to its shoulder-pads in tourists.
And there's a thing: why are Italian restaurants much better in London than they are in Italy, with a couple of honourable Tuscan ex-
ceptions? How come you don't get to dip your bread into a
delicious mixture of olive oil and balsamic vinegar, like you do in
Zilli's in Soho? And, by the way, if you're thinking of a table at
Harry's Bar, Venice, on the recommendation of Michael Winner,
remember: Michael's a millionaire without any children, and you
will have to take out a second mortgage on your house . . . Where
was I? Oh, si, Sorrento, picturesque, stunningly perched on cliffs,
and handy for Pompeii, which was the real reason we were there.
Pompeii, preserved for thousands of years under the volcano ash of

66

the erupting Vesuvius. Once teeming with 20,000 inhabitants, and now teeming with millions of sightseers. So see, and marvel – but not in July nor August, when you may feel that the very stones have turned to lava again 'neath your summer sandals . . .

The choice in Sicily was simplicity itself: a tour to Taormina, and then a luxury lunch in a Sicilian villa, or an invigorating stroll up the slopes of Mount Etna. Exercise in any form being anathema, we plumped for the chance to see Taormina, sitting like an eagle on its Sicilian crag, and the villa lunch. It was a mistake; as a general rule of thumb, any tour that includes the descriptive 'luxury' should be avoided. It never is. Taormina is beautiful, full of Roman and Grecian artefacts, and a magnificent amphitheatre. The views in all directions take the breath away, and there, across the bay, the great volcano – Etna. Even as I looked, it belched forth a huge plume of grey dust, flames licking its rim. Before my very eyes, Etna was seriously erupting, in all its terrifying glory, for the first time in thirty years. It was majestic, awe-inspiring to behold. And then, somebody said: 'What about those people on the Mount Etna tour?' I had an immediate vision of fire and brimstone raining on our friends, leaving nothing behind but a charred Nike or two. There were glitterati among them. Sir Tim Rice and Robert Powell. We offered a silent prayer for the lyricist and the tragedian, and congratulated ourselves on our choice of tour. We needn't have been so smug – apart from picking bits of ash out of their hair, teeth and ears for a couple of days, Tim, Robert and the others were unmarked. We, on the other hand, had the 'luxury' lunch . . .

The Sicilian villa was the very one seen in *The Godfather*, part one, where Michael Corleone (Al Pacino) sees his young bride blown to smithereens. The tour guide said we would be greeted by the Baron. He turned out to be friendly; simply, even cheaply dressed. If he was a baron, I'm Eddie Izzard! A merry band of strolling Sicilian players engaged us with guitar, tambourine and tempestuous head tossing. We drank something fizzy, that reminded me of Babycham. We toured the villa, furnished from Sicilian car boot-sales, and then came the high-point – the 'luxury' lunch, in the Baron's own cellars. The first course was shrivelled vegetables, the main course was boiled meat-loaf, the wine was like swallowing iron filings, and to put the Sicilian tin-hat on it, the strolling players had followed us. I don't know if you have ever attempted meat-loaf to the strains of what I took to be German marching songs of World War II, but it can be hell on a delicate stomach . . .

After we had piled, drained of all emotion, back into our tour bus, the guide asked brightly: 'Well, did you enjoy that?' In crisp Anglo-Saxon, I told her the truth. Mount Etna might have erupted underneath her. 'Nobody's ever complained before,' she muttered, darkly. Given Sicilian reputations, I suppose I was lucky to get off the island with my life . . .

August – The Silly Season

'Why did summer go so quickly? Was it something that you said?' Lines from the song 'The Windmills of your Mind', and don't look now, but it's August already. August gets a mixed press, for what is traditionally a month of high-holiday and begone-dull-care all over the world. Pretty little May-June is bustin' out all over – but August? August is a wicked month. The word for August in my native tongue, is Lunasa, pronounced Loonasa. It's the source of the Gaelic English words Loony, Lunacy, Loonatic. Of course, Lunasa doesn't mean stark, raving bonkers in Gaelic – it means the time, or month of Lugh, a Celtic god who, now that I come to think of it, wasn't the full shilling either . . . Ever seen Brian Friel's marvellous play, *Dancing at Lughnasa*, where a family of spinsters in the furthest recesses of Northwest Ireland are overwhelmed by the madness of dance? And their little cottage becomes the scene of almost-pagan ritual? Doubtless the influence of Mad Lugh of the Long Arm, but perhaps we'll leave the delving into early-Celtic mythology for another day, when you feel more like leaping into the air and hammering the old floorboards. Oh, you do? Women always do; feel like dancing, that is. Men only like to trip the light fantastic during their youth, the years of their courtship. Women are always up for a boogie, the commonest social phenomenon among the over-forties at any event that includes music, is the sight of women dragging men on to the dance floor . . . 'You never want to dance, these days . . .'

I have to confess that evidence is pretty thin on the ground that August is any loonier than other months. There seems no more than the usual complement of the criminally insane walking about the BBC; my listeners' letters, emails and faxes are no more barking than usual. Anybody who travels to France in early August is, of course, displaying certifiable insanity, as every Jacques, Jules et Jim takes out his little Deux-Chevaux, and chases up everybody else's exhaust-pipe . . .

The clearest manifestation of August's supposed loony-inducing qualities used to be the behaviour of what was once called the 'Great British Press'. (Now there's a description you don't hear a lot, these days . . .) In the hoary old days, before Rupert and Robert rewrote the rules, and said that if you hadn't got a story, you could always make one up, August was a hair-tearing, shirt-rending month for editors and their newspaper journalists. Parliament closed, school closed, courts closed, no football. Half the country had left the country, in search of sun, sex and sangria. This included half the criminals. So there wasn't a decent crime to be had for love nor money. August became the month of abandoned puppies, cats saved from mine-holes, and fat men, covered in grease diving off the beach at Dover in the general direction of Cap Gris Nez. Strange, anymore than men over forty dancing of their own free will, swimming the English Channel is rarer than hen's teeth, these days . . .

In those days of yore, August was the month when newspapers discovered strange beetles on our potatoes, unexplained artefacts in the Peruvian desert, unearthly lights over Salisbury Plain, and canals on Mars. Pictures of distorted carrots abounded, and Lady Docker was usually good for an outrage or two on her yacht in Monte Carlo harbour. If you were really stuck, you could always ring up Malcolm Muggeridge for a salty word on Royalty, God or the BBC. By September/October, the madness had abated, and we were back to sobriety and the facts, just the facts. Now, it's August every month, and no newspaper reader can tell fact from fantasy anymore . . .

Anyway, if you wanted someone to do a knocking-job on good old August you've got the wrong man. I was born there. Yep. August the 3rd, that's me, Leo the Lion, not Lugh of the Long Arm. And I'm sane – although you'd probably get an argument about that from my radio listeners, and my daughter, who often leaves the room in high-pitched girlish hysteria at some of my more profound statements. I think I've heard 'Mad old Geezer' in between her shrieks, but I can't be certain . . . What does she know, slip of a girl? August – if it's good enough for the Queen Mum, it's good enough for me. Happy Birthday, Your Majesty!

Tuck Me In . . .

'Mists and mellow fruitfulness'. Sounds good, doesn't it? 'Close bosom-friend to the maturing sun.' Even better, if we didn't know any better. It's the 'image' thing again, the kind of thing that wins elections, keeps Madonna on top, and gives Posh Beckham sleepless nights. Perception beats reality every time; it's what makes the world go round, in the new Millennium. If you can get the nice pictures in the paper, and manipulate the story, who is going to worry about the facts? 'Spin-doctoring', the political commentators call it and generations of poets, painters and proselytisers have done a pretty fair job on us with autumn over the years.

Think autumn, and what do you get as a mental picture? Ripe fruits, russet-coloured leaves, apple-cheeked children merrily on their way to school, the sun setting red and gold, behind the barns of saved hay. For Heaven's sake, when did you last see a barn? And those russet-coloured leaves are going to be all over your lawn, your window box, your footpath and your railway line; even as we speak they're going to hold up your trains, ruin your garden, be dragged into your house on the boots of those same apple-cheeked children, and cause you to nearly break your neck every time you step outside the front door. And another thing: I've got loads of blackberry bushes in the field at the end of my garden, but I'm never in time to get a single blackberry. Every year teams of rascals with buckets get there first. I've thought of guard-dogs and razor wire, but it hardly seems worth it, even for a couple of blackberry and apple crumbles ...

It may not seem all that important to you but surely, gentle reader, you can sympathise, and understand why, when it comes to autumn, you don't find me running round the place with garlands in my hair. The season of autumn has had a wonderful press, and it deserves to be exposed for the pain-in-the-neck that it is. I'm an early riser, for reasons with which I will not detain you here, but let me tell you, it's dark out there now. And it's cold. And everybody's got a cold, flu or double pneumonia. The country's nose is running and the cattle are lying down in a field near me; always a bad sign.

I suppose I should be grateful that there's no sign of rabbits. But then, there's little sign of any wildlife, unless you're a Radio 1 listener. The little swines (other rabbits and Radio 1) have taken a powder, gone to ground, at the first sniff of the people's friend, good old Mr Autumn. Say what you like about the animal kingdom, and some of it can be pretty delicious, but it's got autumn summed up. As soon as the last rays of an August sunset go down behind that aforementioned blasted barn, Mr Fluffykins and his loveable fellow-vermin are out of it. Find a shady nook, pull up the duvet, and out go the lights until spring. If homosapiens are the last word, and if we really are the zenith of animal life on earth, how come mankind didn't think of it? Hibernation is the answer to the nation's woes. Think about it: if we all hit the sack at the first sign of a brown leaf, would not the world be a better, cleaner place? Think of the savings in energy: the earth's precious resources conserved, no greenhouse gases, the environment purified. Alright, there would be no Radio 2, but as against that all manner of unpleasantness would cease (and I'm not just talking about Radio 1 or *Big Brother*). Wars, riots and the stock market would go into suspended animation, Paul Daniels and Debbie McGee would disappear again, Carol Smillie's teeth would go into a glass by her bed for six months, Ainsley Harriott's skillet would be stilled, and who doesn't need a break from Jamie Oliver?

Of course there will be regrets: no more pictures of Posh; Alan Titchmarsh's gentle tones no longer there to thrill; no football for six months; no news of Wills and Harry; no pictures of Posh; no riveting news of IT girls nor panting page-three lovelies; no pictures of Posh . . .

Still, I think I could take it, couldn't you? Wrap me up safe and warm, snug as a bug in a rug, and wake me with a nice cuppa tea with the first daffodil. I might miss Christmas, but trust me, I won't miss autumn . . .

Christmas

And another thing: if anybody else tells me that they hate Christmas, that it's too commercial, that if it wasn't for the kiddies they wouldn't bother, I'll turn my *Star Trek* phaser on to 'Stun', and let them have both barrels. Or, I would, if the batteries had been included . . . If there's a person that gets right up my nostrils this Holy Season of Goodwill to All Men, it's the eejit who ritually intones, every year at this time, 'Christmas? It's not the same, is it?' Not the same as what, you oaf? *Nothing's* the same as it was. Time's winged arrow and all that. And don't give me that line by some old French philosopher (was it Aznavour or Distel?) 'Plus ça change, plus c'est la même chose.' The more things change, the more they remain the same? Tosh mon brave. If there was any truth in that load of old frog's legs, would the present Mrs Wogan have spent a fortune doing the bedroom? And that Morris Minor I bought when I was twenty-one, would still be rattling every bone in my body . . .

Of course Christmas is not the same. Like ourselves it gets older every year. And earlier. And bigger. And better. I got my first Christmas card from a listener in October. Frankly, I thought that they were a little tardy in switching on London's Regent Street lights on the 15th of November; Oxford Street beat them to it by at least a week. Incidentally, since Christmas appears to come around about every three months, why don't they just leave the festive lights up there, and switch 'em on at the appropriate time, say, when the nights begin to draw in? That's the way it works in the townships of France and Spain . . .

I know too well that in the midst of prosperity there is poverty

73

and deprivation, but Christmas has got bigger, more lavish, more expensive, because we *want* it that way.

If we didn't spend the money in indulging our extravagances, do you think Mr Mohamed al Fayed, Mr Harvey or Mr Nichols, Mr Marks or Mr Spencer would be filling their stores to bursting with Christmas Fayre?

Christmas is no time for good husbandry, for counting the bawbees. It's a time for putting your head in the sand, and letting the moths fly from your purse. And it's not a bit of use kidding yourself that this year you're going to be sensible – I know, I do it every year, and every year pay not the slightest attention to myself . . . However, you'll have spent it by now, and damn the torpedoes.

What's with this Scrooge-like, 'Bah! Humbug!' mentality? You'd think Tiny Tim had never got better and grown into Giant Haystacks, for goodness' sake. What kind of a stone-like heart is it that doesn't glow along the High Street lights, that doesn't twinkle at the sight of tinsel, chirrup at a chipolata, burgeon at a brussels sprout or turn handsprings at the merest hint of Gloria Hunniford and her Hampers.

Incidentally, Christmas Hampers; what are they about? A non-vintage sparkler, a couple of bottles of plonk, a tinned ham, bit of fruit cake, lump of cheese with dry biscuits you'll never eat, a couple of tubs of whole-grain mustard and marmalade, that'll be stuffed in the cupboard and thrown out in a couple of years' time by the younger members of the family, being a year over their 'use-by' date. One hundred quid! Most of which is for the finely woven basket with the real leather straps, which in its turn, is conveyed to a corner of the attic, and never seen again. Why not buy your friends, family or business associates the kind of food and booze you know they like, and wrap it up the way you do with other presents? 'You'll get far more for your money,' cried Thrifty Terence.

Anyway, isn't there something 'off' about buying your chums and loved ones food and drink for Christmas? What are you trying to say? Doesn't it smack of food parcels for the needy and less fortunate? Surely buying food for anyone is making it clear that you think: a) They're not eating properly, b) They can't afford to eat properly and c) You do eat well, and properly. Oh, and d) You're better off than they are. What sort of messages are these to be sending to your family and pals at this time of Goodwill to All Men? You would have been better off sending the usual hankies and socks. Yes, they would as usual have been thrown into a drawer, and never seen the light of day, but at least you haven't set alight a spark of resentment that will burn throughout the New Year ...

Christmas; I love it. It's the Real Stuff. Or Stuffing, if you like. And I do. But not the old Sage and Onion, and if it's all the same to you, you can keep your chestnuts (or marrons, Marco-Pierre). The present Mrs Wogan does a mesmeric number not entirely unassociated with garlic and various herbs that would cause any right-thinking turkey to march straight into Bernard Matthews' boudoir, and give himself up.

I love the Old Bird. Turkey's okay by me as well, particularly the skin. Indeed, my attitude to Johnny Turkey is not unlike that of your average Chinese Mandarin to a Peking Duck: keep the crispy skin and throw the rest of the bird away. Ah, the succulence! The greasy glory of it! The memories of Granny Byrne's house in Dublin, and Auntie Nelly's gigantic, and always slightly overcooked Christmas Turkey. Various younger brothers, maiden aunts, parents, cats and dogs on carpets, sofas and beds, sated – nay, bursting. Not our hero. Little Terence is in the kitchen with the carcass, stripping off the last of that golden, glorious skin, and then stuffing it into his capacious maw. Then, to a quiet corner, like some beached whale, deaf to Auntie Nelly's complaints from the kitchen ...'Who's been at the turkey? It's naked! How am I supposed to make sandwiches without any skin? And the stuffing's gone as well ...' They never had the energy to pursue the culprit; had Auntie Nelly known, I was doing them a favour, helping them to avoid all that saturated fat. Probably added years to their lives . . .

I do the same for my family to this day, but they seem strangely lacking in gratitude: 'Get your hands off! I'm trying to let the bird settle! Get him out of the kitchen!' I wouldn't mind, but I'm the Father of the Feast. I'll bet Bob Cratchit got first go at the skin when they grilled the robin, or whatever small bird was on his poor little table, before Old Scrooge stuck his oar in . . .

Talking Turkey, that Grand Cut of a Woman who has insisted on White Meat Only for the past thirty-three years of our married life together, and I, Old Skin and Leg, thought to change the Christmas Menu, a couple of years ago. 'What,' say we, 'about a couple of nice plump pheasants, flavoursome and gamey, in a rich Bordelaise?' The children (sorry, adults) nearly went mad. 'Pheasants? Whaddya mean, pheasants? We have to have turkey! We've always had turkey!' We haven't dared mention the merest hint of change since. Extraordinary, isn't it, how conventional, how traditional, our ground-breaking, forward-looking, modern, cutting-edge young people are, when you get right down the Parson's Nose? . . .

I can't have been more than three or four years of age, because my first memories of Christmas involve looking through bars. It must have been a cot. Either that or the Wogan family were incarcerated over the Festive Season by brokers men, long long ago. However, nobody in the family appears to have a criminal record or rolls their own cigarettes, so it must have been a cot. I'll swear I was awakened by a shadowy figure in bed. I lay transfixed, as he reached into my cot with parcels and shapes that glittered even in the gloom. And that's it. I don't remember so much as a 'Ho, Ho, Ho!' after that, not to mind the impatient click of reindeer's hooves on the roof. I'm not sure it happened, unless it was my Auntie May in a red dressing gown . . .

That's the real magic of Christmas: the mythology of Santa Claus. When your last child stops believing in Father Christmas, it changes. Not necessarily for the worse, but Christmas changes. Parents stop pretending, and the older children, who've kept the marvellous deception going for the sake of their younger brothers or sisters, drop the pretence; and something wonderful, and almost holy, melts away like a snowflake ... No more the slice of cake and glass of sherry left on the dining-room table for a hungry, thirsty Santa ... No more shrieks of delight to wake the dead (or still inebriated) parent, as the children discover their presents at five o'clock in the morning ... No more the blood, sweat and tears of trying to put a Wendy House together at two in the morning, with the alcohol lapping against your back teeth ...

One Christmas, in an attempt to recreate my own experience with the Man in Red, we dressed up a friend of mine in the full Santa gear, and at one in the morning, fortified by a flagon or two of the Late-Bottled Vintage, sent him up to the children's room with the presents. He was to sneak in and deposit the goodies, contenting himself with a kindly smile behind his white beard, if one of the children awoke. Unfortunately, the Late-Bottled brought out the thespian in our friend. From the bottom of the stairs, we heard 'Hello children! Ho! Ho! Ho! I've brought your presents! Have you been good? Tha's good – so have I. I expect Father Christmas will be bringing my presen's shortly ... Well, cheerio! Mus' be off – reindeer, you know ...' He stumbled from the room, and fell down the stairs like a ton of bricks. 'How did it go?' I asked. 'Ver' good,' he burbled. 'They sheemed shurprised ... ' They were. 'What was Leslie doing in our bedroom last night?' they piped on Christmas morning. 'He turned on the light, and woke us up. And he was drunk ...'

It's a long time since anyone in the Wogan family believed in Father Christmas, but we still believe in Christmas – a family Christmas. That's what it's about. That's what it's always been about. And long after we've disappeared, like the snowflake, there'll be a slice of cake and a glass of sherry on the dining-room table ...

Sword Play

As far too many numpties are fond of saying on far too many 'Reality' TV shows, it's been a 'journey' and a half for me over the last few years: Her Majesty granting me an Honorary Knighthood, complimented by the Ordinary Knighthood that allows me to call myself 'Sir', and my wife 'Lady'. And before you ask what an itinerant Irishman is doing taking on such high-fallutin' airs, this 'veteran' broadcaster was born in Ireland when the country was still a member of the British Commonwealth. So there . . . Not that anybody outside of hotels and restaurants calls me by my title. I'm still 'Tel', 'Wogan' or 'Oi!' to all who know, love me, or couldn't care less. Only an eejit would insist on being called 'Sir', but I like Michael Caine's take on it: he never opens letters that are addressed to 'Mr' Michael Caine . . .

It was an enormously proud moment for me and mine, when the Queen's deftly wielded Excalibur whistled past my ears for 'services to broadcasting'. My loyal listeners had been worried sick lest I receive a nasty flesh wound. One offered to tape back my ears, lest the cold steel leave a severed lobe to stain the Royal carpet, while another suggested a device, not unlike a miniature stair-lift, to help me off my creaking knees. After the tense moment was shown on BBC TV News, a worried mother queried how the Queen got away with all that sword play, when her subjects' children were not allowed to play conkers anymore, because of Health and Safety rules . . .

I've been fortunate to shake the Royal hand more than once, but a couple of years ago was held a very grand levee at Buck House to honour the great and the good and the many reformed reprobates of the British music industry, the bringer of much glory to Britain, and much more importantly, much gold to her coffers. Everywhere one looked in the gilded, chandeliered halls, a famous face. As we lined up to meet Her Majesty and Prince Philip, I observed what I call the 'Royal Effect': otherwise confident, successful people begin to behave in a highly-strung, twitchy manner. Dame Shirley Bassey narrowly avoids knocking over an occasional table while curtsying to the Monarch; the only one seemingly unaffected is Dame Vera Lynn, but then she's been an unofficial Royal since the last unpleasantness. The Queen and the Prince are all unaffected warmth and charm, eager to put the most fretful at ease . . . as Her Majesty moves away from our little line-up towards another group, Phil Collins of Genesis and stellar solo musical stardom, whistles the five notes from *Close Encounters of the Third Kind*. The Queen turns back, smiling. 'That was nice,' she says, 'what was it?' Collins has turned into a speechless pillar of salt. 'He was trying to get in touch with ET, Ma'am,' I babble. The Queen smiles, in a kindly, forgiving way, as you might do with children who have been rather silly, and moves away. Phil Collins, when speech returns, whimpers, 'Why did I do that? What in hell's name came over me?' I shudder, then nod safely. 'The Royal Effect,' I reply, and go in search of a stiff drink . . .

Unsurprisingly for someone who had been born and reared there, it was a rainy day in the historic city of Limerick, Ireland, on the day when the youthful Mayor, Joe Leddin and the City Council did me the great honour of conferring on me the freedom of my native city. My flight from London was delayed by a couple of hours, but in that extraordinary, graceful way that the Irish have of dismissing time as an irrelevance, nobody seemed to mind. All my old school friends turned up, and I can now drive a herd of sheep or cattle over Sarsfield Bridge and up and down O'Connell Street as the mood takes me. I'm very proud to be of Limerick, a city and county obsessed with sport. There's a marvellous bronze on the main thoroughfare, O'Connell Street, of rugby players. Elsewhere in Ireland, as it is in Britain, Rugby Union is a middle-class sport, like tennis, badminton, hockey. In my town it's classless. Dockers, cement-factory workers, labourers, solicitors, accountants, doctors all play in the same teams. It's what makes Limerick pre-eminent in Ireland's game. The captain of the British and Irish Lions, Paul O'-Connell, is a Limerick man. It's the very heartland of Munster and Irish Rugby, home to one of the game's greatest arenas, Thomond Park. I played rugby there, and one of my old school-mates recalled the occasion to the audience at my conferring:

'Wogan was a prop, but found himself in the full-back position, as the opposing centre broke through and bore down on one try-line. Only Wogan stood between him and the line. Wogan's alternatives were simple: he could crash-tackle the charging brute, or stand aside and let him score. Wogan stood aside . . . It is said that even as the fellow raced by to touch-down, Wogan whispered to him: "And good luck with the conversion . . ." Was it Dr Johnson who said that the Irish never speak well of each other?'

The Racing-Snake Profile:
Food

Holy Grub

An observant listener has spotted the current vogue for seeing likenesses of the famous in food. Mother Teresa has been seen in a biscuit, and various icons have turned up in everything from rice puddings to a bar of soap. Only last week, someone saw the image of their dead dog in a loaf of bread. As my listener dished up the Sunday roast a week ago, she was astonished to see an uncanny resemblance to myself in a Yorkshire Pudding. I've got first refusal, otherwise it goes on eBay.

Food Glorious Food

First it was DIY. Then came gardening. Then holiday homes in the sun. These days, it's food. There's even more of it about than there was when I wrote the stuff below. Gordon Ramsay had hardly even begun to f and blind, Marco Pierre White and Raymond Blanc were holding themselves aloof from the common herd of Ainslies and Jamies. The only time you ever heard from John Burton-Race was when you went to his restaurant, and listened to the screams of the dead and dying in the kitchen. Now, you can't throw a stone in a country road without hitting a chef . . . Gordon expands and contracts his own restaurant empire on a daily basis, while causing others to close down with good advice. Marco Pierre does his gifted impression of Frankenstein's monster and Raymond's English, I swear, has just got worse over the years . . .

But those are the new kids on the block: *MasterChef*, or as my gang know it, 'MasterShout', brings on amateur cooks, and promises that the show 'will change their lives!' Phrases such as 'a plate of food', 'Bursting with Flavour!' and the immortal 'Cooking Doesn't Get Any Tougher Than This!' from the bellowing John (the chef) and Greg (the green grocer) have gone into folklore. The sad fact that after six series, nobody's life has been changed, is neither here nor there. Then there's the *Great British Menu*, in which Britain's 'best chefs' are pitted against one another on a regional basis, each competition dragged out interminably over five days, while Jennie Bond desperately tries to instil an abrasive spirit of rivalry between the chefs. And fails.

That's not the worst of it. These programmes, in a desperate attempt to add what they consider to be 'colour' to the proceedings, have the unfortunate cooks out in all weathers rustling up grub for soldiers, hungry construction workers, and work canteens. The very jobs that these would-be chefs wouldn't touch with a ten-foot skillet. Best of all, and by far the most entertaining cookery show, is *Come Dine With Me*, where people who can't cook entertain others in the same boat, to dinner. It's a cookery car-crash, but there are no false promises, and you get exactly what it says on the tin . . . Which is more than you can say about 'Chemical Ali', or as we know him, Heston Blumenthal, 'World's Number One Chef'. With him nothing is at it seems – beetroot tastes of orange, porridge of snail. In the Middle Ages, he'd have been done to a turn as a witch . . .

Guess Who's Coming to Dinner?

Now, hard as it may be for you to believe, I am a man who likes his food. 'But,' I hear you cry, 'this cannot be! This six-pack stomach, the racing-snake figure! Where is he putting it all?' Ah, it's probably because I'm highly-strung. Nervous tension, you know, burning off the calories . . . My thoughts are never that far from the trough, despite the best efforts of my sainted mother, Ireland's Worst Cook (mind you, I say that without knowing what others were suffering. When I was a lad, Ireland was a gastronomic desert . . .). I've always loved the old nosebag. People who 'eat to live' are a mystery to me. The late (or so it is thought) Lord Lucan, ate 'Lamb Cutlets Reform' every day of his life at his club. I know a man who has eaten nothing but sausage and mash for lunch for the last thirty years. For these people, food is no fun. It's fuel. What do they do of an evening? The high spot of my day, the hour around which my world revolves, is sitting down to dinner with my wife. And lovely as she is, I will admit freely that her cooking has a lot to do with it. But, if you don't care what or when you eat, what is there to look forward to? The crossword? Your computer? The Scouts? Don't even mention the telly. What is there worth looking at, when Alan Titchmarsh and Carol Vorderman are not on?

Food brings people together. It's the most pleasurable of social activities – alright, if you'd rather be down the pub with your mates, dancing around your handbag at a rave, fine. Just don't come to me for a reference . . . Friends are at their best when eating together, it's food that cements families. It's why the Friday family dinner is sacrosanct among most of my Jewish friends. Over a meal is when families meet, discuss, argue and behave like a family. Helen and my great joy is when our young people join the old folks at home at the weekends, for lunch or dinner. All high days and holidays, birthdays, anniversaries, in my family, are celebrated over meals.

Even the Ewings of blessed *Dallas* memory, came together over food. Breakfast was when you found them at their best. Tables groaning under plates of eggs, bacon, waffles, grits, flapjacks and maple syrup. Nothing ever got eaten, because JR would enter, sip on orange juice, deliver himself of some appalling aside to torpedo everybody's hopes and dreams, and that was that. Still, breakfast brought the family together. Perhaps if the Ewings had ever got together over dinner, rather than a desultory cocktail in the Southfork lounge, it might have been a different story. Talking of dysfunctional families, *Eastenders* is alive with them. And why? Ask yourself, have you ever, over the last twenty-four years of its existence, seen any family on Albert Square enjoy a meal together? Have you ever seen any character enjoy his or her food? It's all down to the Queen Vic for a pint and a pork scratching, or the caff for a nice cuppa tea and a fry up. And how has Pat got that size? I've never seen her eat a thing. Someone should tell her; life is not all earrings . . .

The only time food turns to ashes in my mouth is when I have to sing for my supper. And this is the time of the year when all good fellows, clubs, companies and conglomerates get together for the annual dinner and dance, prize-giving, charity-auction and ball. If I really wanted to, I could spend the next couple of months in a dinner-jacket. Don't think I'm playing the old curmudgeon – these 'dos' are enormous fun. Just so long as you don't have to be the one to make the after-dinner speech. It's a separate art, after-dinner speaking. Some of our brightest comedians won't touch it. It's entirely different from a stand-up comic act. I well remember, as President of the Lords Taverners, a great charitable club, learning the hard way that if there was a cleric, a lawyer, a teacher, or the governor of a jail on the list of speakers, always to speak first, because they always had a humdinger to deliver. I don't know if you know of a Rev. Canon Roger Royle? Oh, you do. Well, take my tip. Never, ever, follow him as an after-dinner speaker. He does a routine to 'The Stripper'. It can ruin your life, not to mention your dinner . . .

Food! Glorious Food!

We're a 'foodie' family. By that, I don't mean that Wogan Towers is like those old Hollywood-Elizabethan movies, with a haunch of venison continually on the go over the kitchen fire, a roast suckling-pig with an apple in its mouth, being rushed to the table by a comely serving-wench; the same table that is already groaning with undersides of beef, loins of lamb, farls of wheaten bread, while I, the father of the feast, in the Charles Laughton/Henry the Eighth role, am attacking an enormous chicken, pausing only to hurl the half-eaten drumsticks over my shoulder with a hearty belch, followed by raucous laughter, and the downing of a small bucket of wine . . . Alright, it's not a million miles from the reality of meals at our house, particularly when the family, with prospective out-laws, come swarming down at the weekend baying for food . . .

We like our food, we Wogans. I blame Herself. I cannot blame my mother, the sainted Rosie, because as has already been established both here and between the pages of my autobiography, *Is It Me?* (will you please stop writing to tell me how you picked it up at a boot-sale, and beat the man down to 50p?) dear Rose Wogan was a desperate cook. It was my Auntie May who said that my mother couldn't boil water, although May was a fine one to talk, leaving the cooking to the Granny or Auntie Nelly all her life. Brought up with love, but in a regime of lumpy potatoes, and meat like shoe-leather, I should by all that any psychologist could tell you, have grown up into a pariah, one of those untouchables that proudly proclaim: 'Oh, don't mind me – I'm not interested in food – I don't live to eat, I eat to live!' as if somebody should strike a medal for them . . . there's nothing wrong with loving food. One of these days, when the public has had enough of my ramblings on the radio and television, I will deliver myself of a small, but forceful booklet, on the glories of food and the glories of those who glory in it. I will give short shrift to those who shy from the joys of the table, making many a pungent point about their questionable ability to enjoy *anything*, if they don't enjoy food . . .

As I say, I blame Herself. This fortunate woman (winner of the coveted title, 'Luckiest Woman in Ireland', on the day she married me) is a sorceress with a skillet; the Queen of the cooking-pot. Always a precocious talent, Helen Wogan has, under my tutelage and unstinting encouragement, become a cook to cause Gordon Ramsay to quiver, Ainsley Harriott to pale, and the Roux Brothers to huddle nervously together. And because of this Maîtresse de Cuisine, all the family not only love their food – they can cook it. Mark Wogan was an Executive Chef, Alan and Katherine are more than talented at the stove, range and grill. I, myself, pour a half-decent glass of wine. Too many cooks, you know . . .

As a matter of fact, there are too many cooks all over the television, like a cheap suit. 'Where do they all come from?' asks Ms Dinah Jutton of Stroud, a discerning reader. She takes particular exception to the New Exoticism: coriander, lemon grass, soy, stem ginger, cumin, basil, balsamic. Her old granny never heard of such stuff, no more than my own. Nor the sun-dried tomatoes. Dinah's old granny was a demon with the boiled beef and carrots with onions. The kind of stuff that stuck to your ribs, and forged an Empire. And 'toast with dripping,' says Dinah. 'I'm drooling at the thought' . . . Now, while good plain cooking is something at which my pert little nose will never be turned up, let me be honest with you Dinah, I'm not averse to the old haute cuisine. The man who said that his idea of Heaven was 'eating foie-gras to the sound of trumpets', was leaning against an open door with me. It's just that, like anything else, it can go too far. Recently, I read a review of, supposedly, the best restaurant in Europe, 'El Bulli' in Girona, Spain. Among Señor Chef's esoteric delights, according to the writer, who was on cloud seven: 'a rose petal in tempura . . . a quail's egg in a caramel sweet . . . parmesan ice cream . . . Rice Krispies that tasted of paella . . . frozen foie gras . . . spaghetti made of soup . . .' And so on, and on . . .

Everybody's trying too hard, and it's putting some foodies, like myself, off. Over the last few years, I've been disturbed by my inability to pack it away as in days of yore. I mind well the Christmases that my children would step gingerly over me, as I lay prostrate on the carpet, after another helping of turkey. Now I am content with a couple of slices of breast, some dark meat, a leg and plenty of moist stuffing. This Christmas, I fell asleep in a chair, rather than on the floor. It's a backward step, and I know who to blame. We've been over-fooded, over-reciped, over restaurant-reviewed. You can't pick up a magazine or a newspaper, without being instructed how to fluff up a roast potato. For too long, Ainsley, Jamie, Gordon and the rest of the demented kitchen brigade, have been clogging up our television screens. And our arteries, if it comes to that . . . . Restaurant-reviewing, once the lonely province of failed gardening correspondents, has taken on the trappings of a minor religion. People actually write to Michael Winner, as if he knew anything about food, when all he claims to know about restaurants is how to get a table. (He waves his hankie and shouts a lot.) The trouble is, on this little island of ours, there is a finite number of restaurants, but an endless number of critics. The results can be bizarre: rave reviews for places that, reading between the lines, nobody sane would be caught dead in: 'Jim and Jonty run this little gem like their own home (which it is!). The kitchen is in full view, and we've scarcely time to sit down on the simple chairs at the gingham-clothed table, before Jonty dishes up two small plates of glazed red cabbage with caraway and figs. Delightful! We can hardly wait for the home-boiled ham hock cooking merrily on the stove . . .' Or, even worse: 'My main course was braised neck of lamb with tomato, flageolet and basil (£17.50).' £17.50 for a cheap old cut of lamb, with a few veggies! And for pudding 'Roasted pink-champagne rhubarb with orange and gin sorbet' . . . What? Your lips would be permanently puckered after a spoonful . . .

All I'm asking is that we get food back on the rails. I'm not averse to a recipe for 'caramel banana tarte tatin', although I can envisage it ending in tears. Why gild a lily? A good old appley, sticky, lovely bramley tarte tatin will do me. As for a recipe for 'smoked eel with potato cakes, beetroot relish and horseradish', who in the name of all that's Holy and Gastronomie Larousse is going to waste their time rustling that up? Who would eat it anyway? And you can keep your 'mountain lentils' as well . . .

Sorry, lads, but that's not cooking, it's a circus act. Fatally, some-one has told the chef that he's 'an artist'. Hopefully, somewhere along the line someone will give him a good slap, and remind him that he's a cook, and all that the rest of us are after is, as they sang in *Oliver* – 'Food, Glorious Food . . .'

More Pavlova, Anyone?

Long before your time, of course, but every so often an old geezer like myself can scarce forbear to look back over those balmy days of courtship and marriage in the sixties and seventies. The naivete and innocence of those early tête-à-têtes and dinner parties; that sparkling Portuguese rosé, and the Chianti in the basket-weave bottles, so useful later on as decorative candle-holders ... I remember being introduced to sparkling red burgundy by a more sophisticated friend; I thought it the very acme of fine drinking. Smoked salmon was the ultimate in fine dining. The first time I ordered it, in Dublin's only chic Italian restaurant at the time, I thought it was disgusting, bearing no resemblance whatsoever to my mother's tasty tinned salmon. I ate it, not wishing to appear an utter eejit up from the country for the day. A friend of mine, on her first modelling assignment in London, on being taken to a swish West End eaterie, in a panic at both the size of the menu and the complete lack of anything on it that she even vaguely recognised, ordered smoked salmon and chips. The memory of it has marked her for life ...

Salmon was a luxury food then, as was chicken. Now, they are virtually staples. We drank Liebfraumilch with our fish, and our fowl, we knew what was what. Luckily, duck was a rarity, and nobody I know had ever heard of guinea-fowl – we would have been totally foxed what to drink with those. Gradually, our tastebuds sharpened, our palates became more refined, we lost our fear of head-waiters, wine lists and menus in French, and even took the bold step of entertaining at home. The seventies were the the great dinner party era: prawn cocktail with a marie rose sauce, steak in a mushroom and red wine ditto, pavlova cake to follow. Talk about soigné ... Dinner parties in Ireland were a risk of course, as indeed, they remain to this day. Only a couple of years ago, Helen and I turned up at the appointed time to a house in the Dublin suburbs, to find ourselves the first guests there. And so we remained, for the next hour. Slowly the other guests trickled in, some of them from as far as two doors away, and within two hours, everyone had assembled. By now, the earlier arrivals were footless with drink, but another couple of rounds were necessary, in case anyone would accuse the host and hostess of running a 'dry old house'. Three hours after we were invited, we sat down to dinner, which of course, by now, was a burnt offering. Not that it made the slightest difference. Irish people don't go to dinner parties to eat; it's the drinking and the talking that matters. At one o'clock in the morning, a guest made his way unsteadily to the door. Nobody joined him, so he sat down again. It was two o'clock before the general company rose as one, and stood at the table, talking and drinking, for another hour. By three o'clock they were in the hall, and by four, the last one had gone out the door. People ask me if I would like to return to live in Ireland; I couldn't stand the pace . . . Mind you, before That Grand Woman and I became Home Counties Softies, and had just moved from Ireland to live here, we invited our new-found English friends to dinner. I was speculatively contemplating a shirt and tie, and Herself was clambering from the bath, when our doorbell rang. Our first guests – right on time. We became Anglicised very quickly in our dinner party habits after that. For me it's one of the glories of British life: people arrive on time. Even better, they leave on time. There's a time to live and a time to die, they say. In my book, it's even more important to know when to go home . . .

Lately, there has been a 'retro' movement on the home-cooking front: a return to the good old prawn cocktail, goulash and chocolate roulade. And the fondue set . . . Anything but the fondue set, pleads a listener of mine. An introductory free gift from a catalogue it was, and she thought a dinner party for her husband's boss and his wife would be just the thing to show it off. A fondue bourguinonne, cubes of steak, rather than predictable old cheese. Unfortunately, only when she fired up the pot, did she learn that white spirit was not the same as methylated. The pot turned black, and so did the entire house, with smoke! Her ever-lasting memory of the evening is of her guests sitting there with streaming eyes, frozen to the marrow due to every window and door in the house having to be opened to disperse the smoke and smell . . . Her fondue set sits in a forgotten corner of the garage now, along with the soda siphon, the trimphone and the exercise bicycle . . .

Barbecues

Even as I write, the smoke rises from another Wogan barbecue, its toxic fumes gently drifting over our neighbours' hedge, asphyxiating animal, bird and plant-life alike, but luckily, not the neighbours. They're indoors, sheltering from the driving rain and freezing wind of another glorious British summer. And before you start with all that, 'it's been lovely up here on the Perthshire coast,' or 'the sun is cracking the stones on the Dawlish Sea Wall,' let me make it abundantly clear that I couldn't be happier for you, but the *only* weather that matters to me is what's happening directly over my head. And for the last three miserable summers, it's been the aforesaid wind and rain in my neck of the woods . . . And down the back of my neck . . . Even when I flee Old Blighty's shores to get away from it, the bad weather follows me. I know it's been wonderful in the Costa del Sol, but I'm sorry, the names Malaga, Marbella, Estepona and Sotogrande cast their own dark shadow. I've been there, seen the gold jewellery, the stiletto heels and the white handbags . . . I spent my honeymoon in Torremolinos thirty-four years ago, but somehow it's lost its elusive charm . . . We used to have a holiday home on the Costa Blanca, but in the end, we couldn't face another five minutes at Alicante airport. I know the sun is guaranteed in more tropical climes, but on the only two occasions the Wogans visited the Caribbean, it rained – and before you say anything, it *was* the high season . . . And anyway, the present Mrs Wogan and I are getting a bit long in the tooth for long-haul flights. Thirteen hours in a plane is about nine hours over our limit. We've promised ourselves a trip to Australia when the dust finally settles on my radio and television career, but it'll have to be kangaroo fashion – a series of short hops.

Australia, of course, is the land of outdoor eating and imbibing. 'Throw another prawn on the barbie!' is the cry from Perth to Canberra, apparently, coupled with the 'tinnies' of cold Fosters or Four X. A roaring fire under a sheet of corrugated iron supported on a few breeze-blocks, and there you go, Bruce and Sheila, a sophisticated evening is off and running. And why wouldn't it be, with the sun hot enough to fry a koala to a crisp? Anybody can have a barbecue in the sunshine, for goodness sake. It takes the sorry inhabitants of these blessed, sceptre'd northern isles to do it in the rain. For Heaven's sake, I've played golf in the snow, swum in a thunderstorm, played tennis in hail stones – you don't think a little wind and rain is going to put me off a barbecue?

It's *man's* work, of course. The average male, faced with the prospect of having to cook something in the kitchen, shies like a polo pony, and ends up with cornflakes, a cheese sandwich, or, at the very outside, a hard-boiled egg. Show him a barbecue, it's a different story; 'Where's my apron? Where are the utensils? This charcoal is damp! Why didn't you buy any firelighters? I'm going to have to throw some petrol over it! Oh God, now one of the legs has fallen off! Well, if you don't want to wait order a pizza! Never, never ask me to do this again, alright! . . .' Not that anybody asked him in the first place. Is it worth it, for a charred snorker, a chicken leg that's burned on the outside and completely undercooked on the inside, a hamburger that has disintegrated into a hundred little bits of charcoal? Why do men think that they can cook outside, when they haven't the smallest idea how to go about it indoors? Doubtless it's something to do with our forebears' discovery of fire, and the first al fresco meal of spatchcocked pterodactyl outside the cave. I'll bet that was burnt to a crisp as well . . .

Yet, with all fathers faffing about, with all the burnt offerings, all the aggravation, admit it: you love it. We *all* love it. Even if, as for the last three summers, we have to eat the results indoors. Food that's cooked outdoors tastes differently, that's all. Not just of burnt firewood with a heavy hint of petrol, either. It tastes *better*, even when it's much, much worse ... And when it works, it's like a breath of the warm south. A barbecue, even in the dingiest backyard, under a rain-soaked umbrella, carries with it the promise of summer; the hope of sunny days – children screaming as they cool off under the spray of a garden hose, Auntie Mary dozing in a deck-chair, stunned by the heat and Pimms; the feeling of well-being, that tomorrow, with all its troubles, is a long way away. A barbecue is as much for the heart and the mind as for the stomach. No matter what it tastes like, it feels good ...

Where the Mangoes, There Go I . . .

As you are aware, my radio listeners look to me for guidance on many aspects of modern life. It is a vale of tears, a 'hard ould station', as my Uncle Charlie put it so succinctly, all those years ago. This modern world is a minefield for the sensitive, for those trying to do the right thing, and conduct themselves at all times in a wholesome manner. The newspapers and magazines are full of 'Advice' columns on how a decent person should comport themselves at social gatherings. There are other 'advice' columns in the popular prints, but these are more along the lines of 'My granny has run off with my transvestite boyfriend', and I will not sully this respectable publication with that kind of low talk. People need help in the vexed matters of mores and ethics, and I'm the very man to give it to them.

Take mangoes for instance. Generations of decent British folk have spurned this delicious, exotic fruit, because they simply don't know how to approach the thing. Hard experience has taught them that sticking a fork in can cover you from head to toe in sticky, yellow goo. Similarly, attacking the succulent beast with a knife can end in disaster for shirt, tie, frock and boots. 'Never eat a mango on a carpet' was one of Mrs Beeton's warnings. Distressed gentlefolk pleaded with me for advice. And, of course, like most good advice, mine is simple, direct and painfully obvious once it has been pointed out. There is, I pontificated, only one way to eat Johnny Mango: naked, while standing in the kitchen sink. You can fling yourself into this fabulous fruit, and let the juice fly where it may. Yes, of course there will be a price to pay, and not just to your scandalised neighbours. A willing helper will be needed to clean the windows and the ceiling, not to mention your good self. It was refreshing to hear how the plain people of Britain took this advice to heart, and I think we can put the few cases of 'indecent exposure' down to an over-zealous constabulary. I retired to my lonely monk's cell, well-satisfied with a job well done.

Picture, if you will then, my astonishment, to read in *The Times*, of a CD issued by an Indian mango farmer, entitled 'How to Eat the King of Fruits'. It offers an array of serving suggestions and recipes for the hitherto mango-less. It boasts that you will learn all you ever wanted to know about Mr Mango, but were afraid to ask. It claims that you don't have to wear protective clothing, or indeed strip down to the buff to enjoy the meaty mango. You simply slice the fruit into halves, score the half-mango in a criss-cross pattern, turn it inside out, and dive in – oh yeah! And what, pray, about the huge stone in the middle. Turn it inside-out? You're havin' a laugh, encha? Turning fruit inside out is a recipe for disaster. The stuff will fly in all directions. We're not surgeons here, ours is a kitchen knife, not a scalpel. If it was a scalpel, we'd have a finger off every time we peeled an apple. This man is talking dangerous nonsense. About the only fruit you could turn inside out with safety is the banana, or possibly rhubarb, but I'm not sure that rhubarb is a fruit . . . .

If the honest Indian mango farmer left it there, we could put it down to sub-continental aberration, or depression brought on by the monsoon, but he goes further. This Mango CD he declares, is for a woman to make mango chutneys, drinks and desserts, and win the love and affection of her in-laws. So that's where you've been going wrong with Mother-in-Law! Quick, a jar of mango chutney, and all that unpleasantness over who paid for the wedding flowers will be forgotten . . .

It's a Wrap

The other morning, before the cocks had even cleared their throats, as is my wont, I reached into the fridge for a shot of friendly bacteria. I've done it for years; its pleasant, sweet smoothness eases me into the day before the hasty cup of coffee and whatever piece of fruit I can find that hasn't gone blue-mouldy overnight. Is it my imagination, or does fruit go off more quickly these days? And if you buy it hard as a rock, expecting it to ripen in a couple of days, how come it never does? I expect it's something to do with our ridiculous desire to eat certain fruits all the year round, whether they're in season or not. Or it may be due to 'global warming', like everything else. A hot summer? Global warming. A wet one? Global warming. Drought? Global warming. Floods? Ditto. A radio listener of mine put forward the interesting idea that the improved standard of 'A' levels demonstrated by Britain's youth, was down to global warming causing the youngsters' brains to expand . . . And while we're touching on the lunatic fringe, and before I get to the main thrust of this polemic, what about the professorial eejit who seriously suggested that before we are wiped out, dinosaur-like, by a passing asteroid, we should send examples of our DNA to the moon. Since we won't be around, to be found by whom, exactly, Professor? Perhaps those aliens who sent us radio signals, 30 million years ago. Some other heavily-subsidised gobdaw in a white coat urged caution on hearing this exciting news: 'Careful!' he said. 'Don't answer back – these beings may be aggressive.' As someone slightly more sane pointed out, it will take the little green swine 30 million years to get our reply, and then another 30 million to do anything about it, so there is no cause for immediate panic . . .

Anyway, there I am, with my package of friendly bacteria. And can I open it? I've been doing this for so long, I don't even try. I know that I'd need the fingernails of Sharon Davies, or a Chinese Empress, to make the necessary incision in the tight plastic wrap. I slice through it with a sharp kitchen knife, in the process cutting also the little container of bacterial goodness, causing it to spill its health-giving colonic charmers all over the kitchen floor. After I've mopped the appalling mess up (how can the contents of one tiny container cover an entire kitchen floor?) and rested for a moment by the sink, while the blood that has rushed to my head subsides, after a brief tussle, I prise another little capsule from the package. Another fruitless struggle, as I try to peel its cover off. No dice. Once more to the knife. I stab the cover to make a hole, causing the ever-friendly bacteria to shoot up my nose, down my chin and on to my Garrick tie, bought yesterday at the Club. I know that I can never use it again. Expensive silk ties are never the same after the launderette . . .

Now, this little plastic bottle of cheery good health is a highly successful product. It sells millions. How many more would it sell if you could get at it? Like those boxes of milk that made the Swedish Rausing family as rich as Croesus. How much richer would they have been, if you could have opened one without covering yourself from head to toe in dairy produce?

I know, I know. I'm leaning against an open door with you, on modern society's greatest curse: packaging. Consider this letter I got the other day from a man driven to the very limits:

> 'I wish to submit the following times for ratification as records for dealing with modern packaging:
>
> *Removing cellophane from audio tape:*
> 5 minutes 10 seconds
>
> *New toothbrush:*
> 4 minutes 25 seconds
>
> *Opening plastic bag in supermarket:*
> 2 minutes 30 seconds

(I'm impressed; after five minutes I normally cry for help from the present Mrs Wogan, who opens the bag in a nano-second.)

> '*Buff-coloured envelope which might contain tax demand:*
> 8½ days . . .'

What about packaging for the next Olympics?

Wrapped Up

Look, no one knows better than me that your busy schedule leaves you little time for pointless reminiscing, but if you will just take a nano-second to cast your keen brain back to a few weeks ago, or is it paragraphs, when I was taking the classic Old Geezer's position on packaging – viz, you can open nothing these days without the use of your teeth, or a sharp instrument. And in the case of tooth-brushes and shaving razors, a chainsaw. As ever, it wasn't the big stuff that got my goat, but a little plastic pot of 'friendly bacteria'. I fulminated on the fiddliness of its little foil lid, and how the people who produce it would add millions to their profits if the public could only get at their product. The 'friendly bacteria' folk were not alone in feeling the lash of my pen; I freely inveighed against the Swedish packaging of milk and if I didn't have a go at the ring-pulls that snap on tins of sardines, I apologise. I must be getting soft . . !

All this might have passed as the idle wind, if the 'friendly bac-teria' giant hadn't got in touch, last week. In the course of an excel-lent letter, they assured me that my complaint was to be taken up at the highest level. They were concerned and as a gesture of good-will, sent me a copy of their latest publication, the fetchingly-titled *Guide to the Fat*, a 'friendly bacteria' T-shirt, and best of all a £5.00 postal order, in order to refund any little plastic pots lost in the struggle to open them. Frankly, I was taken aback. It's entirely to the company's credit that they are alert to their consumers' wants and needs, but a five quid postal order? I could take my family out for a slap-up meal on the proceeds, or lodge the whole thing to my bank account and the delight of my bank manager, but the last few ethical bones in my body tell me I must spend the lot on another load of 'you-know-what'. And somehow, I don't think they'll have fixed the foil-lid problem by then . . . Incidentally, I haven't had a postal order for years, and the £5 one has a fine, charming portrait of Her Majesty, the Queen. Perhaps I'll keep it for my descendants – it would probably fetch a pretty penny on the *Antiques Roadshow* 2505 . . .

Out to Lunch

Amid all the furore over school dinners, unfavourable comparisons were freely drawn with the food enjoyed by pupils of our European neighbours: Italy, Spain and most notably, France. A recent letter from an Anglo-French woman living across the Channel, whose children had been educated there, blew that one out of the water. First of all, like 'em or not, a petit garçon or petite fille must have their school dinners, because lunch-boxes from home are forbidden. Don't ask why; the French have a rule for everything. Not only that – according to this correspondent, school food in France is every bit as filthy as it is here. Tinned vegetables, inedible meat, lumpy potatoes and grey fish. But, I hear you cry, the little ones surely go home to cuisine prepared by maman in the best traditions of her maman, and her maman before her. Another myth I'm afraid. Having been dragged around many a supermarket by the present Mrs Wogan, my keen observation of the average French woman's shopping basket shows just as many convenience foods as the maligned British housewife's trolley. Furthermore, the statistics bear me out. Convenience foods are the popular choice not only in France, but Italy and Spain, as well. Are we surprised, shamed, self-reproached? Of course not. Life has changed, with many housewives and mothers working; some because they want to, others because they need to.

Nobody can argue with Jamie Oliver's campaign to improve school dinners, although there have been some outrageous claims made for the superiority of a diet of vegetables, fruit and a lamb chop over chips and turkey twizzlers. Certainly, the former lacks the fat of the latter dish, but there's just as much protein in a twizzler as there is in a chop, and there's more vitamin C in chips than there is in an apple. Fresh fish is better for anybody than a hamburger, but whether the change of diet will bring a marked improvement to a child's brain power or behaviour is, at present mere conjecture. Anyway, as a headmaster tersely remarked, children only have approximately 120 dinners a year at school. The improvement in the eating habits of our children has to come from home. Meals just like dear old Mother used to make. All well and good, if your mother can cook. As I've admitted here more than once, mine couldn't. She could just about do a sandwich, which is what I took with me to school every day of my scholastic career. Because she knew that hopeless-and-all might be her efforts with the skillet, she was three-rosette Michelin standard compared to the heinous efforts of school kitchens, I never had to endure the depths of a school dinner in my life, cosseted as I was by corned beef, ham and sliced pan.

I note with envy the sainted Jamie Oliver's recipes for 'pukka packed lunches', although it does seem strange that he should be advocating children's lunch-boxes, while at the same time doing ditto for school dinners . . . Jamie's kinda lunch-box has soup, in a thermos flask, half a papaya with a slice of lime, ciabatta with mozzarella and prosciutto, or sun-dried tomato bread. There's salad, with feta cheese or parmesan, some cherry tomatoes and mixed leaves. He suggests a dressing of lemon juice and olive oil, wrapped in a little cling-film. It's at this point that you are convinced that the dear boy is not sharing the same planet as the rest of us. For me, he left sanity behind at the mozzarella and prosciutto stage. Is this lunacy supposed to be a practical suggestion for a harassed housewife trying to drag her children out of bed, and off to school in the morning? And its cloud-cuckoo land for you, Jamie, if you think any child is going to bring this kind of stuff into school, let alone eat it. Can you imagine the kind of jeering and cat-calling a poor little unfortunate would get, opening their little separate bag of salad dressing? And I have spared you the worst, leaving you with the salutary picture of some frazzled mother trying to squeeze a prawn sandwich with basil mayonnaise and cress into her protesting youngster's lunch-box.

Of course, Jamie O is advocating good food from the best possible motives, and he is to be applauded for his splendid campaigning, but anybody who has reared children knows that you've got to be realistic about what the little darlings will eat. And if you've got a brave little soldier, who will eat 'rosemary and raisin' bread with cheese for lunch, go to the top of the class.

Not Everybody's Into Coulis and Jus

I know somebody who, when he orders fish and chips, only eats the batter. And the chips of course. He throws away the fish, because he can't stand the smell of it. He's tried smoked salmon, but didn't think it tasted of anything, and sprinkled it with vinegar to try to give it a bit of flavour. He wouldn't thank you for a prawn or a lobster, and he goes green at the very thought of an oyster. The finest Beluga caviar provokes only derision: 'Fish eggs? You eat fish eggs?'

If it was only fish it wouldn't be so bad. The very idea of liver and kidneys are enough to turn this fine man's stomach, and I haven't had the heart to tell him that there are such things as sweetbreads. He simply wouldn't believe it if I broke it to him about pig's trotters, or calves' brains, frog's legs, or snails. And it's worse, much worse than that: he only eats fried eggs. Poached, scrambled or coddled would only make him throw up. Offer him a hard-boiled seagull's, or quail's egg, and you're likely to get it back in the eye.

This fellow will even turn his retroussé nose up at lamb and pork. He thinks that I'm having him on when I speak of a delicious duck, or a finely-roasted pheasant. I need hardly tell you that pigeon, partridge, grouse and guinea-hen are simply beyond the pale. If he had his way, even chicken would be a protected species . . .

Even from this distance, I hear your strident cries: 'Well, what does he eat? Is he a vegetarian? A vegan? As mad as a box of biscuits?' No, friends, none of the above. He eats fried egg and chips. He eats pie and mash and liquor, although he only eats the crust on the pie. He eats curries. I tell a lie, he eats 'meat' curry. That's all he ever orders in a curry house: Meat Curry . . . I'm sure it's because he can't bring himself to say 'chicken', 'lamb' or 'pork'. It's not that he's squeamish, nor an anthropomorphic animal lover – he often speaks glowingly of the rabbit stew his mother used to make. He'll eat a hamburger, but he doesn't want any 'muck' on it, like cheese, pickle, mustard or ketchup. He loves cakes and sweets. He can't bear the taste of wine, beer or spirits. He doesn't drink hot drinks, like tea or coffee, and he's never tasted soup, and never will: 'What? Liquid food? You're havin' a laugh . . .'

You think I'm making this man up, but you're wrong. His son has the same eating, or non-eating habits as himself. The son may, just possibly, be worse. All I've ever seen him eat is a cheese sandwich. Plenty of butter, no mustard. The man's father has eaten the exact same meal for lunch all his life: sausage and mash . . . they'll all eat a fry-up for breakfast, but they'll leave the fried slice, if it's too greasy . . . These good people are the most fastidious eaters you've ever met; half the time they leave most of their food on their plates because of a too-runny egg, a flaw in a chip, too much fat on the meat. They never complain, nor ask for their money back – they just pay, and leave. They're intimidated in restaurants, embarrassed even in cafés. In eating houses they're like children, because that's what they are, in terms of taste, and food. Their palates have never progressed beyond the simple flavours of childhood. Cakes and soft drinks, chips and soft food, preferably brown in colour . . . and don't you dare knock it, because there are millions like them . . .

We're up to our shoulder-pads in cookery these days: every second television programme, every magazine, with pages and pages of esoteric culinary chicanery in glorious colour. And my friend, his family and millions like them, couldn't give a rattling damn. They'll watch Jamie and Ainsley, but only for their amusing eccentricity. 'Spatchcock Quail with Lemon Tahine Sauce'? Forget it. 'Sea Scallops in Radicchio and Pancetta'? Do me a favour. It's curries and Chinese, ready-meals and pizza to go. That's what they like, and you can hold the coulis and the jus. Pass the gravy . . .

Return of the Racing Snake

Now, stop me if I've mentioned this before – go on, try – but in the early summer, the world's greatest shopper and I were guests of the Sainted Sir Don and the Blessed Ron on a wonderful cruise that took us from Rome to Sorrento, from Sicily to Dubrovnik, from Venice to Corfu. I returned to Blighty's shores several pounds heavier, but bronzed and fresh looking. Within a day of my return, I was in hospital, whey-faced and wan, the victim of a pretty agonising condition of the lower intestine, known as diverticulitis. It wasn't anything I'd eaten or drunk, as I imbibed and munched my way around the Med and Adriatic. The old gut had decided to twist itself into a knot, and only some pretty fierce antibiotics could persuade it to straighten itself out. This, in turn, meant that our Hero was pretty confined in the matter of food and drink. Soup and jelly, that was the height of it. Not that I mind soup, and I'm crazy about jelly. I hadn't had it for years, and when the nurse brought me my first quivering mound, I realised how much I'd missed it. It brought me back to my youth: Knickerbocker Glories in Cafollas Ice Cream Parlour, Dublin. Fruit, cream, ice-cream, hundreds and thousands, and right there in the middle of the tall glass, a lump of strawberry jelly. You kept it in your mouth until it dissolved, then swished it around behind your teeth, until reluctantly releasing it down the 'Little Red Lane' – which, if you want to know, is what my mother used to call my throat when trying to force-feed me stuff I didn't want to eat, which included nearly everything, except jelly . . .

Anyway, soup and jelly, that was me for three or four days. All the weight I put on during the cruise fell away, and more besides. Then not a drop of alcoholic beverage passed my lips for three weeks. It wasn't easy, but as the old *avoirdupois* diminished perceptibly, the resolve stiffened. Trousers slipped on more easily, jackets seemed less form-fitting. I hadn't turned into a racing-snake in a couple of weeks, but others noticed the difference: 'There's nothing of you!' . . . 'You'll want to start eating a bit more, you're fading away!' Clumsy sarcasm of course, but better than: 'Ah! You're looking very well. I thought you were a bit bloated the last time I saw you . . !' Why do some people do that? Don't they realise the damage it can do to the more sensitive soul? You walk away wondering what the hell you must have looked like a couple of weeks ago, and why nobody told you that were a dead ringer for Oliver Hardy . . .

I'm back on the booze now, and eating normally. That's probably a bit more than you, with your bird-like appetite, but as for the demon drink, I never touch beer, rarely spirits, and isn't red wine supposed to be good for you? And yet, and yet, it's creeping back on . . . I can feel it, I can see it . . . Is there anything worse than the insidious regaining of weight? Lower your guard for a nano-second – a slice of toast here, a biscuit there, an irresistible roast potato – and blow me down, that half a stone that you sweated blood and tears and sacrificed the best months of your life to lose, is back again, bringing a couple of extra pounds with it. The collars tighten, the belts have to be let out, the jackets left unbuttoned again. It breaks your heart. I've seen men lose three stone in weight, following a regimen that would have intimidated Sparta. For three months they glory in their new-found svelteness, then three months later, it's back to square, sorry, round one. I've done it myself – I've got the pictures and the video tapes to prove it . . .

Anybody can lose weight, but how do you keep the flab at bay? Exercise? Come on, is there anything more mind-blowingly boring? Have you been to a gym? Why do they do it? How do they do it, without falling into manic depression? Jogging? Running? Just take a look at the faces of the people doing it. Through the summer I tried to swim thirty lengths a day. It may have helped, but I hated the tedium of it. Up and down the pool, mindlessly, like a great goldfish . . .

Sensible eating, that's the answer, they'll tell you. But that's as boring as a running-machine, or swimming until your brain decays. Face it, there is no answer. Who wants to look like Anna Wintour or Jane Fonda anyway? You and I, we weren't born to skin and bone. My doctor has a lovely word for us: bonny. We're 'bonny', you and me. It suits us . . .

Staying Alive:
Ageing Gracefully

Call Me Meldrew

Look, I know that it's probably me, but I'm finding my declining years a bit of a disappointment. Not the old standbys of creaking joints, increasing wrinkles, widening girth or boy scouts offering to help me across the road. Nor the passing disinterest of pretty girls, for whom a man's eye never fades. I passed that particular signpost of decrepitude a good fifteen years ago, when, at a dinner party in Ireland, a beautiful young woman caught my eye. She smiled winningly, and crossed the crowded room to sit beside me. 'Ah,' said a small voice inside my head. 'Good man. You never lost it!' 'Hello Mr Wogan,' said the lovely. 'You knew my mother didn't you?' I don't go back to Ireland much, now days. Too many elderly women, telling me about their grandchildren . . . But it's not that that has driven me disenchanted with time's winged arrow. Nor is it finding myself halfway up the stairs with no idea why I'm going, or what I'm going to do when I get there.

It's just that I was expecting something more from the advancing years: an increase in wisdom; a gentle, all-encompassing tolerance of the world around me; an understanding, at last, of the human condition. Instead I find myself unconvinced and unsure of all the things of which I was absolutely certain when I was thirty. I catch myself agreeing with the most bilious newspaper columnists; and at least part of every day is given over to foaming at the mouth at new Labour, new comedy, new anything. That's when I'm not spewing invective at the television set. There used to be an appalling old curmudgeon of a journalist named Sir John Junor, the worst of his breed, now gone to his eternal reward, I'm sure browning nicely.

Not only am I beginning to sound like him, I'm beginning to *look* like him, in the dark with the light behind me . . .

The passing years ought to bring a mellow kindliness, a viewing of the parade with a warm and gentle eye. However, I find in myself no urge to pat noisy, badly behaved children on the head and send them on their way with an encouraging word. A clip round the ear and a kick in the pants seem to come more naturally. And, of course, I don't believe it when my wife takes me aside to tell me how noisy my own children were at that age . . . Don't you find that everything gets on your nerves these days? Michael Buerk reading the news in a pink tie and a yellow pocket-handkerchief, for Heaven's sake. Those awful people on breakfast television. Anybody commentating on sport, apart from Peter Alliss, Alex Hay and Brendan Foster.

One of life's little bugbears, at least as far as this keen observer of the human condition is concerned, is the phrase 'Research shows'. Scarcely a day goes by without some team of over-funded eejits from some university that ought to have stayed a polytechnic, producing a report of stunning banality on some obscure subject. Some time ago, 'Research showed' that 'fat' was bad. It was smartly followed by a report that 'thin' wasn't so good either, in fact, people were dying of it . . . Research warned us against too much protein, and since then, the late Professor Atkins told us to stuff ourselves with it, if we wanted to lose weight. 'Forget the carbohydrate!' warned the good Professor, which, in turn, flew in the face of all previous advice to athletes and sportsmen to load themselves full of potatoes and pasta at every opportunity. Salt, research informed, was bad for us. People stopped eating it, and not long afterwards, started falling over in the street. Incidentally, the keen-eyed will observe that the aforementioned Professor Atkins, whose sole object in life was to keep us all slim, fit and everlasting, is no longer with us. Nothing to do with his diet, he fell down the stairs, or some other unfortunate accident. It proves something. The mortuaries are full of people pronounced fit as a flea at their annual check-up, who walk in sprightly fashion out of the doctor's door, and under a number 19 bus.

If all the pointless, misleading 'research' we've had to endure over the past years was laid end to end, it would girdle the earth several times over, and still not amount to a row of beans. What about all the stuff we've had for aeons from 'Research scientists' about how we should be gobbling up doses of vitamin C, to combat colds and flu. Now the same fellows in white coats are telling us to watch it with the vitamins, lest we do ourselves mischief. Who told us to swallow them in the first place? And those breakfast cereals, with their kindly pet medical man, who assured us that fibre and roughage was the way to regularity, bright eyes, healthy teeth and strong bones. Failing to mention that the wheaty bangs were full to bursting point with sugar, salt and the odd e-number. Recently, research that must have cost millions, and taken years, showed that those who did not eat a full breakfast were knocking 1.5 years off their lives. Further costly and time-consuming research showed that those who failed to take regular exercise were decreasing their life span by three years. As a shrewd Radio 2 listener pointed out, the solution was there before our very eyes: don't bother with the exercise, and eat two full breakfasts a day . . .

The research is getting us down. One hundred and fifty years ago, there was little or no hay fever in this beloved isle. People got colds, runny noses and wheezy chests; but there were no researchers to tell them they had hay fever. Now the country's overrun with it, according to the papers, quoting researchers. It *could* have been my usual summer cold, but you know the way it is – you don't want to be left out of the swing of things. I bet Liz Hurley gets hay fever. And Elton John and David Furnish. Why? Why are we getting more of the things our grannies and granddads never got a whiff of? Don't blame pollution, there was almost as much of it around in Victorian times, with all the coal-burning going on. And anyway, pollution doesn't bring on stress, and research already shows that every dog and divil in the country is suffering from that.

Doctors are stressed, soldiers are stressed, mothers are stressed, children are stressed. Gordon Brown looks stressed, but you can understand that. I thought life was supposed to be easier in this bright new century. Hasn't everybody, apart from the residents of Albert Square, got a washing machine and spin drier? The pubs, restaurants and supermarkets are heaving with drinkers, scoffers and shoppers. The entire nation flies for at least two weeks every year to a sunnier clime, and the Rich List just gets bigger every year with self-made men and women. And are we contented, happy? Ask a researcher. He'll tell you; the entire country is a-quiver with stress. Where's it all going to end? I'll tell you; when they put away the clipboards, stop asking silly questions, and concentrate on the really important things in life, like, what's the best way to play out of that bunker on the 9th?

New Tricks for the Old Dog

Following the bracing news that old Dickadumdum Des O'Connor was looking forward to the prospect of becoming a father again at the overripe age of seventy-two, I received the following letter, which shrieked volumes not only for the writer but for every male in the country over forty:

'Oi! Tel! Have a word with your mate Des. He's not being exactly fair to the rest of us blokes. It's not so much the bed-room Olympics I'm worried about either. Ever since her indoors read that the blasted 'Connor goes power-walking forty-five minutes every day, washes his hair twice a day, and lives on one meal a day, my life has been hell. She's bought me a new pair of trainers, an extra bottle of shampoo, and yesterday, all I had put in front of me on the table was one lightly boiled egg. It's all very well for Des. He gets to be rampant at seventy-two, and sit next to the beautiful Melanie Sykes. All I get is sore feet, falling hair, and an empty stomach. And the missus now looking at me in the way her mother used to look at Rudolph Valentino . . .

Have a word, Tel. Ask Des to slow down, and act my age.

Mark (Aged 42)'

It's not easy being a man, these days. And blokes like Des O'Connor, who've never outgrown puberty, don't make it any easier. Where does he get the energy anyway? He's skin and bone on one meal a day, and don't tell me he's capable of anything, after forty-five minutes of power-walking. It's the kind of behaviour that has better, younger men, lying back on their pillows, sipping thin broth through a straw. What's the matter with him, is he auditioning for the SAS? The plain people of Britain look to people like Des O'Connor for guidance and leadership, and this is how he repays them; setting impossible standards for old geezers, who were looking forward to a gently paced retirement, with nothing more exerting than an easy stroll to the pub of an evening. Now they're expected to be fit, agile sex-gods with twinkling eyes, a roguish smile, impeccable hair and a dodgy tan. And their womenfolk, happy enough with their lot until now, looking at them with disappointed eyes, tinged with disdain . . .

Not long ago, in my capacity as counsellor to the nation, I drew attention to the sad fact that many long-established messages were being washed up on the rocks from newly-retired husbands following their wives around supermarkets, questioning their purchases: 'Why are you buying that, dear?' . . . 'Do we really need that much kitchen-towel?' . . . 'There's a much cheaper brand one here, dear . . .' Retirement has to be handled gently, if the bond is to survive. Initially, husband and wife must tiptoe around each other, as if on egg-shells, until territorial issues are resolved. Bumping into each other at every turn will test the sturdiest relationship. Now, as if getting older wasn't tough enough, O'Connor shoves his oar in. Next thing you know, we'll be following the old woman around Ann Summers: 'No, not that thong, dear. There's one over here in crushed velvet' . . . 'Do we really need another sex-aid?' . . . 'That's much too big dear, we'll never get it through the door . . .'

As the old World War II slogan put it so forcefully, 'Loose Talk Costs Lives'. It would come as no surprise to me at all if, since Des's triumphant blethering, there was a marked increase among the male population of a certain age of pulled muscles, back strain, chest pain and blood pressure. Not to mention starvation and twisted ankles. People in the public eye need to put a guard on their tongues in the matters of sex and diet. All over the country there are once happy, settled, contented men, attempting to 'DO A DES'. And lots of women laying back and thinking of England, for the first time in years . . .

It's not the sex, 'the hurly-burly of the chaise-longue' as Mrs Patrick Campbell so efficaciously put it, as far as that's concerned, it's a free country, as long as you don't frighten the horses. It's the ONE-MEAL-A-DAY nonsense. I had to burn every newspaper and magazine in the house, in case the present Mrs Wogan caught sight of it.

The Eyes Have It

Recently, I went to the optician to have the Wogan eyeballs given the once-over. After exhaustive tests on various machines, and the reading of small print from varying distances, the optician seemed well-pleased: 'You know,' she said, 'you have the eyes of a twenty-year-old.' I was flattered but puzzled. 'How do you reconcile that with my sixty-year-old eyesight?' I enquired, a tad petulantly. She smiled enigmatically, reminding me of the dentist who consoled his patient with the words: 'Your teeth are fine, but your gums are going to have to come out . . .' Mind you, the concept is not *that* irreconcilable; most of us with bodies in the sixties, have minds in the twenties. Indeed, there appears to be evidence that the more advanced we get, the more our minds go into reverse . . .

My own loss of youthful, hawk-like 20/20 vision followed the classic pattern: somewhere in my forties, my arms suddenly were not long enough to hold books and newspapers far enough away for me to read them. Telephone directories needed a magnifying glass, and a well-struck golf ball literally disappeared out of sight. For a while, I deceived myself into thinking I was hitting the ball thirty yards further. That's an early symptom of loss of binocular vision: self-deception. I know people who continue this foolishness long after everything has become a blur. And, with the greatest respect, and nary a hint of male chauvinism, most of them are ladies. There are good women of my acquaintance who haven't been able to read a restaurant menu properly for years, but who will haughtily disclaim their need for visual aids. All vanity is ultimately foolish, but this particular strain borders on the insane. Playing golf with these fine ladies is an even greater strain; they've no idea where they've hit the ball, and much of the day is spent on fruitless searching. Perhaps they perceive that glasses, or specs, are ageing, and they may be right, but recent sightings of Nicole Kidman in spectacles give the lie to that. Indeed Nicole's plucky move may help to overcome female prejudice. 'Men don't make passes at girls who wear glasses'? Never heard such rubbish! Over here Nicole . . .

Anyway, has nobody ever heard of contact lenses? I first realised something had to be done when, introducing the Variety Club Awards on television, the camera to which I was addressing my polished remarks was on the other side of the room, a good fifty to sixty yards away; and in the lens of this camera was the autocue, with my script. (In case you don't know, anytime you see anybody addressing you fluently on the television, they're not making it up as they go along. They're reading it off an autocue or portaprompt. Sorry.) Anyway, the camera was so far away that my script was but a dancing, hazy blur. That wasn't the easiest telly show I ever did . . . I was reminded of my embarrassment on last year's Children in Need television appeal. (Which, incidentally raised a record £25 million, thank you.) Gaby Roslin and I had just thanked Sir Cliff Richard for coming along and entertaining us, when Gaby had a bright idea: 'Look,' she cried. 'Cliff, why don't you do the next link and tell the viewers how to pay?' 'I can't,' said Cliff, ruefully. 'I can't read it from here . . .' What made it worse was that Gaby had done exactly the same thing to Cliff the previous year, with exactly the same response . . . Good job he knows his songs by heart . . .

I don't blame dear Cliff for not wearing glasses, it doesn't sit with his Peter Pan image, but let me reiterate: contact lenses! I wear them for a couple of reasons: as Cliff will know, people who wear specs on television look like Mr Magoo. Secondly, I've tried glasses . . . I spent most of the day stumbling into the furniture, the children and the dog looking for them . . . I know people who have a pair of glasses in every room of the house, and still walk into doors in their helpless searching. Look, I've got a contact lens in my left eye for reading, and another in my right for distance. Trust me, the brain compensates. I take 'em out every night, and put 'em in every morning. And if a ham-fisted eejit like me can do it, anyone can. Think about it, next time you're forking out £300 for the latest designer frames . . . And here's lookin' at you, kid . . .

And Miles To Go . . .

Age, they say, is only important if you're cheese. Or a wine. They also say, if you're stuck behind one on a golf course, that a tree is 90% air. How come, then, that you invariably send your ball crashing into the remaining 10%? I wish that they'd keep their sayings to themselves, whoever *they* are . . . Age is something you never think about, until you're thirty, and after fifty, you think about little else. I tell a lie; after sixty, you think more about your pension. Birthdays are delightful until you're twenty-five, after that, hold the carousing down to the dull roar. I remember at a dinner in Ireland, when the world was young, some fat-faced eejit pontificating about how your twenties were for finding yourself, your thirties for making your mark, and your forties for building on it. He didn't mention your fifties and sixties, presumably because you're well past it by then.

It's one of the shibboleths of the age we live in: things you *must* do by a certain age, or you might as well pack it in. You must be walking by the time you're one, talking by eighteen months, going to nursery school by the time you're three, and riding a bicycle before you're five. Never mind that the Swedes don't send their children to school until they're seven, and they've never struck anyone as a particularly backward race. How old are the Swedes before they play tennis? Surely they must start earlier – look at the way they beat the pants off us.

There's a generation growing up that has to finish school before it's eighteen, has to have a 'gap' year when it goes to the Far East to catch some awful bug, and then *must* go to university, although it really hasn't a clue what it wants to study. You *must* make your first million before you're thirty, and if you're of a female persuasion, you must have a partner, and a child, before you're thirty-five. No use telling anybody that Baron Thomson of Fleet didn't make his first million until he was fifty, and continued to make it in hatfuls after that. The young put themselves under enormous pressure by these 'use-by' dates. Incidentally, the 'use-by', 'sell-by' thing is the prime indicator of your *real* age-grouping. Those of us of a certain maturity, largely ignore such arbitrary dating on tins, pots and packets. We go by smell, touch, experience. We know that producer/manufacturer is being ultra-cautious. Too much damn hygiene around these days anyway; none of these youngsters have any resistance . . . when our young return home to keep the old folk happy, they go through the refrigerator and pantry with a fine tooth-comb, consigning immediately to the bin anything that's five minutes over its 'use-by' date. They're surprised we haven't killed ourselves years ago . . .

The assumption that certain milestones have to be reached by a certain age is patently ridiculous, yet many businesses will only recruit at thirty-five years of age, or under. Fifty or over, and you're history. It flies in the face of all experience: How old was Churchill during the dark days? Gandhi in his greatest years? Victoria (no, not Beckham: she peaked early)? Chou En-Lai? Freud? Don't let me go on, I can bore a small crowd with this forever. Christ himself was not seen nor heard of until he was thirty-three . . .

Surely it was clear, long before the discovery of DNA, that we are not all cast in the same mould? Some children grow up quicker than others, some adolescents reach maturity long before their peers. Some grown-ups never grow up at all. One of the biggest gobdaws in my class in school, is one of Ireland's most successful men, far more than boys that were considered smarter, brainier. We all follow different paths, run at different speeds. To think that everyone is going to converge at the same time, and at the same points, is just not sensible. All of which is a roundabout way of protesting the newspapers' habit of adding people's age to their name every time they run a story, or a quote. 'Terry Wogan, 63, said today . . . 'Give me a break, I'm still running. As the poet, Robert Frost, puts it: '. . . and miles to go before I sleep . . . '

The Memory Man

You can see him coming, from right across the room. Now he's in your face, eyeing you with a knowing smirk. You know what's coming, because it's happened all too often before. He pokes you in the ribs, none too gently. 'You don't remember me, do you?' He knows that the answer is 'No'. He's actually trying to embarrass you, to make you feel inadequate, to cut you down to size. The last thing he wants to hear is, 'Yes, of course, you're Sean McEntee, a quantity surveyor, and we had a pint of stout together, in the snug of Nearys of Chatham Street, Dublin, between the hours of seven and eight on the evening of the 12th September 1978.' That would certainly soften his cough. What he wants is for you to mumble, 'Yes, of course, I . . . it was . . . weren't we . . . aren't you a friend of eh . . . ', while he sneers at your bemused confusion. Which is why I don't do that anymore. Sorry chum, but the only answer you're going to get from me is 'NO' and I'm not apologising for it. I don't remember you from Adam, and the only reason you remember me, is because you've heard me on the radio or seen me on the television . . .

Of course it's nice to be remembered on this side of the Great Divide, but again, I'd rather be remembered for the right reasons, and not be mixed up with several other people. I can never return to my home country of Ireland, without someone rushing to my side to reminisce on an occasion in which I played no part whatsoever. Recently in Limerick a woman of mature years excitedly grabbed my arm, and cried, 'Ah d'you remember those days we used to be breaking stones, above in Ballinacurra!' I've never broken stones in Ballinacurra, not anywhere else, in my life. She was obviously mixing me up with some other ex-con on the chain-gang. However, she wasn't seeking to discomfort, or embarrass me. So I smiled, nodded and said, 'Those were the days, what?' She went away pleased with a shared memory of youth . . .

People's memories on one's deathless performances on television can be more than a little confused as well. It's not easy to know how to adjust your face, when an avid fan approaches with the congratulatory, 'Oh, will you ever forget your interview with Oliver Reed?' Pretty easily. It wasn't me, it was Michael Aspel. And, before you go even deeper into the mire, Grace Jones slapped Russell Harty, not me. It was Parkinson who interviewed David Niven. I'm the eejit who had problems with George Best . . . Mind you, it's easy enough to get confused by the television. Nobody knows who anybody is. Can you tell Ant from Dec? I thought not. Life must be hell for them. While I was in the throes of *Wogan*, that thrice-weekly monument to incisive chat, I wouldn't have remembered my own name, if it hadn't been plastered in six-foot-high letters, behind my head. One Monday, the producer said, 'Good News! Tom Jones is coming in on Wednesday.' 'Good news indeed, underling,' I reposted merrily. 'I haven't talked to him before.' The producer cast his watery eyes heaven-ward. 'You interviewed him a month ago,' he said, wearily. A good job Tom Jones didn't say to me, 'You don't remember me, do you?' That would really have been embarrassing . . .

I was one of those who used to say, proudly, 'I don't remember names, but I never forget a face.' I forget just as many faces as I do names, these days. I think I may have forgotten my own, because the face that looks out at me from the bathroom mirror, doesn't look like the me I remember. It's more like my father's. At least I'm keeping his memory alive . . .

The Past Is A Foreign Country

Recently I received a distressing letter from a mother: 'The other day I was half-listening to your mindless waffle, when you played a record that featured a clear, young voice shrieking along, as they do. My daughter, late for school as ever, stormed into the kitchen with a face like thunder: "I don't believe it!" she cried. "He's just played my favourite pop song, on Radio 2! That's the pits!"' You can't do right for doing wrong . . . It's *their* music, you see, not yours, ours nor mine. It's part of *their* lifestyle, their cry for attention, their need to reject everything their parents, teachers and anybody over twenty years of age, stand for. If my own long-past teenagers are anything to go by, they'll get over it. But, boy, while it's going on, it seems to last forever . . .

They didn't have teenagers when I was a teenager: it hadn't been invented. You did what you were told, came home when you were expected, did your homework, and while you may not have re-spected *all* your teachers, you never threatened to slit their throats with a knife. Maybe at the weekends you slipped into a leather jacket, and oiled your hair back into a duck's tail, or pulled on an anorak and set off on the back of a pal's Vespa for Brighton, where you mooched moodily up and down the promenade, until it was time to go home. You sneaked a glass of cider if you could find a barman lax enough to pour you one, and you'd never heard of drugs, never met anybody who'd tried them. There were no clubs, no raves until the sun came up. There *were* 'hops', where the boys stood on the side of the hall, and the girls sat on the other, both sides terrified to make the first move. The girls because their peer group would have immediately branded them as 'cheap', and the boys because they were, well, terrified. The best-looking girl in the room would never get a dance; so fearful were all the boys of rejection. Insecurity was big in those days, and low self-esteem rampant. I never saw anybody with a diamond in their nose, and only girls wore earrings. And you'll never guess, my children, where they wore them: in their ears! I didn't see half enough female navels when I was a lad, but I'll bet that few indeed, apart from maharajahs' wives and nautch dancers, wore diamonds in their belly-buttons.

When I was in my teens – although nobody called them that, at least, not *this* side of the herring-pond – parents were never wrong; now they're never right. Back then a policeman or teacher could give you a clip round the ear if you looked sideways at them. I spent much of my formative years queuing for the pictures. In Dublin, you always queued, whether the picture was good or bad. And then, you stood inside the cinema, leaning against the wall, until it was your turn to take a just-vacated seat. Still warm. Nobody of any age ever saw a film from beginning to end. We came in somewhere in the middle, and left where we came in. Which explains why, these days, we can pick up the plot in a soap opera even if we miss a dozen episodes . . .

I didn't intend this to be an old-geezer-type rant but I see that if I don't pull myself up pretty sharpish, I'm not a million miles away from 'I never saw a banana until I was fifteen!' or the dreaded 'They don't know they're born!' You lose it, little by little, the older you get, and, it's natural to think your own generation, its ethics, its morals, its norms of behaviour, superior to both past and future generations. Although I'm bound to say that young eejits with rings in their nostrils and studs in their tongues do reinforce the prejudice.

People of the generation who lived through World War II are the proudest of their era, and no generation, before or since, would gainsay them. And they've got the best stories. Recently, a listener reminisced about his granddad and grandma during an air raid. The sirens went off, and everybody rushed out of the back door to the Anderson shelter, a homemade corrugated-iron job in the back garden, that saved a lot of innocent civilian lives. As they ran, Grandma suddenly stopped, and made to run back to the house. 'Where are you going, woman?' shouted Grandad. 'I've left me teeth indoors,' answered Gran. 'For God's sake, come on,' roared Grandad. 'They're throwin' bombs, not sandwiches . . !'

Lets hope they're still making them like that . . .

Time's Banana Skin

The younger you are, the more time's winged arrow moves like a carthorse. Children, and teenagers, get bored out of their minds by endless hours of 'nothing-to-do'. The most exhausting part of parenting is keeping young ones busy and entertained. The halcyon days of youth are endless, but once you reach middle age, the old winged arrow of time seems to acquire rocket-boosters. Incidentally, anybody know when middle age starts? Now that we're all dodging the coffin for longer and longer, forty would seem reasonable, since the average age for clog-popping is around the late seventies to the early eighties. However, you just try telling somebody in their early forties that they're 'middle-aged'. The least you'll get is a torrent of abuse, and there's every likelihood of fisticuffs. Fifty-year-olds are not that keen on the description either, although there's not that many of us anticipating the Queen's congratulatory telegram, even in these days of increasing longevity. People are middle-aged at sixty nowadays; in my mother and father's time, just a generation ago, that was *old*.

And people of sixty *looked* old. In this new century, the sixty-somethings are getting married again, and haven't quite dismissed the possibility of starting a new family . . . On that subject, I read an article lately that condemned late childbirth, on the grounds that there was nothing more embarrassing for children than being picked up at the school gates by people who looked like their grannies and grandads. This was immediately rebutted by a letter to the editor, which pointed out that with the singular lack of nannies, au-pairs and childminders these days, the people picking up the children *were* their grandparents . . . In any event, what with improved diets, more exercise, physical fitness and aerobic classes, not to mention Botox, these days, who can tell the difference between grannies and mummies?

The old saw about you knows you're getting older when you think Cilla Black looks great in a basque and fishnet stockings; it may well be too true to be funny, but there are more acid tests of declining powers. The 'half-way up the stairs, my mind's a blank' syndrome is, of course, a classic, but what about the 'Of course I remember, we met last year at the Henley festival' thing? When it turns out to be *five* years ago? That one always gets me, right in the mazzard . . . So, on top of days and nights whizzing by, and seasons disappearing over the horizon as soon as they arrive, the years themselves are contracting as I get older. Time doesn't pass; for something to 'pass', you have to notice it go by. I must stop blinking, I'm missing whole months . . .

What is it, do you think, that seems to rev Old Father Time's engine up, as we get older? Well, do you remember when you were younger, something you were really looking forward to took ages to happen? And something rotten, like exams, were on top of you before you knew it? Even now, something nice, like holidays, take ages to come around, while Monday mornings are every couple of days, or so it seems. Maybe it's just an illusion – I'm getting slower, so everything else seems faster. I wouldn't mind, but I'm only middle-aged, you know . . .

Don't Go Changing

A few scant years ago, an old classmate of mine (and I use the word 'old' advisedly) had the grandiose notion of bringing his classmates of forty years ago together for a bit of a hooley in Dublin. From all corners of the globe they came – well alright, most of them from just around the corner, because they'd never left the Ould Sod. But there were a couple of us who had taken the Emigrant ship, and felt that the journey back to the hallowed halls of The Young Offenders Institution which had housed us and de-loused us might be worth our while, if only to see how many of the warders had escaped.

It was a grand 'do', a good 'craic', as they say in Ireland, for reasons that have always escaped me. Only a couple of my classmates had gone to their Heavenly Reward; and these lads being firmly of their generation in Holy Catholic Ireland, only a couple of marriage sep-arations. We were a generation that were in it for life . . . A couple of the old boys looked as if life had dealt them a hard hand, but in general, it was a gathering of prosperous, middle-class, middle-aged men. Extraordinary, isn't it, how people in their late fifties and even sixties, regard themselves as 'middle-aged'. How many people do we know who have lived to be a hundred and fifteen?

The remarkable thing was, I recognised and remembered every one of them. It was easy – they hadn't changed. Of course, they were fatter, balder, wrinklier and a great deal older looking than me; but they were the same crowd of eejits and lousers that I had left behind in the school yard, forty years ago. They spoke the same, they acted the same, they laughed, shouted, moaned, groaned and behaved in the same funny, foolish way that I remembered all those years ago. They were surgeons, doctors, accountants, lawyers, quantity surveyors, account executives – one of them was even a snail farmer – but behind the suits, ties and after-shave, there they were – The Lost Boys. The Boys I'd left behind. Not a day older, not one iota more sensible than when we'd left each other with promises of eternal friendship, our spotty faces aglow with anticipation and ambition, as the school-gates clanged shut for the last time behind us . . .

It brought it home to me that, apart from those unfortunate enough to suffer extremes of ill-health, poverty (and, possibly, wealth) and appalling bad luck, and of course, fame, most people don't change. At least not from the teenage years. Didn't the Jesuits infamously boast that if they got hold of somebody before they were seven, they could mould them for life? Luckily, I was eight before they got hold of me . . . And now, research shows that children's characters are formed by the time they are three!

All I'm saying is, if that's the case, how do you explain the extraordinary changes in character, that go on before our very eyes in Albert Square, virtually every night of the week? Jim Branning, a curmudgeonly old drunk without a thought for anyone or anything beyond his stomach, falls in love with a mad old biddy, marries her, and was last seen reading a Dylan Thomas book of poetry. Lisa, a brow-beaten wreck of a woman in the throes of pitiful self-destruction, re-emerges phoenix-like from the flames, band-box smart, cool, calm, collected and ready to knock seven bells out of the 'ardest nut in Walford. Billy, who arrived on the scene as a bully, sneak, thief and cheat, has turned into a decent, sensitive, loving husband to Mo, possibly the most stupid woman on the planet. I expect him to start an Open University course in the Humanities at any moment . . .

Of course, nobody expects *Eastenders* or any soap opera to reflect real life, do they? Oh no? Don't tell me you don't find yourself shouting at the television at the ungrateful Martin Fowler (there's another whose character underwent a sea-change), or shrieking at Nana Moon to clear off to the nearest Home for the Bewildered . . . As the great Phil Mitchell himself might say – 'Whass going on?' No change there, then . . .

Suits You, Sir

You know that marvellous song from *Robin and the Seven Hoods*, 'You've Either Got, or You Haven't Got, Class', sung by Bing Crosby, Frank Sinatra and Dean Martin? There's a great line in there: 'he gets dressed to get dressed . . .' There's not too much of that around these days, at least as far as the male species is concerned. What happened to the tie? The old hand-knotted silk number appears to be no longer *de rigueur*, even in the ritziest of joints. I've seen jeans in the dining-room of the Ritz itself, zut alors! Old Cesar Ritz must be doing hand-springs in his grave. I know, the tiresome old geezer is ranting on again, but does everything have to be casual, these days? On the young, 'casual' looks great, but from forty on up, it's pathetic. In open-necked shirt and denim, the older man looks ridiculous anywhere else but in the wide open spaces. And forget shorts and a T-shirt . . . anywhere . . . And who wears sandals, apart from the British and the Monks?

When I was a bank clerk, I can't remember putting in more than ten minutes intensive work in a day, in all that time. We started dishing out the cash at ten in the morning, broke for an hour at one o'clock for lunch, and closed up for the day at three. Myself and the other lads played shove ha'penny until we could decently leave, and then it was off to the flesh-pots (well, coffee-bars) of Grafton Street, Dublin. Mind you, we had to work a half-day on Saturday, but we were allowed to wear our club ties and blazers . . . The club tie and the blazer were a dead give-away: they identified your school, your club, your class, even your religion. They still do, I suppose, in some parts of Ireland, and they certainly do in Britain. The Eton tie, the MCC, Sunningdale, the Regimental, I Zingari, The Taverners, the R and A, the Garrick . . . The last named which I am proud to sport at the old place, was apparently designed by du Maurier, the great actor-manager. Smoked salmon and cucumber he thought appropriate as club colours, and generations have cursed him since . . . Every soup stain, every sauce-spot, every dribble shows up on the light colours of the Garrick tie, like a moon-sign. I've never seen a clean one, except on a new member's first day, and then it only lasts as long as his first course . . . Some members wear their old neckties like a badge of courage, the colours long since muted by years of Brown Windsor and Vintage port. They look like they've eaten a hundred lunches *through* the tie, rather than over it . . .

It must be one of the more refreshing aspects of being a woman that you don't have to bother with a tie. Or a blazer, if it comes to that. It was different in Victorian times, and even in the fifties, but since the liberating sixties, you can tell nada, zip, about a woman from the way she dresses. Duchesses are got up like tarts, and vice versa. Taste is in the eye of the beholder, and you certainly can't tell caste, creed or college from the fashion sense of any woman. You can perhaps tell whether she has any common sense, but that's a different story . . . and even then, although you may think it supremely silly to turn up at a premiere bursting out of a frock held

together by safety pins, nobody ever took Elizabeth Hurley for a
fool, and she's built a career on that frock . . . I suppose attention-
seeking was always part and parcel of the actor, but anything goes
all over the place nowadays. And I'm going to sound like an old
geezer ('Why wouldn't you?' I hear you cry . . .) but I don't like it.
Oh, I don't mind how people dress – they can overdo it, undercook
it, look like the fairy on the Christmas tree for all I care, but can I
make a plea for 'appropriate'?

Most women like to get dressed up, lots of men affect not to;
and I think that's what it is – affectation. Maybe it's even inade-
quacy – it's as if some men think it compromises their mankind to
get into a suit. I know plenty of fellas who won't wear a dinner
jacket, they'd rather turn up at a formal occasion, or even a wedding, looking like an insurance salesman who's wandered into the
party by mistake. Don't they know how silly they look?

Have you noticed, nobody does 'dapper' any more? Most of those
men described as 'trendy' or 'fashion-plates' by the glossies, look like
un-made beds. Who told the smaller man that he'd look good in an
Armani suit? It looks as if it's swallowed him . . . While you're there,
who buys Elton John his suits? Whoever it is, they're no friend. In
the same week that he admitted to spending half-a-million on flowers, he was filmed going to court wearing something that looked
like a sack tied in the middle – a right barrel of bread-soda, as the
granny would have put it.

The present Mrs Wogan's (keeps her on her toes . . .) mother, although a quiet woman from Sligo, had a few salty old sayings, too,
among them the very relevant: 'fine feathers make fine birds'. Nothing wrong with that you say, but it's damn near beggared
me . . . But I digress. Back to the preening male: I saw a repeat of
Beau Brummell lately, and you never saw such primping. Not a crease
in sight, and no visible panty line in those tight trousers,
either. What's happened since the sartorial grandeur of the days of
Beau and Prinny? My father's generation, and his father's before

him, gave not a tinker's curse about clothes. Oh, they had a good suit and a working suit, shiny shoes and always wore a tie, but cleanliness was the watchword, and 'fashion' was a female thing. I don't remember caring much about clothes, either, as a young man. My wife soon beat that out of me, of course. However, my young men, my two sons, are very clothes-conscious. They both have a 'look'. Not the same 'look', but each has an individual way of dressing, usually in muted colours: grey, black, dark blue. They both look tremendously smart to me, but then, they would. So do most young men in their late twenties, early thirties, these days.

I think the penny dropped for the British male in the eighties. It can't have been the sixties, with that dreadful Carnaby Street tat, all cheap velvet, beads and Afghan coats. It certainly wasn't the seventies, as I know only too well from watching re-runs of *Blankety-Blank*. What were we like? Tight-fitting suits with huge lapels, flared trousers, matching floral shirts and ties, sideburns – those sideburns!!

The sartorial thing is tough for us older guys. It comes naturally to the younger generation, but we're caught between the cravat and the cardigan. As I've said earlier, denim and jeans are sad, and the open shirt only draws attention to the chicken-neck. The cravat went out the window with Hercule Poirot's button-hole, and the blazer seems to be the province of the seedier golf-club. Val Doonican killed the cardigan, but if they're going to get rid of the tie, we might as well not bother getting out of bed ... I know what you're going to suggest, but sorry, not the Nehru jacket – in fact, anything but the Nehru jacket. What about the hounds-tooth sports coat with the cavalry twills and the suede shoes? You're kidding. That fella who was after Penelope Keith in *To the Manor Born* – Peter Bowles – gave that particular outfit the kiss of death nearly twenty years ago.

I'm giving up. Maybe it's a letter I received the other day that's put the kibosh on it: 'Dear Terry, Thank you for wearing that suit on television last night. My old grandad, who hasn't said a word for thirty years, sat up in his chair, and shouted: "That's my old demob suit!" We haven't seen it since we gave it to Oxfam all those years ago . . .'

The Times they are A-Changing

I get at least 600 emails, faxes and letters every day to my morning Radio 2 show, but it's a rare, and gratifying, occurrence indeed, when the kindly, if aged, editor of *Woman's Weekly* passes on a letter addressed to the publication, and to me. This one came from a gentleman in Sutton Coldfield, who sneaks the odd 'new-man' look over his wife's shoulder at my ramblings.

His letter started: 'I hope you don't mind me writing to you about something that really annoys me' . . . and I thought, here it comes, a mouthful of dog's abuse, a barrage of contumely, a tirade at Terence. What else could it be? When somebody says to you, 'I hope you don't mind me saying this,' you know you're in for it. Similarly, if anybody remarks, 'Well, with the greatest respect . . .' you're going to get it in the neck, and respect is the last thing you can expect. Why do we feel that we have to dress it up, when we want to tell somebody off? There's no point softening the blow before you hit somebody. Wouldn't it be better to save it until after-wards, as in: 'Please stop trying to cut your wrists with that blunt Swiss army penknife, I take it all back . . .'?

Anyway, my doubts and fears about this correspondent were ill-founded. The decent fellow agrees with much of my ranting, and wished to let off steam, with a grouse of his own: 'No one these days has any time for anyone who isn't computer literate.' This chap proudly still uses a pen to write with, and a telephone with which to communicate. And he feels that people are treating him as if he were a dodo, or some other extinct species, such as Light Entertainment on the television. He speaks for his generation. The great golf commentator (and indeed, great golfer) Peter Alliss, recently blanched visibly when I mentioned that I used emails, and surfed the net. He looked at me as if I'd let him down, and not only him, but everybody in the country drawing a pension. He left me with the distinct impression that if I ever mentioned it again, our friendship was at an end. I felt like one of those unfortunates in those great old Bateman cartoons, you know: 'The Man who Entered the Garrick Club Coffee Room Wearing the Wrong Tie' . . . I was a quisling, a traitor to the cause. Shoot me, I'm over sixty, and I can use a computer . . .

I sympathise with my friend from bracing Sutton Coldfield. Television, in particular, is continually inviting the viewer to share their opinions by email or text. They want your opinion, but they want it now, forget your postcard or phone call, and it's a long time since anybody sent a telegram. And by the way, who told them to abolish that? I don't remember being consulted, do you? People of a certain age, anything from fifty to one hundred, have an in-built resistance to new technology. They have to call on the eight-year-old next door to programme the video recorder, they hate mobile 'phones, they don't know what all those wires at the back of the television are for, and words like 'scanner', 'server', 'digital' and 'text' are anathema. It becomes a sticking-point, as it has for my friend the letter writer. 'You can keep your new-fangled ways, it's too late for me to change, even if I could be bothered.' But there's no need to feel either resentful at the pace of change, or guilty because you can't keep up. There's nothing more graceful than a well-written letter, nor more friendly than a leisurely phone call. Personally, I'm resistant to the mobile phone. What, in Heaven's name, did people do before it came along? It's a frenzy of communication; they're sending texts, they're sending photographs, they're watching films, they're listening to music, all on the phone. But is anyone any the wiser? We're better informed, certainly, but are we any better off? Where's the Information Super-Highway going? There have already been some nasty accidents – who can blame those who prefer to take the road at their own pace? Remind me again of that story about the Hare and the Tortoise . . .

Musings

Watch Your Step!

'People sometimes ask me why I married the Queen. I reply, 'Because she was there.' . . . A quote attributed to Prince Philip, though not, I rush to add, by me. I've run into the good Prince a couple of times, and he's not a man to cross. I interviewed him on television, and it was one of the most uncomfortable few minutes of my life. I wanted to ask him about the Royal Family, and he wanted to talk about carriage-driving. Never the twain met. At its root was Prince Philip's failure to grasp the idea that carriage-driving was scarcely of riveting interest to the Man on the Clapham Omnibus. Rather like the occasion when he said that he didn't understand why more people didn't take up polo . . .

Of course the Prince didn't marry Her Majesty 'because she was there', but it is the reason most often given by those who trek across ice-field and steppe, up and down huge mountains, and across stormy seas in rowing boats. Not everybody, mind you. Simon Murray, who at sixty-three became the oldest man to walk to the South Pole, was quoted as saying on arrival: 'I don't give a damn if I never see another snowflake in my life. I feel more like a-hundred-and-three than sixty-three'. He took the 681-mile stroll with Pen Hadow, who became the first Briton to walk to both poles unaided. At the same time that Murray was trekking over the snowy wastes, his wife was attempting to fly around the world in a small helicopter. She crashed in the Antarctic, not too far from her husband's footprints. She assured me that she's going to try it again, now that she's up and about. All she needs is another helicopter . . . Need I mention Ranulph Fiennes, running seven marathons in seven different countries; on frost-bitten toes?

'Not the full shilling,' I hear you cry, and I couldn't agree more. Mind you, you're looking at someone who loses his nerve three rungs up a ladder, and who can't climb to save his life. Someone who has never been in a tent, not to mind a bivouac. Someone who skied backwards down a nursery slope in Val d'Isère, and flung himself into a snowdrift, rather than crash into a café table, occupied at the time by his family, all of whom were hysterical with laughter, and have never let him forget it since. And before you start referring to that yellow streak down my back, let me tell you that I prefer to regard my timidity in the derring-do stakes as an intelligent, finely-honed instinct for self-preservation. Also, as I have pointed out before, I will not leave home if I think that there's the ghost of a chance that I will be less comfortable elsewhere than in my own little bothy.

I'm aware that lots of apparently sane people perform these death-defying deeds to raise money for good causes, and I raise my titfer to them, but what makes anybody want to pull a sled across the Polar ice-cap? Why would you want to row across the Pacific? Hasn't Richard Branson got enough to do without going up in a balloon? It's okay Richard, we've noticed you . . . It's more than a cry for attention, though. These extraordinary people want to test themselves to the limits of their endurance, and beyond, against the elements, against nature itself. I admire them, I applaud them, but I simply don't understand them. An easy life, that's the one for me. If there were more like me, nobody would have ever discovered anything, and we'd still be walking around thinking the world was flat as a pancake. There are worse than me though. I have a slightly-conservative friend, who thinks that the world would be a much safer place if everybody kept to their own side of the street. No risk, you see. Bit like the Nanny-State they're building all around us as we speak. Don't smoke. Don't drive. Don't drink. Don't eat too much. Don't answer the door. Don't go outside. Don't risk it. And don't walk on the cracks in the pavement, it's unlucky. Wear a vest, you'll get a chill. Take care now. Mind how you go. While you're up, make us a cuppa tea ...

Little Women

'Men!' said my maiden aunt Nellie dismissively. 'They're all only after one thing.' My mother, the only married one in a family of five daughters, and the one with the sharpest tongue, replied: 'And how would you know?' Auntie Nellie had 'no time' for men, and spent most of her non-working days in the company of like-thinking women, also named Nellie. Funny how you never hear the name these days, but there must have been a lot of Nellies around in the forties, as well as Roses, Mays, Dinahs and Kitties, the first names of my mother's family. All pretty rare in the new millennium. Edwardian, I'd say – like Maggie. My great aunt Maggie, who dressed exclusively in black, and who would have frightened Dracula, had 'no time' for men either. To Nellie and Maggie, men were self- and sex-obsessed, untidy, lazy and given to drink. Not to mention insensitive and uncaring. I doubt whether Nellie or Maggie had ever been out with a man in their lives, but by shrewd observation, and listening to women foolish enough to have allowed themselves to be linked and then trapped to the wily male, they come to a view of the opposite sex not a million miles from that of their present-day sisters ...

Men have been getting it in the neck from women since time immemorial, but it's only in the last thirty years or so that the ladies have gone public with what they think of old 'all mouth and trousers'. I won't say that it's been hell, but it hasn't been good. The male's self-esteem has been battered to a pulp by the constant demands that he be better: better round the house, with the children, in the kitchen, and most undermining of all, in the bedroom! You'd want to be made of stone not to cast an envious eye back to the baronial style of my late father-in-law, who insisted on his lunch everyday at one o'clock, that his soup be cooled in advance on the window-sill, and that cold meat would never pass his lips. When this king among men went on a picnic, a primus stove had to be brought along, the better that his ham, potatoes and cabbage be served piping hot . . . He was not a man to be disturbed, contradicted, nor ignored. And you could put out of your mind entirely any smutty stuff regarding the bedroom . . .

Men of that generation, and the generation preceding them, had no doubts about themselves, nor where they stood in the pecking order. At the top, with the children at their feet, and their hand patting the little woman's head. From time to time they may have heard rumblings of discontent from the nursery, but they put it down to the vapours, or some other mysterious 'woman's' complaint. I need offer no better example than Mr Barrett of Wimpole Street; like Mr Ben Bolt, women 'trembled with fear at his frown.' . . . not much of that going about these days . . .

Today the male species is the fall-guy. Who gets ridiculed every hour on the hour on countless television adverts? Dear old dad, inept boyfriend, clumsy lad. Who's smart as paint, switched on, effortlessly superior? You've got it: cool mum, glamorous girlfriend, lissom lass! Who falls over his feet in every sit-com? Himself. Who always gets the last laugh? Right. That same little woman who used to get her head patted. On television and film, in the battle of the sexes, there's only one loser. Your man in the trousers . . . They've just revived *My Fair Lady* to great acclaim on the West End stage. When it was first performed, in the sixties on Broadway, nobody would have had any difficulty with the final scene, where Eliza Doolittle comes crawling back to dear old chauvinistic, mysogynistic, bullying Professor Henry Higgins. They still applaud it now, but nobody believes it. In this day and age the only reason Eliza would have returned would be to wrap the good Professor's voice-recording machine around his neck.

How did we let it slip lads? When did it all go pear-shaped? . . . It was happening long before John Wayne popped his Stetson . . . Hang on. You don't think male superiority never really existed, do you? You don't think it was a myth, just started by women, all along? Could it be, that behind every great man, there's a woman, working him with her foot?

The Heart's A Wonder

Recently one of my listeners sent me some cuttings, supposedly culled from 'Lonely Hearts' columns in Irish newspapers:

'Bad-tempered, foul-mouthed old git, living in a damp cottage in the back of beyond, seeks attractive 21-year-old blonde with big chest. Box 40/27' . . .

'Galway man, 50, in desperate need of sex, anything considered. Box 00/03' . . .

'Following recent sad loss, teetotal Tipperary man, 53, seeks replacement mother. Must like biscuits and answer to the name of Minnie. Box 08/73' . . .

'Better, disillusioned Kerry man, lately rejected by long time fiancée, seeks decent, honest, reliable woman, if such thing still exists, in this cruel world of hatchet-faced harridans. Box 53/41' . . .

Call me world-weary, a hardened old geezer if you like – and you wouldn't be the first. I'm the recipient of dog's abuse on a daily basis on the wireless, and have been the butt of people's scorns these many years. Barry Cryer, a raconteur and television and radio poseur, whose grey hairs give him an air of distinction that his louche lifestyle scarce deserves, told me lately that his memories of me as the host of *Blankety-Blank* on television, just after the Relief of Mafeking, are as of a blank page, on which the livelier wits, such as himself, could paint their lugubrious pictures. I don't mind telling you, it cut me, to the quick. And now I've forgotten where I was . . . Senior moment . . . Ah yes, the Irish 'Lonely Hearts': I don't believe they're true. The sentiments expressed, yes. Too true. Particularly of the Irish countryman. But since when did the truth get you anywhere, least of all when seeking a soul mate? You've got to put your best side out and keep it there for ages, or at least until you've secured your prey. Opening doors, rising when she leaves the table, are only the tip of the iceberg. Perfectly natural bodily functions have to be suppressed, sometimes for years. So, 'Lonely Hearts', while not lying, have to be economical with the truth. GSOH for instance. How many times have you seen that? Good Sense Of Humour. Oh yeah? *Everybody* thinks they've a good sense of humour. I'll bet Hitler thought that if he was known for anything, it was his hilarity at the dinner table . . .

Now, before you start, this is not a smart-alec attempt to pour scorn on those who seek love, affection and companionship through the 'Personal' columns of newspapers. I understand how difficult it is to find a soul mate in this frantic, workaday, materialistic, bus-lane ridden world. What else can you do, if you're not the kind of person who sits on a stool in a singles bar, endlessly recycling your chat-up lines? No, I mean it. It's not easy, whatever your age. Very few people have a huge circle of friends from whom they can pick or choose. Not everybody wants to join the local club, be it tennis, golf, bridge or bowls. And only the fortunate few have the kind of confidence that enables them to approach a complete stranger, no matter how attractive they find them across a crowded room. And not everybody is as lucky as I was, to meet the girl of my dreams at a party that only happened at the last minute, and that she only attended because some utter eejit had let her down that evening. Love is a lottery, just as life is, and just as in life, some people don't get the breaks in love. I applaud those who despite rebuff, disappointment, heartbreak, and plain, downright lack of opportunity are still not too disillusioned nor cynical to search for love, wherever they can find it. Personal columns can bring lonely hearts together, and end the sadness of lives blighted by being alone. Mind you, even as I write this, I'm reminded of a remarkable woman I met a few years ago, living in a cottage in the hills of Northern Ireland. A handsome woman, in her late forties, now with a responsible job as librarian in her local town. Intelligent, well-read, she had, literally, given up her chances of love and happiness to care for an ailing father who had lived a great deal longer than anyone could have expected. She had taken on the care of her beloved father, because she saw it as her responsibility on the death of her mother. She had given up her job, and for twenty years lived alone in a remote farm, with a very sick old man. And now, she was alone. I asked her if she felt resentment, if it had all been for nothing. I expected regret, even bitterness at the waste, the chances of love and a family of her own lost to self-sacrifice. I asked her if she was lonely. She answered with a smile and a sparkling eye. 'I'm alone,' she said, 'but never *lonely* . . .'

Trapped Wind

Poor old Michael Fish will never live down that immortal evening on television in 1987, when he dismissed the ravings of a caller who had heard rumours of a Great Wind Coming. Michael didn't exactly scoff, nor did he tell the woman to pull herself together and calm down, but it was implicit in his demeanour, the shrug of the shoulders, the suggestion of a superior smile. With all the quiet confidence of a weather-man who knows his high pressures from his lows, and his troughs from his fronts, Mr Fish assured us that the Great Wind was but a figment of some eejit's overwrought imagination. Some hours later, a hurricane blew over everything that wasn't nailed down, and Sevenoaks became One-oak. I don't know whether that proud town ever recovered, but dear Michael Fish didn't miss a beat. He continues to predict the weather with supreme confidence, and, indeed, his brave efforts have recently been rewarded in Her Majesty's Birthday Honours List. Good man Michael, particularly when you see some of the eejits who receive gongs for doing nothing more than putting their hands in their pockets, and forking out for some political party.

I was put in mind of Fish lately, when another Great Wind blew up from the Bay of Biscay, and sent us all running for cover. This one the forecasters got right, so most people had battened down the hatches in time, and all that had to be done was to sit in the front room, and watch the rain coming down in torrents, while pursuing the traditional British lamentation over the summer, at the same time reminiscing on how much better it all was, when you were young. Actually, in my own case it wasn't, being born in Limerick,

Ireland, in a more or less constant downpour, which persisted throughout my formative years. As I've said before, I spent the greater part of my youth in Wellington boots, up to my ankles in puddles of rainwater. Never did me any harm, apart from the odd wheeze on the chest, and the occasional nasal congestion, but I'm not saying that I could not have done with the odd shaft of sunlight. Weather forecasters in Limerick had it easy. 'Rain', they would predict, and they were always right. 'A soft day', the old farmers would say, or if the rain was slanting down particularly viciously, 'That'll make a good day yet' . . . Which reminds me of the Irish jockey who leapt off a horse named 'Wogan's Wager', of which I owned part of a fetlock. The game little animal (the horse, not the jockey) had finished a distant last in a race at Chester (a long way to travel, to see a horse barely break into a hand-canter). As he landed lightly on his feet, the jockey turned to me with a smile. 'He'll win a race yet,' he said . . . It has a timeless quality, that word 'yet'. 'When Hell freezes over', would be another way of putting it . . .

While we're on the subject of wind, and horses, some years ago, my radio show had a daily horse-racing report, for reasons which escape me now. To give the thing an added frisson, I would pick a likely nag from the list of runners. 'Wogan's Winner', we called it, more in hope than in anger, and it rarely troubled the judge, as they say in racing circles. In fact, I was personally exonerated by the Council of Churches report on gambling, because my daily tip was regarded as a positive disincentive to the punter. In a moment of weakness, I thought of a scheme that might make us all rich, and at the same time, cock a snook at the Council of Churches report. Surely, if there was anything to the power of thought and the theory of transference, millions of listeners concentrating their keen brains on one horse, would surely push it first past the post. 'Mrs Penny' was the horse's name selected for the great experiment, and I duly instructed the loyal listeners to focus their thoughts on Mrs Penny in the 3.30 at Towcester. Picture, if you will, the universal disappointment when the game little trier came in nowhere. 'Ah, well,' I consoled the weeping millions. 'It was worth a try. Another good idea, gone west.' A couple of days later, I received a letter from a listener who said that she had been walking down the main street in Towcester town, going about her legitimate business of an afternoon, when she was suddenly picked up by a Great Wind, and carried six furlongs to the outskirts of town. She wanted to know if I had ever heard anything like it, perhaps it was a sign from Above? She signed herself 'Mrs Penny' ...

The Game of the Name

It was the great Dr Johnson who observed that although the Irish were a pretty rough lot, they had at least one thing going for them: they never spoke well of each other. As in so many of his pensants, the old Doc was spot on. Still is, if you listen in any Dublin pub. Mind you, the Irish are even-handed: few indeed are the people of any nationality who escape the lash of the acid tongue.

I'm sure that it was in no way a riposte to Johnson when an Irishman, George Bernard Shaw, remarked that while the English were a fine, tolerant people, a person had only to open his mouth for an Englishman to despise him. And, dear reader, you know that GBS was right then, nearly a hundred years ago, and he's still right today. The rugged Northerner despises the Southern Softie for his Estuary-speak, and there are plenty of people south of the Watford Gap who still shudder at a plain-spoken Yorkshire burr. Despite Huw Edwards' best efforts, and that of his reporting sidekick Gito Harry (sorry, I'm not sure if that's how you spell it, but what sort of name is that?), rich Welsh tones are regarded in some quarters as suspicious. Particularly at Twickenham on an England v. Wales day. I know that Albert Finney, Tom Courtenay and their ilk, made regional accents acceptable on the West End stage, but *Macbeth* (sorry, *The Scottish Play*) apart, I've yet to hear Shakespeare enunciated in anything but ringing RADA Home Counties tones. And speaking of things Scots, it remains a paradox that although there isn't much love lost between England and Scotland, statistics (bless 'em) prepared by advertising agencies, claim to show that the most trusted accent in Britain is the Scots one: which is why you get so many ads on the telly with voiceovers delivered in gentle Edinburgh tones. No, no, never Glaswegian. Too tough. Not middle-class enough. That's the nub of it really, isn't it? On superficial acquaintance, we still define each other's place in society by how we speak. That's how the Irish slipped under the razor wire. A British ear cannot categorise an Irish accent. Nobody on this sainted isle has any idea to which class an Irishman belongs when he speaks. It accounts, at least in part, for the acceptance in the British media of the late Eamonn Andrews, Val Doonican, Graham Norton, Father Ted, and somebody else whose name escapes me.

Names; that's another way of telling the cut of a man's jib. Notoriously, and unfortunately, in Northern Ireland, you can tell a person's religion, and probably their political inclination, by their name alone. I know that sounds preposterous to everybody on mainland, secular Britain, but trust me ... It's not a lot more ridiculous than *our* innate ability to tell the nobs from the others by *their* first names. From just one page of the *Tatler*: Camilla, Natasha, Matilda, Amanda, Emilia, Bettina, Octavia, Sienna. From another page: Nick, Jake, Ben, Max, Joss, Boris, Angus, Casper, Mungo ... Let's face it, they're not going to hail from Heckmondwike, and they haven't been to a comprehensive.

I prefer nicknames. Throughout my youth, mine was 'Bawky'. I never knew what it meant, but I preferred it to 'Terry'. You can't make a snap judgement on a nickname. The great John Eales, captain of the Australian Rugby Union side, was known as 'Nobody'. Because, 'Nobody's perfect'. A friend of mine in Dublin is called, simply, 'Crime'. He's a bit slow to buy a round of drinks, and as you know 'crime doesn't pay'. My all-time favourite is 'Exorcist'. He's called that because after he leaves, there's not a spirit left in the house . . .

Words to the wise

I worry about women's magazines. It's the advice. I've just read 'how to throw a stress-free party without breaking the bank'. These wise words include serving a cheap Italian sparkler instead of champagne. And who, pray, do you think you'll be fooling? Prosecco isn't champagne, and everybody will know it on the first sip. It's got a vague, peachy taste; why not serve 'em individual little bottles of Babycham, and be done with it? If you can't afford champagne (and it's getting cheaper all the time), you can get a very decent bottle of Sauvignon Blanc or Chardonnay for the same price as some filthy cheap sparkler.

More advice on the 'stress-free party'. Get this: 'I have a strict "no red wine" rule at my parties, and no one has ever complained. Well, well brought-up British people don't complain – they just never go to that restaurant or that person's party, ever again. Has this adviser any friends left? I doubt it: 'Food doesn't have to be elaborate. I once went to a party for which everything had been bought that morning from a farmers' market – stunning cheese and bread, figs and quince jelly. Wonderfully simple, but absolutely delicious.'

I can just picture that party, and the people there. Men called Barty and Jonty, in rugby sweaters and open-toed sandals, women called Melissa or Nikki in gypsy skirts and no stockings, and help yourself from the scrubbed pine table. Figs, quince jelly and cheese? Try eating that while you're standing around making small talk and trying to get a swig of that revolting sparkling stuff.

Actually my father might have liked that party – he wouldn't have touched the booze or the quince jelly, but he had a passion for figs. He loved them, but they didn't like him. The little seeds got in amongst his false teeth, and he would always have to pay a visit to the men's room after a feed of figs, to sluice the little beggars out from behind his plates. He caused many a diner to flee the loo in confusion, at the unwholesome sight of my father's top set of dentures getting a brisk scrub under the tap.

The final piece of 'advice' puts the tin-hat on this excuse for a party. 'I refuse to wash-up scores of glasses, so I order fabulous plastic ones.' Great. Honestly, if you're not prepared to spend a few quid, taking time and trouble to throw a decent party, what in Heaven's name are you doing it for in the first place? Who but a cheapskate would throw a cheap party? And who, but the desperate and hopeless, would bother going?

The obsession with food, fitness and fat is universal, as is the tosh written about them in every newspaper and magazine. A beauty I came across recently was '12 Reasons French Women Don't Get Fat'. These include: They eat smaller portions. They make sure they have lots of little 'pleasures'. They have three meals a day, but never seconds. They don't weigh themselves. They drink water. They love to laugh. And so on. The biggest load of old cobblers I have read in many a long day. Oh, and French women walk wherever they can, and take the stairs whenever possible. Well, as Tony Hancock used to say, 'Stone me!'

This kind of nonsense takes up two whole pages of the magazine, but please don't tell me any woman with half a brain is supposed to read it without kicking the soft furnishings. French women come in all shapes and sizes, the same as every nationality under the sun. In the south west of France, where I have spent a good deal of time, they all tend to come in much the same shape – comfortable. The ladies of 'Boul Mich' and St Germain are no more chic nor slim than those of Knightsbridge and Sloane Street. It's all mythology, and it's in the interests of French tourism and commerce to keep the myth alive.

An Italian friend of mine chokes on his pasta (and he wouldn't thank you for Prosecco) whenever he hears people talking about the 'fashion-conscious' Italians, how smartly dressed every self-respecting male and female is, in Milano, Torino and Roma. How Italians are so obsessed with the 'bella figura' that they would die, rather than lose their figures. My friend lived in Milano for fifteen years, and he says most of the people he knew were overweight and bursting out of their cheap suits.

Here's my advice: 1. Let somebody else throw the party; 2. Don't worry about your figure in France; and 3. Don't bother with Harry's Bar in Venice. It's ridiculously expensive, and you might bump into Michael Winner.

More Awards, Anyone?

Now, right away, just in case you think you're dealing with somebody suffering from a bad case of sour grapes, let me say that I'm no stranger myself to the accolade and the award. I have mounted the podium on several occasions, to say a few graceful, modest words upon receipt of a statuette or plaque. You're looking at a former 'Tie-Man of the Year' here, not to mention 'Britain's Best-Dressed Man'. I daresay I could have aspired to the greatness of 'Pipe-Man of the Year', had I been bothered to smoke one of the filthy things. I have been awarded gongs, and innumerable lumps of plastic and tin, for my services to radio and television, charity, variety and ballroom dancing and these articles. I'm even on the judging panel of *The Oldie* magazine that makes awards every year to the most disreputable old codgers in the country. So the following isn't sour grapes, more sour gripes.

Many years ago when, if I wasn't winning awards, I was presenting them, I made a resolution to ignore them. I don't mean refuse to accept them a la Marlon Brando and his Oscar, because to do that is both ungracious to the people who have voted for you, and ungrateful. By 'ignore' I mean pay no attention, treat as the idle wind. Because, slip of a lad though I was, I knew that the day would come when the awards with which I was being swamped would silently slip away, and if I believed the hype when I was winning, I must perforce believe it when the well ran dry. So it's with no great heartscald that I see others carry off Variety Club, Television and Radio Industries Club, Sonys, National TVs, and Bafta awards. Good luck to them. I just hope they don't attach any importance to getting the gongs. It's undeniably gratifying that the public, or your peers, think that you're worth voting for, pay you the compliment of placing you above others in their esteem, but that's the holy all of it. Next year, next week, it will be somebody else receiving the accolades. What's the old showbiz line? 'Next day on your dressing room they hung a star . . . The day after that, no one knows who you are . . .'

From the late seventies until the late eighties, I won the *TV Times* award (now The National TV Awards) for the most popular Male Personality on Television; ten years in succession. Down the staircase I'd merrily trip, smile winningly, mouth a few banalities, and off, with a small plinth under my arm. It must have been such a pain in the butt to every other male TV presenter, but that thought never even occurred to me, then. The awards were nice, and I was flattered by them, but only for the moment, and I assumed everybody else felt the same. Now, I'm not so sure. It's easy to be cavalier, when you're winning . . . Anyway, I was convinced that the only reason I was winning every award was because I was 'there'; I was everywhere, all over the radio and the television, like a rash. When the public were asked to pick a name, mine was the one which came first to mind. And I'd won it last year, and the year before that, and the year before that, and, well, you get the picture . . . After my tenth successive win, I asked to be taken off the list of contenders, because I knew that eventually, the public would vote for somebody else, and the press would delight in my dumping. I shouldn't have bothered. Although I had deliberately excluded myself from the poll, the morning after the awards ceremony was televised, the headlines screamed 'Wogan Defeated!' . . .

You can't throw a stone in the street nowadays, without hitting an award-winner. About this time of year, every thinking person knows and expects that we are going to be up to our shoulder-pads in award ceremonies. The holy Oscars, the blessed Baftas, we're used to them now, and take the appropriate evasive action. If we can't find some excuse to hide in a darkened room, at least we know to busy ourselves in the kitchen, if we catch the sight of Gwyneth Paltrow or Halle Berry making their way to the stage. The knowledgeable keep a wary eye out for the likes of Tom Hanks and Michael Caine, too. Neither minds delivering themselves of a fifteen-minute encomium on their life and times. And there are always those who take the opportunity of thanking not only their parents, their families, the world and his wife, but God, as if the Creator wasn't there to help every aspiring talent in the auditorium, but had singled out this particular eejit for special praise . . .

Of course, awards ceremonies exert a fascination for the viewer; here's the glitz, the glamour of the stars, the triumph and the tragedy of the opening of the envelope, the hysteria of the winner and friends, the crestfallen, brave smiles of the losers. Then there's the added bonus of the fashion disasters to cheer the heart of every decent woman watching. Priceless gowns that don't fit, cleavages that are just too low, frocks that are just a little bit too tight. Mutton dressed as lamb, collagened lips and Botoxed foreheads as far as the eye can see. And that's only the fellas . . .

As I've said, at this time of the year, we expect these excesses, and gird our loins for the ordeal. It's the rest of the year that's got me worried. Is it me, or have you noticed that there appears to be an awards ceremony every week? I know that Andy Warhol promised us that we'd all eventually be famous for fifteen minutes, but the way things are going, it looks as if everybody in the country is going to collect an *award* as well. It can only be a matter of time before we have Eyebrow Plucker of the Year, Dog-walker of the Year, Best Performer in a Karaoke Bar. Pick your own accolade and somebody, somewhere will fashion a little plastic medallion for you to hang in the loo . . .

Let's not be curmudgeonly – if it adds to the gaiety of the nation in cheerless times, let's welcome it. There is an up side, apart from the happy jeering at Hollywood monsters. Where would we be without our own dear soap stars making a show of themselves at our own, slightly down-market occasions? How refreshing it is to see the characters in *Eastenders* are only playing themselves, and that foul-mouthed actors and comedians are not pretending. They *really* are like that . . .

I have a little rule of thumb that may help, when it comes to *your* turn to collect your award. When I'm informed that I'm in the running, I ask the organisers if I have won or not. If they say no, I don't go. If they won't say, I don't go. It's a wonderful way to avoid those brave little smiles of disappointment that gets on everybody's nerves, and that nobody believes for a moment anyway. Everybody knows that the losers are seething with jealousy and envy. Don't cheapen yourself. Your time will come. How do you think that I won the grand title of 'Britain's Best-Dressed Man'? I turned up, when nobody else could be bothered . . . Put your name down – you're next . . .

Pomp & Circumstance

The highly successful and blood-boltered movie, *Gladiator*, was a reminder that in Roman times the sovereign way to keep a firm grip on the hearts and minds of the people was 'Bread and Circuses'. An Emperor of Ancient Rome might be making a fearful hash of holding back the Hun and the Visigoth, but as long as he kept the Roman mob howling for more, with skin and hair flying in all directions in the Colosseum, his laurel wreath was safe. For 150 days in the year, lions, tigers, giraffes, elephants and, of course, humans, were done to death in the most savage manner possible to assuage the blood lust of the crowd. Then Plebus would take the early evening chariot back to his villa in a popular development just off the Appian Way. As she peeled him his grapes, his wife, Attractacus, would enquire: 'Had a good day, dear?' 'Oh, bit disappointing really, only a couple of hundred killed . . . Still, you can't blame Caesar . . .' This is where poor old Marie Antoinette got it so wrong. 'Let 'em eat cake', she said, and the next thing the tumbrils were rolling, the old biddies were getting out their knitting, and Madame La Guillotine was off and running. It's not outside the bounds of possibility that had Marie Antoinette read her Roman history, she might have said, 'Let 'em eat cake, and throw in a firework display', and easily kept her head. Thereby changing the course of history, and depriving us of *A Tale of Two Cities* and *The Scarlet Pimpernel* . . . I'll go further: Give 'em a damned good circus, and they'll forget about the bread, not to mind the cakes . . .

Personally, I can't abide circuses. Even as a child, I failed to clap my hands in boyish glee when the circus came to town. It wasn't the smell nor the tacky costumes. It was the clowns. Come on! Who thinks clowns are funny? You'll be telling me you like Marcel Marceau, next . . . Look I know it wasn't the circus as we know it, that Marcus Aurelius and the other old Romans meant. They meant pageantry, spectacle, parades, pomp and circumstance. And I love all that! Who doesn't? Grand spectaculars are no longer used to keep regal heads on shoulders, nor even unpopular governments in office, but they undeniably add to the gaiety of the nation.

The flowing plumes and gorgeous uniforms of the Lifeguards may cause congestion as they make their stately way from Hyde Park to Buckingham Palace during rush-hour, but I doubt if even the grumpiest London taxi-driver begrudges them . . . When it comes to pageantry, the British are best, up there with the ancient Romans . . . Now, it's gleaming horseflesh, glittering carriages, swords and breastplates glinting in the sun. Although the brilliant British talent for parades doesn't go back all that far into the mists of time. It was a Marquis of Reading, returning from watching the spectacular durbars of India around the turn of the century, that persuaded the powers-that-be of the time to put a bit of zing into things. Unfortunately, the first chance they got was Queen Victoria's funeral . . . However, it went well, and the idea of grand, particularly royal, spectacles was born.

I was privileged to be part of one of the greatest, when I linked the BBC Radio coverage of the wedding of Prince Charles and Lady Diana. A day I'll never forget, with Richard Burton declaiming sonorously as the sun shone down on the almost impossibly glamorous couple. The richness of the spectacle as it unfolded, the grandeur and the glory of it all was only matched for me by the people, the ones who had been sleeping for nights on the cold pavements, just to be part of the pageantry, to catch just a glimpse . . . They were the happiest crowd I had ever encountered – no jostling nor pushing, just good cheer and good humour. People at their best, happy to pay their simple tribute. They waved their flags and cheered everything, from passing pigeons to perambulating police-men. And such an out-pouring of love and loyalty, as the great parade passed by!

I can only imagine what the reception will be for the most beloved person in the land as the pageant for the Queen Mother makes its way through the crowd! This time I won't be there, on the ground, to taste, to feel, what should be the greatest display of public affection ever seen in this sceptre'd isle. But I'll be there, in spirit, along with most of you, cheering at the television, and feeling, if only for a little while, that the world's a better, brighter place . . .

For The Birds

Just when you think it's safe to raise your head above the parapet, the call of the loony-bird is heard once again in the land! The Royal Society for the Protection of Birds, which normally contents itself in fretting over the habitat of the nesting dunlin, the apparent disappearance of the golden eagle and the fish-hunting osprey, (laudable indeed, in a world given over to crass materialism) has recently asked us to start collecting flies. Not just flies – ants, bugs, insects of every shape and size. The RSPB is worried, you see, over the diminishing number of small birds in our green and pleasant hedgerows and trees. I don't know how their figures are collated, and far be it for me to doubt the researches of such a distinguished quango, but there doesn't seem to be any reduction in the raucous racket from my garden, as soon as rosy-fingered dawn peeps over the horizon. Blackbird, thrush, robin and wren are positively hysterical over their proprietorial rights, and have you heard the cockatiels? And how come this non-indigenous interloper is multiplying and prospering, while the humble native sparrow seems to be taking a powder? Green, graceful and beautiful, the cockatiel has been screeching around my neck of the woods for some years now, and although our climate can't be to its liking, it's thriving.

And while you're there – isn't it strange that the more beautiful the bird, the more discordant its song? Nobody could accuse the goose, the duck, the heron, the swan, of tuneful trilling. The glorious peacock, most stunning of all to the eye, makes a noise that offends the ear. The predators, the carrion eaters – crow, rook, magpie, jackdaw, seagull, hawk and jay, all betray their carnivorous nature by their aggressive cawing and mewing. Just a minute: you don't think that this non-ability of our beautiful feathered friends to carry a tune, can possibly be translated to homo sapiens, do you? I mean, hold hard there, but have you ever heard Naomi Campbell, Kate Moss or any other supermodel, burst into song? Have Johnny Depp, Brad Pitt, or Orlando Bloom got a note in their heads? And if so, why haven't we heard it? Does Becks ever sing in the bath? Have you heard Posh? All right, all right, let's not go there . . . Neither Sinatra nor Crosby was an oil-painting, and the same goes for Justin Timberlake. Actually, if you don't mind, I won't pursue this particular thesis – I've just remembered Elvis . . . And Kylie . . . And Doris Day . . .

Where were we? Oh yes, fly-catching for the RSPB. They want to know if the reason the birds are missing, is because the bugs have gone away. They suggest that sympathetic motorists count the dead insects on their bonnets, windscreens and number plates after a journey, and let the RSPB know the result. My listeners on Radio 2 of a morn' have readily leapt to the challenge. Well, anything as barmy as this always brings them out from behind the chaise longue. Hardly had this nugget made the 7.30 am headlines, before someone claimed that in response to the RSPB's plea, they had strapped a railway sleeper to the front of their Reliant Robin, 18 feet long by 5 feet wide, and in a journey round the block, had assassinated 11,310 assorted beetles and bugs, two traffic wardens, a milkfloat, several bins, a boy scout who was attempting to help an old lady across the road, and the old lady. Another claimed to have downed some 4,000 flies on his number plate, scraped them off, and put them between two slices of bread, on the bird table. A seagull had the lot in seconds. A keen cyclist wanted to know if the greenfly that he regularly caught in his teeth while a-wheel would be of any use to the statisticians? One listener, who was paying attention more keenly than was necessary, or even desirable, made the point that wiping out all these little flying creatures, was not going to be doing our few remaining birds any favours ...

The waning of certain species, while others wax and grow strong, has been a fact of life on this planet since Adam and Eve, or the Big Bang, whichever you believe. Don't panic if you can't catch enough bugs, or you haven't seen a sparrow lately. Something tells me it'll be okay. Look at the Great Bustard. We thought it had departed these shores forever, and look! The old Bustard's back.

A bit like Bruce Forsyth, really ...

All Things American

It may be just another day, another dollar, to you pal, but the 4th July is Big Stuff across the old Herring Pond. It marks the American Declaration of Independence and subsequent Constitution, that magnificent document masterminded by Thomas Jefferson, proclaiming the secession of the thirteen colonies of America from the yoke of the British Empire. Two-hundred-and-twenty-four years ago to the day, if you're counting. Given the couple of thousand years that Britain and Europe can look back, two-hundred-odd years of history isn't a lot to shout about, even if our friends the Americans seemed to have packed a good deal into that short span. It reminds me of a visit to San Francisco, when I overheard one American saying to another: 'You know, some of this stuff is a hundred years old!' . . .

So 'Independence Day' has little to do with that blockbuster movie where Will Smith as a pilot and Bill Pullman as the US President saved the Planet (again!) from some particularly repulsive aliens, and made the world safe for the rest of us to live in (again!). It's all about the Declaration of Independence, and the American Constitution and the first affirmation of freedom and the rights of man ever drafted. And yet the same declaration carries within it the seed that is at the root of much of America's suffering. Enshrined in the declaration and the constitution, is every American's 'right to bear arms'. And we all know how many innocents have died in the streets and classrooms of America, because of people's stubborn refusal to give up that 'right' . . .

It may be only an apocryphal tale, but at the time of the Declaration, the founding fathers of America had to decide what was to be the official language of their melting pot of a country. So many nationalities, so many different tongues – another tower of Babel. Linguistic order had to be brought to bear on the teaming masses. The boys got together and eventually it came down to a straight fight: English or German. The final votes were cast, and English won. By one vote! It doesn't take much imagination to work out what might have been, if German had got the nod. For a start, we'd all be talking German now, as a second, if not a first language. German would be the 'lingua franca' of the developed world, just as English is. I doubt very much if German-speaking America would have fought on our side in either World War. That one vote, in favour of English, changed the history of the world . . .

Not that most Americans give much of a hoot for the rest of the world, or its history. Americans are completely isolated from us, in their ivory tower on the other side of the Herring Pond. The *Los Angeles Times* daily newspaper is about three inches thick. News of the rest of America may be found on the back page, and it would take Sherlock Holmes himself to find anything about the rest of the world. For the inhabitants of Los Angeles, the world ends at the San Fernando Valley. Mind you, some of the inhabitants of the City of Angels are not too clear about their immediate environs. Climbing into a taxi on Sunset Boulevard, I civilly requested to be carried with all speed to the Buena Vista Studios, Burbank. 'Burbank?' inquired the driver. 'How do you get there?' Now, Burbank is Hollywood's nerve-centre where all the film and television studios are located. Without Burbank, no Hollywood – simple as that. 'It's over the hill,' I explained. 'Follow the signs.' 'I'd better ring the office for directions,' he said, in what (admittedly) was somewhat fractured English. He got out of the taxi, and entered a phone box . . . Not all of the States is on the cutting edge . . .

Their peculiar insularity breeds a strange intolerance among Americans – there's only one way, the good ol' American way. I read of an inhabitant of Park Avenue, New York, strolling down the sidewalk of that wide boulevard, enjoying a cigar. He did this every day, because his wife wouldn't allow him to smoke in their apartment. Fair enough. But on this day, as he walked down the Avenue, at peace with all creation, or as much as you can be in New York, a woman sitting at a table outside a café accosted him as he passed. 'You're destroying my environment with that disgusting cigar!' she shrieked. 'Put it out!' It ruined your man's day. It could have ruined his life, for all I know. It's the unreasonable, fundamentalist zeal with which Americans approach everything, from political correctness, to feminism, to aerobics, to dieting, that's frightening to those of us who can pick out more colours in life's spectrum than just black and white. Their attitude to we pariahs who smoke just about sums it up: the scene, once again, is a Hollywood restaurant. Myself and a colleague, having eaten and supped lightly and well, thought we might light up the old post-prandial cigar. Had we walked into the place with leprosy, we couldn't have provoked a more horrified reaction:'You can't smoke in here! There's a room for smokers!' And there was. A little cubby-hole where we sat, puffing self-consciously away, while the other diners peered at us, like the dogs we were, before they exited, noses in the air, into the Los Angeles smog . . .

It's extraordinary for a people whose roots are so disparate, whose ancestors come from every corner of the globe, to find the Americans so parochial, so narrow in their view, not only of the world, but of their own country. Maybe it's the size of the place, but Americans rarely wander from their own state. People from the Eastern states would die rather than go West, and vice versa. And the rest of the world? Last year in a Nashville, Tennessee restaurant, where they serve you the main course before you've finished your starter, I fell into conversation with an up-and-coming country music star! 'Where d'you all come from?' he asked. 'Oh, Great Britain, but I'm originally from Ireland.' He thought for a minute. 'Yeah – Ireland – that's the same as Scotland, right?' . . .

That's the Americans. They may not be quite sure where we are, but whenever we've really needed them, they've been there . . .

This Is For The Birds

As I write, the swallows dip and swoop above, recklessly diving to skim the pond for insects. At least, I *think* they're swallows . . . They could be swifts, or house martins . . . There are people who know the difference, and regularly explain it to me; as soon as they tell me, I forget it – so don't bother to write in. Something to do with the tail, isn't it? They're all swallows to me, and the sight of them never fails to lift my spirits. In the distance I can hear a cuckoo, another lovely, life-enhancing sound, but why are they always in the distance? I've never seen a cuckoo, close-up. I've seen robins and wrens, hoopoes, cardinals and flamingos on one leg, but I've never got near a cuckoo. Pheasants regularly try to commit suicide under the wheels of my car, and pigeons are everywhere, with their irritating whooping cry. Just don't get me started on magpies; they seem to have taken over the world. And, like Anne Robinson, do you know anyone who likes them?

In Ireland, where I grew up, the crow was the dominant bird. Or maybe it was a rook. And tell me how you know the difference? I know, I know – crows fly around in pairs, rooks form gangs, but can you tell 'em apart? Then, there's the raven, just to complicate the big black bird scene. Whatever they were, they were everywhere in Ireland, when I was a garsoon. They thought they owned the place, nonchalantly strutting in the middle of the road, rising at the last minute above the roof of your car, and settling back down in the middle of the road as soon as you'd passed on. They ignored bicycles; you had to swerve around them, the crows made you feel like an unwelcome intruder in your own country – I can hear their sneering cawing to this day . . .

Is it me, or are there more woodpeckers around? The green ones, with the little red topknot? I think I know the reason for their success in nature's endless battle for survival: they've stopped beating their brains out against trees. I don't know when the first woodpecker realised that it was a mug's game to go on blunting your beak against the unrelenting trunk of some oak, ash or beech, in the search for a tasty morsel, but I can imagine him up there, high in the branches, hammering away, on the off chance of a beetle 'neath the bark, when suddenly, like all the best revelations, it comes to him in a flash, 'What am I doing here? Are there any starlings, jackdaws, sparrows or jays banging their heads against trees? No wonder they've been looking at me strangely for all these years . . . So how do other birds keep body and soul together?' He watches in astonishment, as the others simply dig their beaks into the soft, yielding earth, pulling out plump, tasty worms. The rest is history, the word spreads among the woodpeckers like wildfire: so long tradition – elbow the tree, get down and dirty . . . Your average green woodpecker wouldn't give you tuppence for a lump of wood these days. Thriving and well fed, they stroll about the green fields, hoovering up the worms, and doubtless wondering why it took them so long to see the light . . . A classic tale of survival – the only surprise is that the Blessed Attenborough hasn't stuck his nose in yet to enquire about the creatures' mating habits . . .

I don't care if you do call me a sissy; I'm a fan of our feathered friends. It's hard to beat a perfectly roasted chicken, as Fatty Soames so memorably said. Yet, before you dive into that bucket of Colonel Saunders' best, let me remind you that birds display some disturbingly human traits: recently, an osprey returned to her nesting ground, but without the mate that had accompanied her for years. However, within days, another male osprey appeared, and seemed an ideal substitute. He hunted for fish, returning every day to deposit his catch. The perfect family man. Then, he got chased off by a younger, bigger bird. Big, strong and no idea, he bought the fish home and ate it himself. Worse still, despite a deal of wing flapping and squawking, he hadn't a clue about the vital 'me male, you female' business. He was so clueless, even Saint David couldn't have egged him on . . .

I hate to let down my own side, but give that bird a pair of trousers and a couple of apposite thumbs, and you've got the story of a lot of unfortunate women's lives . . .

Smuts Get in Your Eyes

You won't remember steam trains? No, I didn't think so. Too young, eh! Great big iron monsters, that chugged, hissed and steamed their way up and down the country, leaving a trail of smoke, and a reek of oil and coal, as they traversed the green and pleasant land. Power, speed, excitement, romance – *Brief Encounter*, *Murder on the Orient Express*, *Strangers on a Train*, *The Railway Children*, *Thomas the Tank Engine* – all as nothing without the hiss of the steam, the rattle of the wheels, the triumphant screech of the whistle, the smut in your eye . . .

'Don't look out the window!' your mother would cry, as you stuck your little head out, to feel the thrill of sheer speed, the wind howling in your face. 'You'll get a smut in your eye!' And despite all the warnings, all previous experience, out went your head, and in went the smut. It was as if the tiny flake of coal dust had been waiting for you. Pin-point accuracy, straight in the eye. 'Ow!' A sigh of resignation from your mother: 'What did I tell you? How many more times?' The handkerchief was already in her hand. It had been there long before you stuck your head out the window. Mothers of the Steam Age knew about trains and smuts. 'Here,' she would say, 'open your eye – which one is it?' None too gently, the corner of the handkerchief would be set to rummage around the watery eye, to your groans of protest. With uncanny accuracy, the offending fragment of coal would be prised forth, scarcely visible on the pristine hankie. Then, the real object of the exercise would begin: 'Look at you! The dirt on your face!' Your kindly mother, holding you all the while in a vice-like grip, would then moisten the handkerchief with

166

her tongue, and briskly set to rubbing three layers of skin off your face. 'OW! OW! OW!' 'There,' your mother would say. 'That's better, now sit down and read your book.' Eyes smarting, and face numbed by pain, you didn't move for the rest of the journey . . .

And do you know the really strange thing about this true-to-life tale? Everybody you tell it to, thinks that the same thing happened to them. Everybody remembers a smut in their eye, even those born and raised long after the demise of the steam train. Everybody remembers their mother spitting in her hankie, and rubbing their face red raw, even if it never happened. It must be a folk-memory, a tiny flicker from the distant past, that has been carried through the generations, almost to the time when we crawled from the primeval slime, or the Garden of Eden, or when there was something worth looking at on the television.

Mothers today simply wouldn't lick their handkerchiefs and rub their little darlings' faces in it, would they? No! Unhygienic, germ-laden hankie, covered in spit? Get Esther Rantzen and ChildLine immediately! Where are the Social Services Police when you need them? In this Nanny Society, obsessed with Health, Hygiene, Too Fat, Too Thin, No Salt, No Losers, Mind How You Go, and If I Were You, I Wouldn't Get Out Of Bed, there is no place for the mothers of yesteryear. It's not that they didn't know about 'Clean', they just didn't think that a bit of dirt would do you any harm.

So, are children today healthier than we were? No, they're fatter. Happier? Well, cleanliness is next to Godliness, but not necessarily Happiness. Sometimes, I swear I can still feel that wet hankie rubbing off layers of skin. But I'd still stick my head out of a steam train window, if I got half the chance . . .

Eat Something!

Now, you'll know well enough that I have no particular axe to grind on the trying subject of 'figure'. My own racing-snake profile is well known, and the privileged few lucky enough to have seen my six-pack, have remarked that Brad Pitt should be so lucky. So it's not out of misplaced envy that I can be found pointing the finger at the number of beanstalks that I see walking the streets in the guise of young women.

When you haven't got a proper job, you spend much of your day surfing the satellite. Richard and Judy can only fill up so much time. Satellite surf for long enough amidst wrestling, Australian Rules Football, shopping channels, reruns of *Poirot* and *Sherlock Holmes*, black-and-white sci-fi and old soap, and you will find something called 'The Fashion Channel'. There you will see an endless procession of models, super and otherwise, trolling in a slovenly fashion up and down a ramp in front of audiences that seem to be composed mostly of the undernourished and escapees from a loony-bin. The girls themselves resemble nothing so much as garden rakes, and bad-tempered, pouting garden rakes at that. The kind of garden rake that springs back to hit you on the nose when you haven't even touched it. These swaggering, arrogant garden rakes are hardly wearing a stitch, but the sex appeal remains that of a garden rake. I know you'll put my indifference down to declining powers, and too much cocoa before bedtime, but trust me, I still have enough of my senses about me to detect a flying pheromone, and there ain't no buzz.

I wasn't really expecting any: you and I know by now that fashion

168

is not now, if it ever was, designed to please the simple, heterosexual male. Quite the opposite . . . and we all know that none of this far-out stuff is ever going to make the high street. You may catch a passing glimpse at film premieres, but rarely elsewhere. Never mind all that, I know that I'm leaning against an open door; it's those poor girls themselves. I find myself shouting at the television screen: 'Eat something!' Have they neither mother nor granny to feed them up? Those poor emaciated bodies, those legs, oh, those legs. The last time I saw legs like those, they were standing in a nest . . . These girls look like ragged refugees – who or what are they doing it for? Not the opposite sex; how many men do you know who want to dance (to use a euphemism) with a bag of bones? Skeletons are no turn-on, for those of us still wearing trousers.

Ladies, the finger of suspicion points to you. You're the ones who've bought the confidence trick. Every newspaper, every magazine promotes the woman without a pick on her frame as the ideal, and, be honest ladies – there are very few who don't look on with envy. The diet and slimming business has boomed as a result, not to mention aerobics, weight lifting, yoga, sauna, running, jumping, boxing, pressure pads, and any other device legal or otherwise that may whittle off the excess avoirdupois, and enable the average woman to bear a passing resemblance to Schiffer or Moss. Ally McBeal seems to be a bridge too far, or am I clutching at straws here?

Even I am too young to remember when the Rubenesque figure was the *belle idéale*, when men would stand transfixed for days before paintings of jolly, apple-cheeked, ample ladies frolicking like mad with nymphs and satyrs. Plump was good then – I well remember an old Irish love song that featured the line:' . . . She's a fine big lump of an agricultural Irish girl . . . ' Well-nourished was the fashion then, maybe the present obsession with looking like a stick of celery will pass too. I'm not suggesting that everybody should be walking around looking like a barrel of bread-soda, but can a happy medium be struck somewhere? And have wannabe skinnies thought it through, to those years when slim becomes scrawny, and the swan-like neck turns into a chicken's? Fowl, isn't it?

Mirror Mirror on the Wall

It was the great Scot, Rabbie Burns, who said that the greatest gift of all was self-knowledge: 'Tae see oursells as others see us.' He wasn't talking about physical appearance, or outwards show, but how other people judge us, what they think of our behaviour, what kind of people they think we are. However, even if you 'can't judge a book by its cover', first impressions are important. Most of us do our best to look our best, to make a favourable impression on boyfriend, wife or boss – but here's the rub: the great majority of us don't know what we look like. We go by the opinions of girlfriend, husband, pals or work-mates. And unless your friends are Trinny and Susannah, they're going to tell you what they think you want to hear. (Incidentally, can you imagine Trinny and Susannah having any friends?)

Nobody since man crawled from the primeval slime, has ever answered the query 'Does my Bum look Big in This?' with anything other than a ringing denial. When it comes to physical appearance, the closer you are to someone the more difficult it becomes to tell the truth. Relationships are delicate flowers, and nothing makes a friendship shrivel and die more speedily than an honest, unvarnished opinion. And trust me, the little white lie is a vital ingredient of the happiest marriages . . . Anyway, you and I are too conscious of our own deformities to begin to criticise, knowing all too well than an answer in the affirmative to a query such as the above, will elicit a tart response along the lines of, 'Oh Yeah? Well, let me tell you it's time you started dressing your age . . .'

So it's no use looking to others for a clinical dissection of yourself, or your wardrobe. The pity of it is, when we ask for an opinion of our appearance, we're not even looking for the truth. All we want is a ringing endorsement of our figure and fashion sense. No need to feel guilty about it, everybody's the same. And I mean everybody. Nobody ever told Her Majesty, the late Queen Mother, that she looked like a birthday cake. A wrong word from the Lady of the Bedchamber, and she'd be down in the kitchen blackening the grate. Why do you think that the fashions on display on the ramps of London, Paris or Milan resemble nothing so much as a freak-show? Who's going to tell Alexander, Karl or Stella that they're wrong? They ask for your opinion of something that looks as if it came straight out of the Hammer House of Horror, you'd better be up-beat, unless you want to find yourself behind a sewing machine in Taiwan . . .

It's up to you. You're on your own. There's always the mirror, and the mirror never lies. Wrong. Mirrors differ, of course; some flatter the fuller figure, others can make you look like a beached whale. The one thing you can be sure of – that mirror is not telling you the truth. It's telling you what you want to hear, showing you what you want to see. Nobody looks at themselves in a mirror dispassionately, objectively, or without prejudice. 'Mirror, Mirror on the wall, who is the fairest of them all?' was the incessant question of The Wicked Stepmother, and she always got the answer she was looking for. The old bat's mirror was a downright liar – just like yours, and mine.

We're not fools, we know that it's not Brad Pitt nor Gisele Bündchen looking back at us, but only a real eejit would deny that our mirrors are rose-tinted. How else can you explain the people you see in the street every day? How many times have you muttered to yourself, 'Who let him out dressed like that?' or, 'She must have got dressed in the dark,' or, 'How can anybody think that outfit looks good?', or even, 'They're not all locked up yet . . . ' People in colours that scream at each other, men in vests, girls with their plump bare midriffs bulging out over their low-slung jeans, women with corn-coloured hair, like haystacks in the wind, middle-aged men apeing the young with their shirts outside their trousers. Greasy hair, dirty shirts, open-toed sandals with black ankle-socks. The list of visual offences is all around us, yet all of these people have a mirror, which they undoubtedly looked at before they went out the front door. What did they see? Certainly not what the rest of us can see, or they would never have left home. They saw what they wanted to see, an idealised picture of themselves. Nobody is without ego. Nobody deliberately sets out to look a fright. People may aspire to be diferent, to seek attention by their looks or dress, but they're not going out into the great wide world to be rejected or sneered at.

It's the camera that never lies, and nobody knows that better than anybody who has appeared on television! That's when you learn the truth, the real truth, when you do see yourself as others see you. It's never a pretty sight, because nobody looks as good as they think they do. I'll bet you anything you like that Nicole Kidman and Jude Law recoil in horror when they see themselves on the screen: 'You never told me I looked like that! Why didn't somebody say something?' These people look in the mirror every day, the same as everybody else. But, like the rest of us, they don't see reality. The anorexic sees that they're too overweight, the overweight can't see that they're bursting out all over.

How many times do you hear people say, 'Oh, I hate having my photograph taken. I look like nothing on earth!' What they mean is they don't think the camera does them justice. I hate to tell you this, but it does. That's what you look like. Alright, I allow you a little leeway with passport photographs. Everybody looks like the Phantom of the Rue Morgue in them . . .

There's no need for tears. Go out and face the world, secure in the knowledge that everybody else thinks they're better-looking than they are as well. But now, you're one up on them: you know it, and they don't . . .

It's a Sell-Out

In the good old days, when you and I were young, Maggie, you knew where you were. For instance, if the Sales were on, it was January. It's January now, in case you've been up the Hindu Kush or down a hole in the ground for the last six months, but you'd never know it from watching the shop windows. Or if you did believe everything you saw in a shop window, you'd be pardoned for thinking it was January all the year round. It's 'Sales' twelve months of the year these days. There's a bed shop I pass at an unearthly hour every morning of my life that has had a 'Sale' every single day since it opened over a year ago. So, obviously it has never sold a 'horse-hair' nor a bed-post at their proper retail price. And it's not just bed-knobs and broomsticks: have you ever seen a crockery store over the last ten years that hasn't had a 'Sale' sign up? Or a purveyor of three-piece suites and sofas? Nobody sells a book at the price on the cover, nor cassettes, nor videos. Persian carpets have been at a discount since before the Shah left in a marked manner, and there appears to be no price structure at all for mobile phones. Computers are permanently On Sale, as are televisions and second-hand cars. I could bore a small crowd with an endless list of 'For Sale' items, but I see that I already am, so I'll desist . . .

Your keen intelligence has already discerned that I'm not a big 'Sales' fan. Too true. Firstly because, in common with most men, I'm not big on shopping. I blame my mother – why not? Mothers and fathers are blamed for everything these days, from truancy to first-degree murder. I blame my mother, because 'Roughhouse Rosie', as she was known to all who knew and loved her, was a ruthless berserker of a shopper. She would rush around like something on wheels, from shop to shop, department to department, picking up, discarding, trying on, going back for another look, looking, feeling, testing, all at a hundred miles an hour, dragging an unfortunate, exhausted child in her wake. That child was me, and it marked me. Just as your male partners, and husbands, have been marked for life by their mothers. Just as you are, probably even as we speak, marking the unfortunate little males in your family. You're a hard woman . . . So, for me shopping will always be a chore, not a pleasure. Blessed with my mother's impatience, I can be in and out of a department store in half an hour, with six parcels under my arms. It's like everything else I do: I may not be very good, but I'm quick . . .

My second objection to 'Sales', is that they're a con; a great big loss-leader to lure you in, and entice you to spend three times what you intended, because everything is a third of the price. If my bed-shop has had a 'Sale' sign since the day it opened, how can anybody work out the original price? How can you know whether you're getting a bargain or not? So they put a line through the original price, and knock a hundred quid off; how do you know that they didn't add a hundred quid on in the first place?

I don't know why I'm shouting at you – you know all this, but you're still lured in, like bees to nectar: 'It's the Sales! Let me at 'em!' You're not put off by those horrendous scenes on the 6 o'clock news, as people charge through the doors, trampling on the weak and infirm underfoot, as they seek their own special bargain. You want to be in there, pushing and shoving with the rest of them – the thrill of the chase – the beating of the other woman to it – 'Gimme that! I saw it first!' Man is supposed to be the hunter-gatherer, but Sales give the lie to that. Sales show Woman for what she really is – red in tooth and claw . . . All that male jostling and shouting on the football terraces is only in the ha'penny place. The Kop can't hold a candle to Harrods escalators at Sales-time . . .

As the old saw has it: 'You can always get out by paying.' Here! Take it all! I'll wait outside, with the engine running . . .

This Sporting Life

Sport, it's all over us, like a rash, these days. Every sport had its season when I was a games-mad lad: the mud thud and blunder of the winter sports, football and rugby, then the flannelled-fools stuff of summer: tennis and cricket. Of course, there were others, for the truly obsessed sports-fanatic: netball, hockey, swimming, athletics, table-tennis, badminton, the Eton Wall game; the list is endless, and will only tire you. But even these, and the more esoteric pursuits with which I will not trouble you, had their seasons. Nobody played hockey in the summer, nor went swimming in the winter. Nobody played indoor sports like ping-pong or badminton in the summer. There was a bit of order to the whole business. Everything in its place, and a place for everything.

Nowadays, intoned the old curmudgeon, as his audience slipped into unconsciousness, sport is all over the place. Your radios, televisions and newspapers are bursting, e'en as we speak, with tennis, cricket, horse-racing, swimming, running, jumping and everything but standing still. Fair-enoughski, it's summer, and they have a right to be there. Although whether they have a right to totally dominate the media is something that causes my Radio 2 listeners, and particularly the ladies, to jump up and down a good deal. And golf, that's okay for summer. Except that golf is with us all the year round. Rugby – that never seems to stop. Football? They give that a rest for about six weeks and then we're back to the kick-and-rush, virtually every day of the week. Ah, those long-lost days when football was played only on a Saturday. These days, dear old Des Lynam has to give the moustache a trim every couple of days . . . Cricket, a perennial as well: in the darkest days of winter you can see Australians bounding down the crease, their noses and lips smeared with sun-block. I know that it's summer in the southern hemisphere when we're scraping the ice off our windscreens here, but it seems to fly in the face of the great English game. What would the great Edwardian poet Sir Henry Newbolt ('Play up, play up, and play the game!') make of it? CB Fry and the other Corinthian Casuals? Football in summer? I think not . . . Rugger in the sunshine? Are you mad?

It's mammon, of course. The old moolah, the mazumah, the cash. Sport's awash with money because the public, with more time on their hands, and seemingly plenty to spend, can't get enough. 'If you've got the money, we've got the sport' is the watchword. The advertisers of health-drinks, cars and sports goods want to sell their stuff all the year round – so, let the good times roll; pay the players fortunes, get 'em out there, rain or shine; let's sell those products! So, in the space of less than twenty years, virtually all sport has become professional. It all makes for fitter, faster, win-at-all-costs sport, and I suppose for the punter in the pub, or on the settee with the six-pack, it's more eventful, more exciting. They say that basketball is the most popular televised sport in the US because the viewer can see the whole court, there's a score every five seconds, and plenty of time-outs for commercials. And the average attention-span of the viewer is seven seconds . . .

Am I alone in preferring sport the way it was? Has it to do with my age, or are there young people out there who prefer to play a game for the love of it, for the exhilaration and the fun? Is it me, or weren't the Olympics better without drug scandals and huge hype?

Who would you rather have on the Centre Court, Little Mo and Gorgeous Gussie, or the Williams Sisters? Sorry, I'd still prefer the Irish Rugby team to tie their boots with hairy twine, and run out on the pitch having just stubbed out their cigarettes in the tunnel ... To paraphrase George Orwell: 'Serious sport has nothing to do with fair play ... it is war minus the shooting ...'

Bring back the baggy shorts!

French Leave

I write this from the middle of nowhere: deep in the French country-side with not a soul stirring. The faraway sound of a tractor amid the vines has died away. It's close to lunchtime, and everything here stops for food. Don't run out of fuel between one and half-two: even the petrol stations close for lunch. All I can hear is the chirrup of the little birds that inhabit the vines, the cooing of the boring pigeons, and the squawk of the collared-dove. I've just seen a hoopoe, which would lift the glummest of spirits, and a kingfisher has flashed across the pond, which has left me positively exhilarated. It's quiet here in the southwest of La Belle France. Compared to the crowded isle on which I live and work, it's deserted. They used to call it Aquitaine, and many a battle was fought over it, between the English and the French. It was also known as Gascony and Gascon bowmen fought as mercenaries for the English King, Henry the Second. Gascony has long been known as the heartland, the very core of rural France. And as the Common Agricultural Policy which they designed makes very clear, the French are deeply attached to their agricultural roots. This has not prevented the Parisian from referring to the Gascon disparagingly as what the

Americans call 'Rube', or the Irish call 'bogman'. Which is why the clumsy, unsophisticated D'Artagnan was portrayed as a Gascon, in Dumas' classic *The Three Musketeers*. According to Parisians, the Gascon is famously mean and grasping; yet in the little villages and towns here, people look you in the eye, and greet you as they never do in Paris. They say hello to everybody in the restaurant as they enter, and bid everyone 'au revoir' as they leave. It takes a while before they invite you into their homes, those tightly shuttered houses that you see in every hamlet as you pass through France. I'm sure that you've felt the same as I do, if you've driven through this country. There's nobody here.

It was a long-held theory of mine that it was a cunning French plan, to gain international prestige and financial backing, by telling the world that the population was fifty million, when in fact, the entire country was empty, save for half-a-dozen old blokes from Central Casting, Paris, who were employed to walk up and down the streets of various French towns, wearing a beret, and carrying a baguette. But having parked here for a bit, I'm here to tell you that there is life behind the shutters. They close the shutters to keep out the heat, and the cold. They are undeniably thrifty – air conditioning is as rare as hen's teeth, and central heating is sparingly applied. But they come out for high-days and holidays. It seems that wherever you go here, there's a village 'en fête', and everybody's welcome. For about a fiver a head, you can have an aperitif, the leg of a duck, as much wine as you can drink, and an armagnac to settle your stomach. I've seen little hamlets with about five houses, and as quiet as the tomb for 364 days of the year, heaving with people and unrestrained joie de vivre, for their annual fête. Where all these people come from remains a mystery known only to the French. Maybe it's the French underground . . .

They've had a bad press this year, our neighbours across the Channel. Despite a half-a-million British expatriates living in France, the old enmities still remain, notwithstanding Tony Blair's fluency in French. Perhaps it's got something to do with M. Chirac's equal fluency in English, but his reluctance to speak it. Or possibly Napoleon . . . It's the Americans that have really taken umbrage, however. Following French non-cooperation over the Iraq War, American tourists have given France the *épaule froide*. French restaurants have gone belly-up in New York and San Francisco, and even the beloved American 'French Fries' have been renamed 'Freedom Fries', in retaliation. French wines, particularly the expensive Bordeaux clarets, have got the elbow from their biggest market. What the Americans don't realise is that this distaste is mutual. The French have disliked the Americans for far longer. And it's nothing to do with the sale of Louisiana for tuppence. It's because the Americans speak English, and because of that, the French language has diminished in international importance. It has even been replaced by Spanish, as the most important 'second' language. The only place you'll hear French offered as an alternative to English is the Eurovision Song Contest, and that's only to stop them making a fuss . . .

The French are difficult, you see. So are the British. And the Chinese. And everybody else, when their national interests and pride are challenged. Nationality's just the piece of the planet we were born on. Individuality is what makes us all different. No two Frenchmen are the same. No two Englishmen are the same. Well, maybe Ant and Dec.

The Haunted Fish-Tank:
Television

Don't Look Now . . .

'*There's nothing on the telly!* the constant, poignant moan of the grown-up viewer, is the most frequent complaint I get every morning among the hundreds of emails, faxes and letters to my daily Radio 2 show. And it's an unfair calumny. There's shed-loads on the telly, particularly if you're watching digital, cable or satellite, as well as the five terrestrial channels. You could make a strong case for the opposite argument; that there's too *much* on the telly. That's the real problem: you can spend an entire evening surfing through a sea of programmes, without finding a single one that you can be bothered looking at. More is not better, if all you have to pick from is mediocrity. That's the cause of the 'There's nothing on the telly!' whine. Whole evenings go by, particularly, it seems, on weekends that offer nothing but dross. Early evenings on the weekend seem sacrificed on the altar of 'yoof'. Peculiar, in view of the fact that 'yoof' itself is not watching. If they're not down the pub already, they're tarting themselves up, getting ready to go. No, it's you and me, the sad old geezers, who are expected to endure the cheeky cheesiness, the witless, shameless vulgarity of it all. We're the lost generation of television. As a perceptive pal of mine said: 'When we were in our teens and twenties, there was nothing to watch; television was being made then, by people in their forties, fifties and sixties. Now, when we're in our forties, fifties and sixties, television is being made by people in their twenties and thirties . . . We've never had anything to look at . . .'

Maybe a hint of the old hyperbole there, but every viewer of a certain age will get the point. They'll also know, only too well, that if they start complaining, they'll be dismissed as 'behind the times', curmudgeonly old misanthropes, bemoaning their lost youth. So, was television better, when you and I were young, Maggie? Was there *always* something worth looking at, in the sixties, seventies, and eighties? Let's be fair. Maybe not. Looking back, some of the sitcoms and light entertainment programmes that we thought amusing at the time, look insipid now, and yet, and yet . . . I still watch *The Good Life, Rising Damp, To The Manor Born, Open All Hours, Morcambe and Wise*, and a host of others, on satellite television, in preference to what's currently on offer on BBC and ITV. Tell me it's my age, by all means, and then explain why I (in an age-group that makes up the great majority of viewers) can find nothing of interest, particularly in 'light entertainment', on the major channels.

It's TV Light Entertainment that's at the root of the matter, the heart of the complaint. 'Light Entertainment' comes in waves: In the sixties and early seventies, it was quiz shows. Then it was 'people' shows (*Game For A Laugh, Blind Date*), then 'makeovers' (*Changing Rooms*), cookery, gardening and holiday programmes. Then 'reality' took over, with *The Cruise, Driving School, Airport* and their ever-proliferating ilk. Mercifully, these, with their discovery of mediocre, talentless people, appear to be on the wane. However, they've been replaced by something worse, far worse. 'Reality' has transmuted into 'true-life'. I think it started with *Survivor*, then came *Pop Idol* and *Big Brother*, followed by their teeming, cringe-making spawn: *I'm A Celebrity Get Me Out Of Here, Celebrity Big Brother, Popstar: The Rivals, Fame Academy*. Sorry, I could never watch any of them without blushing with shame for everybody concerned. And I hate to break it to you, but it's going to get even more unwatchable. In the States, they've come up with *Joe Millionaire*, a group of women competing for a rich bachelor. Except, and here's the really amusing twist, he's actually a poor construction worker! Then, there's *The Bachelorette*, in which a girl gets to pick a winner from twenty eejits clamouring for her charms . . . *High School Reunion*, seventeen people who attended High School together reunite in Hawaii, ten years on . . .

There's more, lots more. Don't think our television executives won't be watching, and copying, every last embarrassing, demeaning idea. I've seen the television light-entertainment future . . . It looks like I'll *still* be watching the past . . .

Stick to the Script

The BBC is universally acclaimed as the greatest national broadcasting service in the world, which is why a simple Irish lad, brought up on *Dick Barton Special Agent*, *The Goons*, and the multitude of delights that was the BBC Light Programme, will always be proud to work for the Grand Old Lady of Portland Place, or 'Auntie', as my sadly-missed friend Kenny Everett used to call it. The BBC's game is communication, not only to its British licence-payers, but to every corner of the known world, through radio (The BBC World Service) and television (BBC World, BBC Prime). I may have already recounted to you the groundswell of Danish hatred that took the feet from under me six years ago, because of my gentle joshing at the expense of the two Danish presenters of the Eurovision Song Contest, staged that year in Copenhagen. I hadn't allowed for the fact that most Danes watch BBC TV in preference to their own TV stations. The Danes took my ribbing as a foul slur on their proud nation, and I can never now enter Copenhagen airport without a paper bag over my head . . .

The BBC is the world's greatest international and national communicator. You should be proud to own it. Does the Corporation not bring this slogan to your eager ear, and eye, every hour on the hour? 'It's Your BBC!' Actually, listeners to my Radio 2 show will know that I apply a codicil: 'Well, it's not really yours. It's ours – you're just paying for it . . . .'

I have yet to receive the ceremonial sixth-floor hanging, drawing and quartering for this appalling heresy. The Big Boys Up There only listen to Radio 4. Poor old John Humphrys has only got to make a passing comment on the price of fish before he's dragged before the Inquisition and has his epaulettes torn off. I get away with the Awful Truth because I'm a mere performer, a hobble-de-hoy, little better than a strolling player. I have more listeners than any radio show in Europe, and possibly even more than any broadcaster in the USA but who, the Big Cheeses reason, is going to take me seriously? After all, I'm not a journalist steeped in world and home affairs, trained to a hair to separate the wheat from the chaff. My opinion has the weight of a ton of feathers. They're probably right, although wasn't it the great American politician, Adlai Stevenson, who said that in his experience, journalists, when separating the wheat from the chaff, tended to throw away the wheat?

Recently, we suffered the unseemly sight of a BBC journalist throwing his papers in the air, and leaving in a marked manner, because he couldn't be in the same newsroom as his co-presenter, who seemed, I'm bound to say, no strain to look upon over a plywood newsdesk. The main thrust of his pique appeared to be that he was a serious journalist, and she had somehow sneaked in under the razor-wire as a mere presenter of 'make-over' shows. Journalists have a high opinion of themselves and their profession, despite the fact that every poll puts the noble profession a close second to pensions salesmen as the least trustworthy of callings. Why your man left in such a huff is a mystery. News reading is not something to get self-important or petulant about, it's a piece of cake, the easiest job in the media. Get your good suit and tie on, a quick dab in make-up (in Fiona Bruce's case, the lippy is going to take a tad longer) make yourself comfy, and here comes the six o'clock news, all written nice and clearly before your very eyes. Read it clearly and distinctly, ask the reporter the questions you have written down in front of you, and there! As soon as that silly weather-man shuts up, it's time to go home ...

And before you start with the 'fair play, old boy, there's more to it than that!' I was a radio and television newsreader, and there isn't. Mind you, I wasn't a journalist, and thereby hangs a tale: for neither was Angela Rippon, the most iconic TV newsreader of the seventies. She told me that one evening, at the close of the six o'clock bulletin, she ad-libbed 'Good Evening'. Her sub-editor screamed at her for a full half-hour, and had he been carrying something more lethal than a pencil, she'd have been off to Accident and Emergency. He hadn't written 'Good Evening' in the script. She'd added it on – and she wasn't a journalist! Shortly afterwards, Ms Rippon took herself and her legs off to *Morecambe and Wise*, and said 'Good Evening' whenever she pleased ...

Eurovisions

Just when you thought it was safe to turn on your television again, here it comes, the blessed Eurovision Song Contest. Like the Horse of the Year Show, the thing seems to turn up like the proverbial bad penny every six weeks or so ... For years, it was the done thing among the cognoscenti to deny vehemently ever watching it: 'Eurovision Song Contest! God no! Miranda and I were at that Ibsen thing at the Donmar ...' For years, it was a programme that only the public liked. In the BBC itself, influential figures doubted whether Auntie should bother continuing with the show. In fact, it's my theory that they only continued with it to spite London Weekend TV, who would still die for it ...

Then, quite suddenly, attitudes changed amongst the 6th floor Armanis. Eurovision was no longer a dirty word. It was okay to like it. It was even street-smart trendy. What brought about this volte-face? Well, somebody must have whispered into the suits' ears that Richard Curtis, he of *Four Weddings and a Funeral*, not to mention Comic Relief, was not only an aficionado of the good old Song Fest, but he actually held a party to celebrate it every May! Lenny Henry did the same. Must be okay then . . .

In my book, it's always been okay, since the very first time I watched it, in glorious black and white, on a rather fuzzy set in Dublin. Everybody's set was fuzzy in Dublin, in those far off days of the late fifties and early sixties. Ireland had no television service of its own, so Dublin's Fair City presented an extraordinary prospect to the unwary traveller; a forest of 20 foot-tall TV aerials reaching for the fringe reception of BBC and ITV. It can't be said, therefore, that I ever saw Pearl Carr and Teddy Johnson at their best with the crowd-pleasing 'Sing Little Birdie', although I have a keen recollection of Kenneth McKellar's kilt, with no memory whatsoever of his song.

A couple of years later, all had changed; changed utterly. At least for Irish viewers of the sainted contest. There she was, the virginal Dana, all that was best in Irish girlhood, walking away with it with 'All Kinds of Everything'. Ireland went mad. It hasn't been the full shilling ever since. At least as far as the Eurosong is concerned. Indeed, many trace Ireland's transformation from Europe's Poor Relation to the Celtic Tiger Economy that it is today to that momentous victory all those years ago. Such is its talismanic qualities, that the Irish have been loathe to let the trophy go ever since. They seem to win it every second year, with the UK gamely trotting in as runner-up. Whatever you think about the quality of the songs, and let's face it, we're not talking La Scala here, it has to be admitted that Ireland provided the all-time high-spot a couple of years ago with the *Riverdance* interval act. It's so right somehow, that the outstanding event of the Eurovision so far has been the interval . . .

You're right, that's a cheap shot. What about Abba? Ah, me lost youth . . . Well I remember that balmy evening in Brighton when they pulled the house down with 'Waterloo'. Olivia Newton-John, for the UK, was an also-ran. At the time, she was a very big star on the British pop scene, and it had been a calculated risk which hadn't come off . . . 'That's it!', I said, at my pontifical worst. 'She gambled, and lost! I warned her . . . ' Of course, Olivia went off to Hollywood and became a huge star, with *Grease* and a hatful of international hits . . . Shows how much I know . . . You'd think I ought to know something, after hundreds of years of doing the thing. Nada, zip, nothing. I start with a clear head, but by the time the third rehearsal is done, so am I: the once-keen brain has been reduced to the consistency of porridge. It's all right for you – you only have to listen to them once . . .

I've been criticised for this admittedly cavalier attitude, particularly by the other European countries' commentators; 'If you don't like the Eurovision, why do you do it?' They don't get it. I love the Song Contest. I love it for its awfulness; the dreadful songs, the terrible outfits, the choreography, the schlocky grandeur of it all . . . The greatest thrill of my life in television was to walk out on that stage last year at the Birmingham Arena to present the Contest, and this year, in Jerusalem, it'll be my privilege and pleasure to commentate yet again. And just for you, dear reader, since you didn't ask; this could be another winning year for the UK . . . But then, what do I know?

What about this prophetic little piece I wrote, before last year's contest, in Belgrade? 'I won't be troubling you for the next couple of weeks, as I gird my loins and indulge in a little dry-stone walling to calm myself for the challenge of the Eurovision Song Contest. From what I've seen of the forty-five participants (did you know that there were forty-five countries in Europe?) the thread of musical lunacy is as strong as ever. I would have predicted Russia to win, since everybody in the former Eastern Bloc is terrified of losing their oil and gas, but in the end, it will depend on who's got the most representatives in the Final, the Baltic or the Balkans. And France, Germany, Spain and ourselves? We just pay for most of it, otherwise we'd never qualify for the Final . . . If we'd only thrown the Cold War . . .

Russia Won

Then in the finest 'poacher turned game-keeper' tradition, I was asked to deliver the keynote address at the European Broadcasting Union's Convention this year, in Lucerne. This is it:

> My long and happy journey with the Eurovision Song Contest began in Dublin, in 1971. Probably before many of you here tonight were born. I had left Ireland, and Radio Telefis Eireann in late 1969, to begin a daily radio show for the BBC. I had been the Senior Announcer on RTE radio, but from 1966, worked occasionally for BBC Radio. Eventually, the DG of RTE called for me. I knocked on his door. 'Come in! Ah, Wogan. Where the carpet starts, you stop!' I knew then that my future was elsewhere . . . Although when I began to work for BBC TV, I realised that attitudes to mere presenters were no different. We were as hobble-de-hoys, strolling players, who ought to be grateful for the work. My first contract off-ered me third-class rail travel to the outside broadcast. The producer and his secretary travelled first class. I suspect that many executives in the BBC, and many of you here tonight wish that it was still so . . . Presenters, the talent,

they've got too big for their boots! Take that damned Wogan, sending up and making fun of our Great Eurovision Song Contest every year. Who does he think he is? Why doesn't the BBC control him, tell him what to say, get rid of him? Well, I thought I'd leave, before they did . . .

Back in 1971, the Contest was staged in a small Dublin music hall, the Gaiety Theatre. For an ordinary play or show, it had seating for no more than a thousand people. For the Eurovision, with all the paraphernalia of cameras, sound, lighting, commentary booths, and an orchestra, there couldn't have been more than four- to five-hundred in the audience. About fifteen countries took part, the presenters were confined to a box overlooking the stage. What a contrast to last year in Belgrade, or Athens, and Copenhagen in a football stadium, with 30,000 people, vodka shots being sold in the aisles, and the commentary positions so far away from the stage I might as well have done it from a monitor in London . . . Perhaps it might have been just as well if I had . . . A Danish journalist had caught my commentary on BBC Prime, and it seemed that I had insulted Denmark's honour by not taking the production seriously, and referring to the two presenters as 'Dr Death and the Tooth Fairy'. But they were like two characters from a fairy tale, making all their announcements in rhyming couplets. What commentator wouldn't see the silly side of that? Well, only me, apparently . . . Now, whenever I pass through Copenhagen Airport, I have to wear a paper bag over my head . . . countries can be very sensitive about how they're seen on the Eurovision. A couple of years ago, the entry from Hungary had dancers cavorting round a campfire, and in passing, I commented 'Play gypsy, play!' I was inundated within hours with insulted emails from Hungary, accusing me of calling all Hungarians 'gypsies'. Several of them described in lurid detail what would happen to me if I ever showed my face in Budapest . . . Dangerous work, commentating. I remember the Contest staged in

Luxembourg, when the terrorist threat of Black September meant that the hall was ringed by armoured cars and heavily armed troops. Inside, just before the show started, the floor manager announced: 'Do not stand up to applaud during the show, or you may be shot by security.' It had a slightly depressing effect on the show ... There were moments of real history as well: that memorable evening in Stockholm in the seventies when the Portuguese entry came on stage with carnations in the barrels of guns, and signalled the revolution that overthrew Salazar ... And the moments of high drama: in Jerusalem, the previous year's winner, Dana International, awarding the Grand Prix, tripped over his/her six-inch heels, and fell flat on the stage. Immediately three members of Mossad flung themselves on top of the unfortunate Dana, thinking it was an assassination attempt ... I had presented the song contest from Birmingham, UK, the year Dana International won, and I'm bound to say that I did laugh heartily, remembering how Dana had decided to change her dress when it was announced that she/he was the winner, leaving me standing speechless in front of one hundred million viewers, while she changed ... That was tough, particularly as I had not only presented the show, but after every announcement, had to jump off the stage and run round the back to do the commentary. I lost weight that evening ... Presenting the Eurovision's a hard job, usually requiring more than three languages, and it's interesting to see how different nations see the job. Was it Estonia where the two presenters sang into each others faces like Nelson Eddy and Jeanette MacDonald, while pretending to fall in love? Why, for goodness sake? It's not romance, it's not a musical comedy. The only chemistry necessary between the two presenters ought to be pleasant good humour ... It was Kiev where the female had an American accent and a voice that would strip paint, it was definitely Rome, Italy, where the male presenter, who had been behaving all evening as if he was auditioning for a part in a Quentin Tarantino movie, decided to argue from the stage with the invigilator, the great Frank Naef. Italy hasn't taken part since. Which is a shame for the home of opera, and the great San Remo Festival, which I think was the inspiration for the Eurovision ... And it can only have been Sweden where the lady pretended that her skirt had been torn off by the scenery, as she announced the next song in her knickers ... Ah, if only I could remember half the foolishness ... And you ask me if I love the Eurovision? How could I not? The French entry last year had the singer coming on stage in a golf buggy; another, whose nationality escapes me, had washing hanging out on a line ... Ireland's entry, a puppet turkey ... surely nobody in their right mind can take deliberate silliness seriously. The interval acts, which over the years have ranged from the sublime to the ridiculous: Ireland's magnificent *Riverdance*, which went on to be a hugely successful international show in its own right. And then I remember a night, I think it was Malmo, Sweden, when an elaborate routine involving tubes and tunnels that took ten minutes to set up, and was supposed to culminate, as in the legend of William Tell, with an arrow piercing an apple on a young boy's head, culminated instead, after all the preparation and the flashing lights, with the arrow missing the apple ... As to interval acts, could I make a plea on behalf of all radio commentators? Could you make sure that they're musical? Trying to commentate for fifteen minutes on mime acts, jugglers or clowns or any kind of silent performance that the listeners can't see is not easy, to say the least, and usually results in the radio commentator handing back to his home network for a selection of Eurosong hits ...

I'm not here to criticise, I'm here to extoll the virtues of the world's greatest international television event, but if I might make just one little professional point: please, producers, don't try to be funnier than the Contest. I'm thinking particularly of the Green Room section of the show, when the votes are coming in. Every year, it's an unfunny, unmitigated disaster, as two other presenters try to inject a spirit of knockabout, spontaneous humour into the event. Look, the Eurovision is exciting, camp, foolish, spectacular fun. You can't top it. You can't top it with amateurish, unstructured, silliness. Just talk to the performers. Let their excitement and laughter speak for itself . . . Because, ladies and gentlemen, that's what the Eurovision Song Contest is about: fun. It's Light Entertainment, the biggest of its kind anywhere in the world, and certainly over the last few years, the most brilliantly produced three-and-a-half hours of live television ever seen . . . But, it's not about politics, it's not about asserting your place in the Community, it's not about national pride. It's not about flag-waving. It's not a war. It's a Song Contest. It's great to celebrate when your country's song wins. Just remember, the following day, every other country has forgotten about it. It's a marvellous, colourful occasion, but it's a one-night wonder, like all television programmes; in one eye, and out the other, and what's new on the box tonight . . . It's not an opportunity to show your next-door neighbour how much you love them, it's not an opportunity to show some more distant country how much you dislike them. It's about picking the best popular song in Europe, and having as much fun as we can in the process of doing it.

That's what I've tried to bring to the Contest that I love: a spirit of joy, the sheer fun of it. Through the many years I've been accused of not taking the Contest seriously enough, of sending it up, of jeering it, of not showing enough respect. Wrong. I'm a friend of this Contest, possibly its oldest friend. How do friends behave to each other? Do they flatter each other, like lovers? Are they sycophantic? Do they constantly tell each other what they want to hear? Do real friends pretend? Do they tell each other little white lies? No. Real friends tell each other the truth. They don't indulge in idle flattery. They send each other up, they make fun of each other. If a friend does something silly, you tell him so, and you laugh at him, just as he would at you. Friends may laugh at your expense, but never hurtfully. That's the spirit in which this Contest should take place every year, the spirit in which I've been presenting it since 1971. It's that spirit of unity and friendship among the nations of Europe that was behind the beginning of this great enterprise. You must never, no matter how big this Contest may become in the future, never forget what it's really about: nations coming together in friendly, musical competition . . . I'm immensely flattered that you have invited me to speak to you. It's a memory I will carry with me as warmly as my memories of all the Eurovisions that I was privileged to attend. I've already made my farewells to the great British public, and now I must make them to you. Keep the flames of friendship and song burning. I'll be watching.

Holiday Special

When we're not up to our shoulder-pads in gardening, cookery, makeovers, airports, hospitals and 'we'll make you famous for ten minutes' programmes on the television, what have we got for light relief? Holiday Homes in Foreign Parts! The daytime and early evening schedules are full-to-bursting with amiable young ladies, steering eager British couples to their Dream Homes in The Sun. These are not to be confused with the profusion of Holiday and Travel programmes, that tell you absolutely nothing remotely critical of the places they visit, and are simply glorified brochures that enable Craig Doyle to speak in a language only his mother can understand.

Now, before you start having a go at me for my apparently curmudgeonly stance, let me ask you this: have you ever seen anybody, any one of these desperately searching couples, buy anything? I thought not. Every hour on the hour, on every channel, on every television in the land, Vernon and Dolly, Kevin and Maria,

Norman and Katie, are being led around by some bimbo, into beachhouses in Turkey, cottages in Croatia, apartments in Algiers, deserted farmhouses in the Aveyron, and ruined churches in Latvia. And they love them all! All you ever hear from the questing couples is effusive praise: 'Isn't this lovely?' 'Ooh, that's delightful', 'Beautiful, absolutely beautiful' . . . Not a word of criticism, not a smidgen of good old Anglo-Saxon contrariness about the appalling décor, the dreadful plumbing, the kitchen from the Stone Age, and bedrooms built with Little Jimmy Clitheroe in mind. On all of these programmes, our intrepid searchers after a Better Life Abroad Away From The Rat Race, are exhibited at least four different properties, all of them individual: a cottage, a townhouse, an apartment, a dilapidated wreck in need of repair. And without exception, our couples are ecstatic about every one of them. Over a farewell drink with the Blonde Who's Pretending To Be A Saleswoman, enthusiasm reigns. It can only be a matter of days before contracts are exchanged, the deal is done, and Tim and Josie say farewell to Boring Old Blighty, and 'Hola' to the Costa Calida. Except that they never do. Nothing happens. The desperately searching, wildly enthusiastic couples board the plane, head for home, and are never heard from again. And all that's left for our hostess to do is announce, brightly: 'Sadly, Brian and Tracey were unable to move quickly enough and the home of their dreams was sold to another buyer' . . . 'Unfortunately Sarah and James couldn't find á buyer for their home in Guildford, so the lovely stone cottage they so wanted in Crete, went to someone else' . . . 'Derek and Carmen couldn't make up their minds between the townhouse and the old barn, so they will wait until next year, and once again search the Algarve for their home in the sun . . .' Give us a break!

Who are these people? Where do they come from? How do they get on these programmes? Have you ever been asked if you and your husband/wife/partner would like to have a look around some properties on the Cote D'Azur, free, gratis and for nothing? Do you know anybody who has? Exactly. It's like the endless Polls and Lists that we are subjected to: Most Popular, Most Attractive, Best-Dressed, Greatest Pop Tune Ever, on and on. Do you ever bother to vote in any of these polls? Do you know anybody who does? Yes, we'll talk about them, discuss them, but vote? If less than 50% of us can be bothered to vote in a General Election, what can be the miniscule percentage of voters in these polls, and how can they possibly be represented as 'the people's choice'? (Falls off soap-box.)

So, to return to these arbitrarily chosen sun-seekers; has anybody you know ever met one of these couples in real life? I thought not. I can't pretend to know the complete answer, but let one leave you with a couple of thoughts: Crop Circles. Flying Saucers. We are not alone . . .

I'm A Celebrity . . . Hang Me

Whenever I turn on the television these days, I see young people posturing, prostrating or degrading themselves in the pursuit of fame, and what's worse, older folk, who have been briefly kissed by fame before the fickle jade flitted by, attempting to rekindle the flame by similar degradation in Big House, Jungle or Kitchen. If only they knew . . . This week, at a Christmas party, a distinguished-looking woman gave me more than a passing glance. I responded, as any gentleman would, with a winsome smile. She came over to me. 'Do I know you?' she said. I told her my name. A faint glimmer of recognition crept over her fine features. 'Ah,' she said, 'I don't watch the television, apart from the news' . . . She then went on to lament the fate of Edward Stourton, with a passing reference to Jonathan Ross, whom she claimed never to have seen, but read about in the papers. Like most who claim 'never to watch television', had we continued our discourse, she would doubtless have expressed forthright opinion on *Strictly*, *X-Factor* and Carol Vordeman's exit from *Countdown*, but a tide of hungry lunch-seekers swept us apart.

Those 'a cut above' seem to watch popular television by accident, or osmosis. It's been my experience that a well-known face is not all that it's cracked up to be, and my theory, yet to be exploded, that the public think that everybody who appears on television is freely interchangeable, is backed up by the hard fact that for years, Parkinson, Aspel, Harty and I were thought to be one and the same person. Time without number, people would sympathise with me for Oliver Reed's appalling behaviour (Aspel), Rod Hull's Emu attempting to strangle me (Parkinson) or Grace Jones giving me a right-hander across the chops (Harty). For years, when I first arrived from Erin's Isle without a shoe on my foot, people never knew the difference between Eamonn Andrews, Val Doonican and myself. I first found that cruel mistress, Fame, when but a boy broadcaster in Ireland. Within months, I found that I could no longer frequent my favourite pub, without someone either fawning over me, or inviting me outside for a bout of fisticuffs. Where in the past I could walk down O'Connell Street without a Grecian bend, now I had old biddies calling after me: 'Terry Wogan. Thinks he's f****** gorgeous!' I thought it would be different in Britain, more reserved, until stopped in Carnaby Street by a gent, who said, 'Here! Sign this would you? It's for my wife. I can't stand you myself.'

Fame. Footprints on the sands of time? I don't think so.

In the Good Old Days, high-days and holidays were few and far between. The average man in the British street had little respite from his workaday drudgery, and his opportunities for leisure, rest and recreation were rare indeed. There was always the tavern of course, and the gin-palace, but relaxation was at a premium. Hard, unrelenting work and tedium were the watchwords, a monotony broken only if you were unfortunate enough to get knocked on the head by a passing press-gang, and forcibly recruited into their Majesty's Navy, where you spent the rest of your life dodging cannon-balls, eating weevil-infested biscuits, catching scurvy. That's if you weren't being keel hauled, walking the plank, or dying of swamp fever in the Indies. You could always join their Majesty's Army, of course, and see how long you could stay alive under musket fire, bayonet-charges and the hooves of the French cavalry.

In those good old days, nobody went on holidays, anywhere, for two good reasons: there were no holidays, and there was nowhere to go. Unless you were Jane Austen, in which case there was always a horse and cart to take you to Bath, where you walked about a lot, talked the most inconsequential rubbish, watched the elderly and infirm choking themselves to death on the waters, and were in bed by ten hoping that you'd never wake up. There were no sun-kissed Costas – *Blackpool* hadn't been invented, for goodness sake. Nobody went to France, except the Scarlet Pimpernel, a trip to the Mediterranean, and you were a certainty for some Sultan's harem. Anyone who went to Florida had their scalp hanging from a Seminole totem pole before sunset.

There was the theatre, of course, the haunt of mountebanks, charlatans, drunkenness and moral decay. No change there then . . . Of spectacle, the great day out, there was none. Unless you count a rollicking good night at the cockfight, or the occasional bare-knuckle fisticuffs over thirty-five rounds. Bear baiting too alleviated the gloom from time to time; but for a real bit of a do, and a jolly good day's entertainment, you couldn't beat a public execution. People flocked in their thousands to Tyburn Hill in London to see some unfortunate swing from the gibbet. They made a day of it, eating, drinking, singing, roistering. Not much difference from *Proms in the Park*, really. I do confess to a certain apprehension, particularly as the stage is only a few hundred yards from where they used to swing on Tyburn Hill. It helps to keep 'dying' on-stage in proportion, love.

We're not like that these days, though, are we? Although some may support execution for a capital crime, nobody would want to go to a *public* hanging, would they? No, we're more enlightened, more civilised these days ... or are we? When I watch what is generically called 'reality' TV, I do wonder. For what are *Big Brother*, *Pop Idol* and *Fame Academy*, if they're not about our voyeuristic pleasure in seeing our fellow humans, if not exactly executed, degraded, dumped, and, yes, destroyed? What did we feel as we watched Ann Diamond's and Les Dennis's insecurities and inadequacies paraded before us and then further dragged painfully through the mud of the tabloids? What about those poor unfortunate *Pop Idol* and *Fame Academy* hopefuls, encouraged to parade their fantasies and hopeless dreams before us, only to have them dashed to smithereens by some 'judge', whose only interest is their own over-weening ego? And the final rejection, by public vote.

Let's admit to at least a frisson at seeing our fellow man brought down. Particularly if they're famous, or even a 'celebrity'. It has become a bonanza for those who enjoyed watching 'celebs' press the self-destruct button, or having it pressed for them, by the ever-vindictive press. Celebrity-hood, at least in Britain, has become a minefield. People get elevated to the stars, and shot from the skies in almost the same breath. Their feelings, their personal lives, their families are ploughed into the dust, all dignity torn from them. The price of fame? Who, in their right mind, would want to pay it? You can perhaps excuse the young, reaching for the unreachable on *Pop Idol*, but the grown men and women who queue up for *Big Brother*? Pass.

And as for *I'm A Celebrity . . . Get Me Out Of Here*? It restored a body's faith in the good sense of The Great British Public, giving the elbow to the chancers and fakers, and honouring the honest yeoman qualities of Christine Hamilton, Tara Palmer-Tomkinson and Tony Blackburn. Only a matter of time before another hand-picked selection of attention-seeking sacrificial lambs are led to the slaughter, and the tender mercies of Ant and Dec. Incidentally, did anyone ever find out which one was which? I'm pretty sure one of them was working the other with his foot, because when he (either Ant or Dec) wasn't talking, a rictus grin would take over his face, while at the same time his eyes glazed over. And these are the two-some who can't decide whether they're going to be the new likely lads, or the all-new Morecambe and Wise. It's me again, isn't it?

Shortly after they prised Tony Blackburn from his hat, and re-placed it with a tiara (as distinct from a Tarara) someone sent a robot into one of the pyramids, to probe the inner recesses and mysterious fortress of Tutankhamen's, or possibly, Rameses' tomb. R2D2 was supposed to go where no man had gone before – well, not for 5000 years anyway – rummage about a bit, and come up with something new in the way of papyrus, mummies or scarabs. Unfortunately the little mechanical marvel, having breached one door, found itself faced with another. Some more ancient Egyptian trickery. Back to the old drawing board . . . It didn't fool my loyal lis-tener: 'I know what that robot will find after it's drilled through half a dozen more doors in that pyramid. It'll find a pile of logs in a corner, and a skeleton holding a notice (written in hieroglyphics, naturally) saying 'I'm a Pharaoh . . . Get me out of here . . .'

If I'm repeating myself, don't bother to stop me, it's my age, but I may have mentioned before how the phenomenally successful *Big Brother* series of voyeur-driven television provoked little or no reac-tion from my seven million radio listeners. I've always assumed this was due to a combination of factors: my own indifference to what I regard as exploitative and degrading television, and the fact that the average age of my radio audience is over forty-five. The participants in *Big Brother* are mostly under thirty, with a mental age and IQ well below that. *I'm a Celebrity etc. etc.*, has dispatched my fond delusions.

I neither watched the awful thing, nor commented on it, for the same pompous reasons that I never watch *Big Brother*. Yet my listeners leapt upon it like ravening wolves. They write to me in their hundred, nay, thousands. Who was I to gainsay the people's choice? So I watched it too – well, a couple of episodes, for a couple of minutes. Enough, already . . . and I think my listeners watched it because, for a change, they could watch people on the television who were actually over thirty. Who won? The oldest inhabitant, bless him . . . and his logs.

Most of my listeners, cynics that they are, were convinced that *I'm A Celebrity, I can't believe it's not butter* was shot on a back-lot at Pinewood studios. Where were the flies? The duck-billed platypuses? Those spiders that climb up the loo and bite your bum? Anybody spot a koala? A kangaroo, even? A member of the cast of *Neighbours*? Rolf Harris? Who bathes in a lake in a tropical country? There are things there that can kill you just by looking at you. Well, it *wasn't* the back-lot of Pinewood, merely the back garden of a luxury hotel, which had been sanitised and cleansed of every known animal and creepy-crawly in the Antipodes. The celebrities would have been in more danger in Disneyland.

Before I leave you, panting for more, let's look at this vexed question of 'celebrity'. The participants in the above-mentioned debacle were dismissed by the press as 'D-', even 'E-list' celebs. Be fair lads. It's only the media that makes those distinctions. As far as the plain people of Britain are concerned when you've seen one celeb, you've seen them all. The public make no 'A', 'B', 'C' etc., list distinctions. We're all the same – some people who appear on the telly, the wireless, the screen, the theatre, the football field, and get our pictures in the paper. They'd have a hard time in telling Brian Conley from Billy Connolly if one of them didn't dye his beard purple. And they used to think that I was Des O'Connor. Now, they can't tell me apart from Tony Blackburn.

Don't put your daughter on stage, Mrs Worthington.

Play the Game You Cads

Some time ago, somebody must have whispered in the shapely ear of ITV's Programme Director: 'Psst! Forget Light Entertainment! Elbow Cilla! Ditto Bruce/Lily/even Jamie! Football! Footie! It's the new rock'n'roll!' I suppose, with all our experience, we should never be astonished by the Twilight Zone that is the inner sanctum of television, but, slap me vitals if the Programme Director didn't swallow it. Hook, line and sinker, 'neath the jackboot of Herr Flick, otherwise known as Anne Robinson . . . Not even the old Lounge Lizard himself, Des Lynam, could save football at seven o'clock on a Saturday evening. Sixty per cent of the population are female, and the only footballer they've ever heard of is David Beckham. Indeed, it's worth noting that the Great Posh herself had never heard of Becks until their eyes met across a crowded room. Football may be the new religion, but its temple is the pub, its altar is the widescreen and its faithful are the lads.

The devotion of the England football fan to his club and country, is comparable only to the fierce faith of the Fundamentalist believer. It's medieval; no it goes back much further than the Dark Ages: the football fan paints his face like an aboriginal, works himself up into a frenzy with firewater and ritual chanting, and then attacks the rival tribe. We haven't come that far from the trees and the caves . . . Football inspires the blind faith that used to be the preserve of religion, an unquestioning loyalty to club and country that regards all others as without honour, without the true belief – Heretics, to be scorned, nay, crushed. In parts of Scotland and Nothern Ireland where, unfortunately, the ranting voice of the medieval preacher can still be heard, religious intolerance and downright hatred is still part and parcel of some football matches. However, these are mere extensions of established churches and their prejudices, not the pure, unsullied faith of the Engerland fan.

Sure, what's the harm in it? Wave the flag, stick in on to the back of your white van, cheer on the lads. What's wrong with loyalty to the country, a bit of national pride? Look at the fuss the Irish make over St Patrick's Day, and the Scots on Burns Night. Well, let me say that when I was growing up in Ireland, nobody made a fuss over St Patrick's Day. It was a holiday, a day off in Lent when you could eat and drink what you liked, and apart from a sprig of shamrock in your lapel, and the odd pipe-band marching out-of-step up O'Connell Street, Limerick, in the driving rain, nothing to write home about. In New York, of course, they'd be painting Fifth Avenue green. But those were people who thought Ireland was still white-washed thatched cottages and Maureen O'Hara tending sheep in a red petticoat. I will not comment on Burns Night as the Scots are easily inflamed, apart from saying that my first night in Beijing, China, was on Burns Night. I saw tartan, haggis, suffered all that 'chieftain of the pudding race' stuff, drank my fill of the waters of the Tain, danced four-hand reels, Dashing White Sergeants and Gay Gordons, and never saw a single oriental face for the entire evening . . . .

Why can't the English do the same for St George? is the cry. Of course there can be nothing wrong with following the banner of the national saint of England, even if he was Greek. So's Prince Philip. It's me. I'm wary of blind faith, that's all, whether it be football or religion. I've seen what the religious variety can do in my own country, and here, the footballing faith seems just as harmful, at its fundamentalist worst. It breeds a mob culture, a violent intolerance for anyone not of the same persuasion. Loyalty to the flag turns into jingoism and xenophobia. Then, it's turn your faith-filled hatred on anyone who doesn't look like you, talk like you, or wear the same shirt as you. And as long as the print media continues to whip its readers to frenzies of false hopes, to fantastic dreams of Holy Grails of European Championships and World Cups, to elevate footballers to the status of gods, so will the blind faithful follow the Great Crusade. As earlier faithful followers found, Crusades don't end well, and the most recent Football Crusade, to Portugal, ended in disappointment, recrimination and tears. The Age of Enlightenment brought reason to religious faith; anyone see a light at the end of footy's tunnel?

Noddy and Big Ears . . .

I have my mother's ears. I'm also the proud possessor of that dear, departed lady's eyes, nose and temperament, but it's the ears that stand out. Well, not so much stand out as *loom*. They're large and they're getting larger. It's sad, but true, and probably all-too-well-known already to those of you a certain age, but the only physical adornments that grow bigger with passing years are the nose and ears. The rest, regrettably, diminishes. In men's cases even the old bum disappears! Not that I ever had much of a view of it, but I'll be sad to see it go.

Never mind. Big ears are a good sign in a man. No, I have no medical, scientific or even cabalistic reasons for saying that – it just makes me feel good. 'Lucky lobes', that's what my son, Mark, used to call his granny. 'Cheers, Big Ears!', is now how he greets me . . . a faintly superior smile plays about my mobile, slightly dangerous, lips . . . Clark Gable had big ears – precious little harm they ever did him. Bing Crosby had jug-handles for ears – few enough complaints there. Julius Caesar must have had a mighty pair – how else to keep that laurel wreath securely in position?

We of the Super Shell-Likes then, have nothing to be ashamed of, but it was a welcome boost all the same, to read of good old Noddy's recent triumphs on American television. Because, of course, what's good for Noddy is good for Big Ears. Not *this* particular Big Ears, silly. This particular Big Ears had *his* chance at American television some years ago, but he passed. The people frightened him. Not the American people. American *television* people, who generally behaved like disciples of the Church of Latter Day Saints . . . But I digress . . . It's Noddy's chum, Big Ears, I'm referring to. What's good for old Nod, is good for the Big E.

Success is no stranger to Noddy; he's been a biggie since 1949, and he and his little banger, and Big Ears, of course, have coined it in books, magazines, comics, theatre and television since then. There was a bit of trouble with the thought-police in the eighties, when accusations of racism and sexism were levelled at our hero by the apparently sane, but obviously barking inhabitants of the padded cells of political correctness. Old Nods was forced to change. He was no longer allowed to feel 'gay', and certainly not 'queer'. The gollywogs – Toytown's things – were replaced by monkeys and goblins. Big Ears, bless him, remained unmoved by the winds of change. We aurally challenged folk take a liberal view . . . Noddy and his little yellow car have travelled the world successfully for years, from France to Japan, from Australia to Portugal. Unlike the pound sterling, the little chap is a British institution that readily adapts to the whims and the quiddities of Johnny Foreigner. He's multi-lingual, as well as multi-national. In France he is 'Oui, Oui' in Germany, 'Purzelknirps', in Sweden, 'Kvartetten', and in Iceland, 'Doddi'. For my money, the last name is the only one that comes close . . .

So, we shouldn't be too surprised that our boy with the bells made it big Stateside. On the other hand, the last British character to create a stir on American TV was Benny Hill . . . Thomas the Tank Engine has done pretty well, too – but what does this tell us of the valuation that American TV puts on *our* television products? They give us *The Simpsons*, we give them *Noddy*. They give us *Friends, Frasier, Cheers, Seinfeld* – we give them Benny Hill . . . And before we go *too* crazy over Noddy's big bucks, let's remember that he features solely on the American PBS, the Public Broadcast System, with an audience of 2.5 million out of a population of 250 million. *South Park* he ain't . . .

You see, the American viewing public is the most parochial, narrow-minded, in the whole wide world. If you haven't got an American accent, or at least a mid-atlantic one, you're dead. Benny Hill's extraordinary success was almost entirely down to the fact that his American TV shows were edited to be mostly mime. The only British artist/presenter to crack popular TV in the States remains David Frost. Otherwise, a British accent is an anathema. When you read of various British TV presenters being approached to work in the States, take it with a pinch of salt. They wouldn't touch an 'Estuary' accent with a barge-pole. A 'toffee-nosed' one won't cut the mustard, either. Peter Alliss's success as a commentator on American television golf-coverage, is due to their genuflection towards the great game as 'British'. He gives their coverage its gravitas, the 'bottom' they think it needs. The fact that he also gives American TV golf its only glimmerings of wit and humour is a bonus . . .

When we read of the American success of the likes of *Are You Being Served?* and *Upstairs, Downstairs*, we shouldn't confuse it with great popular success. Almost all British TV exports to the States feature on their PBS channel, which only commands 1% to 2% of the potential audience.

My experience of American television executives is that they don't think we know anything about television. We might have invented it, but we don't know how to do it. When they take a series like *Cracker*, or a character like Alf Garnett, they Americanise them until the original character has disappeared. The British characters in the *Friends* episode when they visited London weren't characters – they were caricatures . . .

But *Noddy*'s a cartoon, a rosy-cheeked little doll. They've given him an American accent. He says 'Gee Whiz!', instead of 'I say!' PC Plod is Officer Plod now, and Golly is Gobbo the Goblin, little rascal. And Big Ears? Just good ol' Big Ears. On second thoughts, isn't that 'sizeist'? Who do I complain to?

There Goes the Kids' Inheritance

If, like yours truly, you haven't got a proper job, the occasional afternoon may find you slumped in a near-catatonic state in front of the old Haunted Fish-Tank, otherwise known as The Telly. As the endless dripping of children's serials, quizzes, and couples getting free holidays in Florida, while pretending to be interested in buying a home there, drift by your dazed gaze, only the ads, the commercials, catch the eye, and cause the drooping lids to lift for just a moment. Some are old friends, like the ear-drops: Christopher Timothy encouraging us to take out insurance, so that we can eat Sunday lunch in the pub, 'til we drop; June Whitfield, advising us to have a care, lest we kick the bucket without a penny to pay for the funeral; Frank Windsor with his kindly offer of a carriage clock, and the promise that 'No salesman will call'; stair-lifts, walk-in baths that you enter in your dressing gown, cunning devices that lower and raise you in the bath, as long as you're wearing a bathing-suit. All of them more familiar, and, yes, more beloved, than any soap star . . .

Talking of soap stars – did it give you pause to read that the name 'Alfie', has jumped thirty-one places into the Top 20 Most Popular Boys' Names list? All because of 'Alfie Moon', the kindly host of the Queen Vic Pub in *Eastenders*. Alfie Moon started out as a wide boy, but has ended up as a slightly gormless Mr Pickwick, who loves his old Nana, and a bulging old boiler named Kat. Obviously, there are people out there, lots of them, who think he is a good role model for their little baby boys. The actor who plays 'Alfie' is Shane Ritchie. And where does the name 'Shane' come, in the Most Popular list? Nowhere. Is it Life Imitating Art, or vice versa? 'Chardonnay' is well up on the list of Favourite Girls' Names. And where does that come from? Followers of the well-known grape that plays such an important role in the blending of champagne? An oaky, buttery Australian white wine? Give over. They're naming their little daughters after a busty beauty from the raunchy series *Footballers' Wives* . . . When you think of what Bob Geldof, Jonathan Ross, David Bowie and Jamie Oliver have called their kids, you have to agree with PG Wodehouse's Bertie Wooster: 'There's some rum work done at the baptismal font' . . .

I see that I have wandered from my main thrust yet again. You really must keep a closer eye on me. I suppose it's the writer's equivalent of a 'senior moment'. It could also be that I am a product of my 'butterfly' education: I know a little about a lot, and a lot about nothing . . .

To return to these afternoon, early evening ads on television, am I alone in detecting a Rift in the lute? Who are all those people shouting 'I have the Right!'? What's 'Quote Me Happy!' all about? A listener wrote to tell me that they actually rang up the insurance company who sponsor the ad, shouting 'Quote Me Happy!' The girl on the other end had no idea what he was talking about . . . Obviously working while the ad was on the telly . . . It's the 'finance' ads that have changed the tune for me. It's as if they have scoured the country for the fattest, plainest, worst-dressed people they could find, to tell us how pleased they are that all their financial burdens have been lifted, at a stroke, by this kindly loan company. Debts of £1000 a month? Zip! Reduced in a trice to an easily manageable £200! Need a car, but no money, no prospects, no credit? Ha! Get behind the wheel of this spanking new saloon, and drive off now, into the wide blue yonder . . . And people believe it . . . They actually believe that the loan company is going to give them something for nothing . . . The sad fact that they will be paying off the debt, at a usurious rate, until hell freezes over, doesn't seem to have occurred to the borrowers.

Or maybe it has, and they just don't care. 'Let the kids, and the kids' kids, and the kids' kids' kids, pay off the debt when we're gone.' I don't like it. It's in flagrant renunciation of all we've grown to know and love on our afternoon telly. Where does the 'spend now, pay later' philosophy leave our funeral expenses? And who's going to pay for Sunday lunch? I'm worried. Get me Gordon Brown.

Soap Less

Recently, a character in that jolly tale of everyday country folk, *Emmerdale*, took a break from the mundane and the bucolic, and went off to Spain. He returned a changed man. Mandie-serning-Viewer of Skegness, an eagle-eyed observer was taken aback. Am I the only one who noticed? His father didn't. His sister didn't. His foster brother didn't. Robert has undergone a complete metamorphosis: he doesn't look like Robert. He doesn't act like Robert. Well, I thought, who's rattled our Mandie's cage? It can happen: people often return from holiday with a different perspective, a new take on life – at least for a couple of weeks, until the euphoria and the sun-tan fade . . . And then, Wily Gofar (a lorry-driver listener) joined Mandie at the barricades: 'Jack Sugden (*Emmerdale*) isn't very observant is he? His son Robert goes off to Spain, comes back a completely different kid, and Jack never notices a thing. Mind you, that happened to his wife a while back and he didn't notice then either' . . . Even allowing for Jack not being the brightest button in the box, I was forced to the inescapable conclusion (unless the *X-Files* is right and the aliens are up to their old tricks, that the Soap Czars have done it again: given a character a new head, a new body, a new voice and a new personality, secure in the knowledge that nobody would notice, or if they did would have forgotten about it by the first commercial break. They're not wrong, another of my lorry-driving friends, Phil Cowle, observed: 'what about *Coronation Street?* Nicky Platt went away as a spotty Herbert, and reappeared as a muscle-bound sex god, and his mother Gail never even remarked upon it. Tracy Barlow went upstairs in 1994 to listen to her tapes and wasn't seen for years . . . '

These out-of-body experiences and these mysterious disappearances are old hat to the true suds connoisseur. I blame *Crossroads*, in the sin-filled seventies, when Benny the brain-dead handyman exited stage left in search of a monkey wrench and never came back. In our innocence of the machinations of Soaps, we counted the hours until his return, assuming that the poor sap had got lost in the extensive grounds of the luxury motel. 'Crossroads' burned to the ground and disappeared down the plug hole. It's come back from the grave lately, but there's still no sign of Benny and his bobble hat . . . And we've all become a great deal more cynical in the meantime. I don't know about you, but the scales fell from my innocent eyes when Miss Ellie changed heads in *Dallas*. Within weeks, Digger Barnes had done ditto . . . Then came the ultimate whammy: six months of Stetsons and shoulder-pads, passion and intrigue 'neath the hot Texan sun turned out to be nothing more than a bad dream that Bobby Ewing had while in the shower. It mightn't have been so bad if he'd at least been in bed – but the shower? You try sleeping in one . . .

Soap operas dominate our television viewing. People identify with the characters, live with the plots. For millions, the bars of the Rovers Return, the Queen Vic and the Woolpack are real places, with real people. Many people were astounded to see Madge Bishop from *Neighbours* appear on a BBC TV quiz, when all and sundry had seen her kick the bucket in a Melbourne hospital a couple of days previously . . .

Yet, if there's one thing to which soap operas bear absolutely no relation, it's real life. Have you ever heard a single expletive in any of the fore-mentioned pubs? Take a stroll round to your local, and tell me if you can hear any conversation at all above the roar of the f-ing and blinding! And when you do hear a couple of words strung together, what will the topics be? Inevitably football and last night's telly! In the heart of the East End have you ever heard anybody in the Queen Vic mention West Ham? Anybody in the Rovers Return ever make a passing reference to Manchester United? Anybody in Walford watch *Coronation Street*? If the whole country was talking about it when Phil Mitchell was shot, why did nobody mention it in Rita's Kabin?

Bring back *Eldorado*. Now that was unbelievable . . .

The World According
to Wogan:
A Guide for the
Bewildered

When Did It All Go Pear-Shaped?

Be of good cheer, gentle reader! This is not some sorry tale of excess adipose tissue, nor of a once firmly honed body gone sadly to flesh. There's quite enough of that class of thing about – indeed, a sight too much. You couldn't throw a stone in the Gobi Desert these days without hitting a weight-watcher. The world is obsessed with fat and fitness, cellulite and cholesterol. Young and beautiful are the watchwords. Growing old disgracefully is a thing of the past. We're all going to live forever, with nary a wrinkle nor a gram of excess poundage between us. It's going to get very crowded, we'd *better* stay slim . . .

Courage Camille! This poor excuse for a column is more of a desperate, last-ditch attempt to identify just when, in this island nation's proud history, it all went pear-shaped. Or to pot, if you like. When did the rot set in? Where did it all go wrong? If we can just identify where the slippage began, we might be able to take steps to arrest the nation's headlong rush to moral turpitude, and the abandonment of all that's best in British life. Oh, for a return to tweeny-maids in pinafores and bonnets, to Just William and Violet-Elizabeth Bott, to people playing up and playing the game, to Corinthian Casuals in baggy shorts, to John Snagge and the boat race, to Dick Barton, Special Agent, and, oh, to Mrs Dale and her diary, where Sally (pronounced Selly) had a hat shop, Doctor Dale called his mother-in-law 'mother-in-law', and Mrs Dale was always 'worried about Jim' . . . The snows of yesteryear . . . my lost youth . . . ah, there, dash away that tear; we can't hold back the winds of change, but we could batten down the hatches, if we could just identify the culprits, name the guilty, apportion blame, pass the buck. I know it's not *your* fault – and it's certainly not *mine* . . .

Many steady thinkers put the beginning of the decline down to the easy availability of ready-grated cheese, and the stopping of the sale of loose sweets, but that's a tad too facile. Plausible, certainly, but it must go deeper than that. And it can't have all started to go pear-shaped on the day that Albert Tatlock first took his cap off in the Rovers Return. There must be more to it than that! And yet, and yet . . . Many a radio listener of mine is content to identify the rot-setting moment with the awful day that Nicholas Parsons was axed, along with *Sale of the Century*. Many go back even further, to that dreadful day in 1975, when Bruce Forsyth recorded 'I'm Backing Britain'.

Personally, I'm loathe to put it down to any one event, to any one person, no matter how big or influential. It's all too easy to blame the decline of modern television on Richard Whiteley, although you could certainly make a strong case for it. I expect in years to come they'll blame David Beckham and Posh Spice. 'Brooklyn', eh? I did have a letter from a listener explaining that it was tradition in the Adams family: Victoria apparently has a brother called Paddington, and another named Waterloo. Indeed, she might have had a sister called St Pancras, but a surly guard moved her parents along the carriage . . . I might have doubted the provenance of the letter, had it not come from David's brother, Peckham Beckham . . .

The rot set in because of a combination of factors. You simply can't put it all down to the day they started having newsreaders on television who had to understand the news, instead of just people with nice legs who could do a dance routine on the *Morecambe and Wise Show*. Nor can the BBC be blamed for everything, just because they replaced Valerie Singleton with Lesley Judd on *Blue Peter*. (Although I have to say that I think it was a major factor in the malaise that began to affect the country's youth at that time.)

It was an accumulation of unprecedented disasters that ate away at the nation's moral fibre: the weather went into a decline when Bert Foord left, probably under a cloud. Amy Turtle remembered her lines on *Crossroads*. Policemen got off their bicycles. RAC men stopped saluting. National Service was abolished, but Elvis was drafted. And then 'Crossroads Motel' burned to the ground! How could anything have remained the same?

'Watch Out! It's a Potato!'

My recent piece about 'bad science' – the public being gulled into believing, by newspaper campaigns and half-baked, unscientific research, that everything synthetically modified was 'bad', while everything natural was 'good', found a familiar echo in a recent announcement by the Co-op that they were banning all GM foods from their shelves. This, the Co-op trumpeted, was because of a survey carried out among their customers, sixty odd per cent of whom stated that they were distrustful of GM foods. Whether the Co-op actually took the trouble to find out if those surveyed actually had the vaguest notion of what GM foods were, or what Genetic Modification actually means, is not recorded, but I would be prepared to stake my children's inheritance that a good 99.9% of them hadn't a clue. They were going by what they'd read in the papers: GM bad, Natural good. The fact that the natural world has been trying to kill us ever since we crawled from the primeval slime, is neither here nor there. Neither was the result of a three-year government trial, that GM corn production was less harmful to the environment than conventional farming. Pardon me, while I leave the room for a moment, for a good scream . . .

There, that's better. Anyway, I'm the last one to be criticising anybody for distrusting scientific reports. Hardly a day goes by on my Radio 2 morning meander, that I'm not scoffing at the ubiquitous 'recent research shows'. For instance, recent research has shown that teenagers prefer junk food. Well, I'll go to the foot of our stairs! This research further, surprisingly, found that very few teen-agers have ever made a pasta sauce, or anything more complicated than toast. Catch me, somebody, I've gone quite faint with shock . . . No sensible, nor even half-bewildered person needs research to tell them this kind of simplistic stuff. If you want some really startling evidence of the state of teenagers today, cogitate on this, from one of my listeners.

At the check-out of her local supermarket, she is faced by a 'management trainee', a youth somewhat surprised to find himself on the check-out counter, when he had expected to be taking more senior decisions in an air-conditioned office. He checks through my loyal listener's purchases, until he comes to a bag of vegetables. He is instantly on the *qui-vive*. 'These haven't got a bar-code,' he says, suspiciously. 'I just picked them up at the vegetable counter,' replies my listener, mildly. 'Well,' says the management trainee, 'I've never seen these kind of things before. What are they, anyway?' My listener lets out a sigh. 'They're potatoes,' she says . . . The poor eejit had never seen a potato in its natural state. He probably thought they came out of the ground ready-chipped, or in deep-frozen packets of mash. Where does he think chicken-breasts are grown? I'll bet my diminishing children's inheritance that he doesn't know that Bernard Matthews' turkeys once had feathers. And what does he know of brussels sprouts? It doesn't bear thinking about . . . For some reason, that little story worried me more than speculation over herbicide-resistant oil-seed rape.

Talking about what's coming to my children has reminded me of my splendid next-door neighbour, a stalwart of the old school, in his eighties. Over a chota-peg the other evening, he chortled merrily: ' 'Never had a vegetable throughout my youth.' 'What did you eat?' 'Oh, beef, lamb, game, Mars bars. Oh, and little fruit, although there wasn't much of that during the war. Never saw a banana until I was twenty.' 'And now,' I asked. 'What do you eat these days?' 'Oh, much the same thing, you know. Beef, lamb, game, Mars bars. Bit more fish, but I'm not mad about it. Never really got the hang of fruit.' 'But you do eat vegetables, nowadays, don't you?' 'Goodness, no. Can't bear 'em . . .'

So, let us be of good cheer. It's not only spotty-faced teenagers who wouldn't know a potato from a pickle, or a head of cabbage from a stick of rock. There's at least a couple of generations of a very distinguished old family who've never knowingly looked a vegetable in the face. I'd like to know what 'recent research' would make of them . . .

A Shriek In Time

You know me. Easy-going to a fault. Too nice, some would say, too even-tempered, a tad too overflowing with the milk of human kindness for my own good. Yet, every so often, say once in a millennium, or when the moon turns blue, you will hear from me a high-pitched shriek, accompanied by the time-honoured cry of the loyal TOG (Terry's Old Geezers): 'Is it *me*?' This cry is not easily wrung from the Wogan epiglottis, but it's becoming more frequent of late. It is not precipitated by the state of the NHS, the breakdown of law and order, education, television, nor three-putting at golf. There is but one aspect of British life that cracks the façade of my iron self-control: Transport. Trains and boats and planes. Road and rail. Bus and Underground.

Let's take the roads first, mainly because the car is my mode of transport. I'll be honest, I haven't been on a bus in thirty years, and I don't feel I've missed anything. Most of my formative years, before I borrowed £200 from the Da to buy my Morris Minor, were spent on buses, so I feel I've done my time. And while I'm at it, it's about the same length of time since I've taken the tube. If that makes me an elitist swine, so be it, but I'm not going down there. I've heard tales and I've seen the state of the unfortunates coming up from the depths of Oxford Circus underground in the rush-hour. I know that thousands, nay millions, have no choice, but we're not the trog-lodytes, and surely the Underground can be made more comfortable, cleaner, more efficient, more user-friendly for those who *have* to use it. Have the useless powers-that-be seen Moscow's underground? The Paris Metro? Even, believe it or not, New York? And am I right in thinking that they're thinking of *privatising* London Underground? (Pause for a shriek.) Isn't that what happened to the railways? No, I don't take the train much, either. Neither does anybody else who can help it. The average train service is expensive, late, or non-existent. The only one I can be bothered taking is the one you put your car on that takes you under the Channel to France, where you can enjoy the delights of a motorway system that actually *works* . . .

Ah, the British motorway. The latest, and the one that swiftly became the most infamous, is the London Outer Ring Road, the benighted M25. Oh, I know you all have your favourites: 'What about the blasted M6 outside Birmingham?' I hear you shriek. 'What about the damned M5? The M11? The M1? The M4? Any blistering M you like?' Fair enoughski, it's just that every week I see thousands of poor, downtrodden, over-taxed motorists, in cars that they paid thousands of pounds more for than their fellow motorists in Europe, sitting motionless on the M25. Mind you, according to the statisticians, that's the quickest way to go. Yes, they have the immortal gall to try to tell us that the slower we go, the quicker we get there. So, logically, if you come to a grinding halt, that'll get you there quickest of all. (Shriek!)

I used to travel the M4 from my bothy in the West to the bright lights of the Metropolis. No more. It is not worth the shrieking, since old Johnny Two-Jags masterminded the Great Bus Lane Scam. The rascal simply took a lane off the motorway and reserved it for buses, crushing the traffic of the busiest motorway in Europe into two lanes, and causing consistent traffic jams that stretch for miles and, of course, out pop the statisticians to tell us once again that being stationary will get us there all the quicker. But it's not that that makes me shriek. It's that fact that in all my time contemplating the perfectly-still back window of the car in front of me, I've never seen more than two buses in that God forsaken bus lane . . . So I took to the M40. And guess what? They stuck a bus lane on the end of that as well . . . And then they put the tin-hat on it. A loyal listener sent me a cutting, clipped from the *Engineering Times* or some such paper that keeps the profession up to date on itself and its doings. The kindly listener had underlined a passage, which stated that the unmitigated eejit who had masterminded the M4 Bus Lane, had received on OBE from Her Majesty, for his excellent work in the services of transport . . .

Shrieking's no good any more. Play the music. Open the cage . . .

What's The Answer?

The sexes have always had problems interpreting what the other really means when they ask a question, and even our friend the 'New Man', so readily in touch with his feminine side, can be foxed by the simple female question, 'Does my bum look big in this?' Those of us who have been tried and tested, nay toasted, in the fires of matrimony, know that this is an easy one, to which there is only one answer, a resounding denial: 'NO!' This must be delivered without pause, hesitation or deviation of any kind, otherwise it will lead to further, more intense, questioning and inevitably end up as a nasty domestic incident, or at best the female of the species flouncing from the room, followed by a slamming of the bedroom door . . .

It must be obvious to even the most guileless, insensitive male that the question 'Does my bum look big in this?' is not being asked in a spirit of innocent inquiry; no discussion is required, and an answer that implies doubt, or even a suggestion of an affirmative 'Yes' will end in tears and a rancorous division of the household's assets. However, as I have indicated, the above question is a piece of cake compared to the other mantraps laid by ostensibly innocent female questions. Recently I had a pained letter from a chap working in an office with six women. He leaves every evening drained of all emotion, having had to tread warily on verbal egg-shells all day. The question that really leaves him for dead is when one of his female colleagues walks into the room, and says 'Well?' His mind races frantically – is it the dress? The hair? Shoes? Work? A gentle inquiry as to the state of his health? Should the answer be 'Yes', 'No', 'Er,um'? Every one is a potential minefield. Again, there is only one possible riposte; a smartly delivered 'Well!' will usually meet the case, and have the added benefit of not only mollifying the questioner, but leaving her as puzzled as the unfortunate male . . .

It gets worse. What about when the little woman with the tiny bum confronts you with a red dress over the arm, and a little black number over the other, and the dreaded, loaded query, 'Well, which do you prefer?' Knowing that hesitation is death by a thousand dagger-like looks, you reply smartly 'The red one.' You may even add that you particularly like my lady in red. Then the other dress is pushed forward. Seeing the error of your ways you quickly change your tune. 'No! I meant the black one,' quickly commenting how well she always looks in basic black. Exit the good lady to dress, while you dash the perspiration from your brow and head for the drinks cabinet. It's only later, perhaps on the way home from the party, that you realise that this is a game no man can win. She turns to you with a disappointed look, and says: 'What was wrong with the red dress, then?' . . .

A lady from Macclesfield heard my dissertation on 'Bums, Big, Small or Keep Your Mouth Shut' conducted on the radio, and she wrote that since her bum looks big in everything she has long since given up asking the old answerless question by substituting, 'Does my fat look like a bum in this?' Her husband always replies favourably, 'Oh yes, dear, it looks fine . . .'

There's a popular song that goes 'There are more questions than answers', and while this is undoubtedly true of more serious stuff, such as 'What's the meaning of life?' or 'Where did I put my drink?', as far as what has been shrewdly called 'the battle of the sexes', it's certainly the truth. And I'll tell you something else: it's been game, set and match to women, since time began . . .

We Was . . .

A shrewd marketing ploy, no doubt, and it provoked a welcome blast of publicity for Mr Collins and his estimable dictionary, but for those who hold the English language dear, the insertion of 'Delia' as a new word to enhance the same vocabulary as that of Shakespeare, Milton and Wodehouse, was a body-blow. 'To Delia', 'a Delia', 'Well, I'll be Deliaed', 'What the Delia?!?' Verb, noun, adjective, adverb, and for all I know, conjunction and proposition, too.

Of course it precipitated a barrage of contumely from those acid-tongued scamps who listen to me on Radio 2 every morning, only awaiting an opportunity such as this:

'I don't believe that Delia Smith is the first celebrity cook to have her name listed in the dictionary. What about Mrs Craddock?'...

'As I stand Deliaing my breakfast, I'm looking out the window, and it's extremely wet and Winton. I'll be glad when this inclemency has Robinsoned off. Must go now, the bacon's ready and I have to trim the Wogan off the edge, as I'm on a diet...'

'As I sat musing, as opposed to amusing, which is what you fail so signally to do, it struck me that the public perception of people can be judged by how they are referred to: For example, the popularity of Cilla, Elvis, Des, Maggie, Delia, all acclaimed by their first name. Then I thought of how unpopular people, or those with no redeeming feature, are referred to by their surname: Hitler, Mussolini, Crippen, Wogan...'

I'm supposed to have no feelings of course. A neck like the proverbial jockey's vitals, that's what you need, in this business... By now, this abuse is like water off a duck's back – it's the abuse of the English language that has me *well* furious. I slipped that in there to see if you were paying attention and everybody noticed. Not!... I'm sure a phrase like...'well good' started out as a mild verbal jape, but enough people didn't get the joke for it to have slipped into common parlance. Nobody seems to know the difference between an adjective and an adverb anymore, least of all golfers. Tiger Woods and his acolytes are forever 'hitting the ball solid'. Meanwhile in a corner of Buckinghamshire that will be forever England, there's a grown man screaming at the television: 'Solidly, you oaf! Solid-ly!'... Do I hear a cry of 'what does it matter, you pathetic old fool?' Well, maybe not, when you consider that half the presenters, personalities and other oafs on the television and radio are speaking with a glottal stop. Nobody seems to be able to pronounce an 'r' anymore, nor an 'l'. Estuary rules, as the No. 1 Estate Hair Shave rules the football field. People have 'acctidents', their cars have 'injins', they watch a funeral 'hearst' go slowly by. They worry at the prospect of 'nuculer' war. The great Richard Whiteley said 'becos' instead of 'because', the even greater Sir Trevor McDonald cannot pronounce 'ear' as in lug-hole. Instead of the word 'appear', out from under the imperturbable moustache comes 'appare'. I can't say 'gas' properly, and 'phantom' becomes 'phantham'. I've just about mastered 'Thames'. Mind you the Irish have always had problems with their 'th's'; poor old Diarmuid Gavin has such trouble with his, that he's barely speaking English at all: 'You're nearer to Goth in de garten dan anywhere else on Eart . . .' 'R' is not 'or', it's 'are'. 'H' is 'aitch', not 'haitch'.

Mispronunciation, like the poor and Carol Vorderman, is always with us, but it's the distortion and abuse of English that are growing apace. What about that very Ally McBeal Americanism: 'I so do not agree . . .', 'I so am not enjoying this . . . ' Thanks to American movies, a perfectly good word such as 'momentarily' is not only being widely mispronounced, it has come to mean 'immediately'. No use blaming Johnny Foreigner though, we're more than capable of murdering the world's most descriptive language ourselves. Ever listen to Radio 1? Ever heard a footballer being interviewed? Singular becomes plural, past and present tense are both up for grabs: 'We was . . .'

Look, I know you think this is the ranting of an old curmudgeon, and nobody under thirty gives a rattling damn, but this beautiful, greatest of all languages will imperceptibly slip away into sloppy slang if we don't keep our ears out. The price of English is eternal vigilance. Next time you hear anybody abusing it, give 'em a good slap. There isn't an old curmudgeon of a judge in the country that will convict you.

Can I Buffalo?

I know that I'm leaning against an open door with those of you who claim to be the full shilling, but things are not what they seem; and it's getting worse. Things are less than they seem than ever before. Years ago, people knew nothing; but they knew where they stood. Nowadays we're up to our shoulder-pads in information, news and gossip: papers, magazines, radio, television and the internet. We think we know everything – but all we really know is what we're told. And what we're told – by the great, the good, the magnate, the tyrant and the gossip-monger, is only what they think will keep us buying their product – their newspapers, their programmes, their shares, their services. Like Manuel in *Fawlty Towers*, we know nothing . . . Trouble is, apart from yourself and the present writer, people don't know it. They're in complete ignorance about their ignorance. They're intelligent, educated, well read, kind to children and animals; but they *still* believe what they read in the papers. With complacency and laziness, even you and I fall into the trap from time to time. Then sanity is restored, when I read myself quoted in the *Sunday Times*. Now it's no small thing to be quoted in the *Sunday Times*. It beats a kick in the vitals. But not by much, when you haven't said it. In case you missed it: 'I'm the only one who can put the ratings up and can I get a decent primetime show? Can I buffalo.'

Maybe you can tell me: what does that mean – the buffalo bit? It doesn't have a question mark for a start. It would make more sense, and perhaps be even more believable, if I was supposed to have said: 'Can I have some buffalo (steak, mozzarella, ears, tail,

hooves for glue)? Can I buffalo what? Which? Or who? The buffalo
bit is bizarre enough, but can *anybody* hear me claiming to be the
only one who can put up ratings? When did I last display symptoms
of megalomania? Okay, yes, I know, the last time you heard me
on the radio – but that aside . . . And finally, as dear old Trev
McDonald used to say, who did I say these loony words to? When?
Where? Don't ask, don't enquire. The old Royal family motto still
rings true: never explain, never complain. Well I have had a bit of a
whinge, but I shan't be looking for legal redress. Many years ago, a
dear departed friend of mine, Sir David Napley, one of the wisest
men I've ever met, advised: 'Never go to court. No matter how right
you think you are, and how guilty the other fellow, *never*. You can
never tell how a judge or a jury is going to jump. They could take a
dislike to your ears, or the colour of your socks, and no matter what
the strength of your case, you're done for . . . !' And David was probably the most distinguished solicitor of his day . . .

Everything's done by mirrors these days. No wonder Paul Daniels
is making a comeback. Everything is image, appearance, spin. For
Heaven's sake, even that wonderful picture of Neil and Christine
Hamilton go Adam and Eve in the Garden of Eden wasn't really
them. Well, it was their heads, but the bodies belonged to other,
younger, more supple people. The trouble was that Jeremy Bowen
believed it. I saw him, battle-hardened, hard-nosed reporter and
early morning newsreader, pick up a newspaper with the aforementioned Adam and Eve tableau on the front page, and heard him say:
'Their bodies are in pretty good shape . . . ' That's the worst of it.
Journalists believe what they read in the papers. Extraordinary.
They, of all people, know what *really* goes on, and yet, they're the
ones most ready to swallow it. Whenever I do an interview for a
magazine or newspaper, broadsheet or tabloid, the interviewer inevitably quotes at me the most ridiculous rubbish that I'm supposed
to have said over the last thirty years. Now, we all have weak
moments, and rushes of blood to the head, but lots of it is up there

with the buffalo I mentioned earlier. And I know that buffalo will cast its long shadow over every interview I do in the future . . .

Does *anybody* say *anything* they're supposed to have said? Does anybody really think that the Queen said of Cherie Blair's legs: 'They stiffen but they do not curtsey'? To whom did Her Majesty say it? The Lady of the Bedchamber, I suppose, who then rang up the *Sun* with the good news . . . Or perhaps Prince Phillip confided the bon mot to a groom at Windsor . . . Trust me. There is smoke without fire. It's there before your very eyes, everyday – just open a newspaper . . .

Buffalo'd Again . . .

Naturally, you will remember my meanderings of some weeks ago, when I tetchily queried a quotation mis-applied to me by the *Sunday Times*, in which I was supposed to have said: 'Can I buffalo', without even a question mark. As I pointed out with some shrewdness, not only did I not say it, I hadn't a clue what it meant. Many of my Radio 2 listeners were quick to offer explanations, not one of which was repeatable after, not to mind before, the watershed. Incidentally, not a morning goes by, but I don't receive a couple of racy, not to say disgraceful stories from my listeners. Do they seriously expect me to repeat such filth? Of course not. They know that I'll just repeat the stories to Paulie, my producer, and he'll use them to cheer up the bar at Mid-Herts Golf Club on Friday night. Which is why I specialise in punch-lines. I give my listeners the punch-line – they have to supply the rest of the story. For example: ' . . . Yeth, and I'm only thirteen . . . ' or '. . . well, move over, there's a sixpence of mine down there . . . ' Don't ask: I have no idea.

But I see that I have strayed a bit from the 'buffalo' motif. My moanings caught the eye of an observant listener, George Bingley, and he came up with a theory: 'The Buffalo Theory'. A theory of such blinding good sense and irrefutable logic, that I must share it with you. Okay George?

'The buffalo herd can only move as fast as the slowest buffalo. When the herd is hunted it is the slowest and weakest ones at the back that are killed first. Thus the general speed and health of the herd keeps improving by the regular killing of the weakest members. It's pure Darwin: the survival of the fittest.

'In much the same way the human brain can only operate as fast as the slowest brain cells, and excessive intake of alcohol as we know, kills brain cells. But, naturally, it attacks the slowest and the weakest brain cell first. In this way regular consumption of beer eliminates the weaker brain cells, making the brain a faster and more efficient machine. That's why you're always smarter after a few beers . . .'

I should buffalo, but I received this welcome piece of honest good sense just as some apparatchik of the Nanny State produced yet another small tome advising us of how many 'units' of the demon drink we should hurl down our gullets on any given day. It appears that earlier estimates were overly generous. Further, unscrupulous topers were using larger glasses for their 'unit' imbibing. Research showed that instead of four units, three would be closer to the mark. And that was only the men. A mere woman was risking everything with a drop more than two-and-a-half units. Unless, of course, she was knocking back hers from a sherry glass, in which case, a point might be stretched to three. Where do these anoraks get off with this 'poor weak female' stuff? My personal experience gives the lie to that tosh. I grew to vibrant, throbbing manhood in Dublin's fair city, and most of the women of my acquaintance could drink Lough Erne dry. A Friday night in Davy Byrnes with any one of them would leave you beggared for a week. The present Mrs

Wogan could still drink any three stevedores of your acquaintance under the table. As a friend of mine cannily remarked: 'All that happens is that her eyes become more like seagulls'...'

As we know, 'research suggests' has become the watchword of the age. A thought has just struck me: do you think anybody would put up a couple of million for some in depth research into our friend the buffalo? I'll give it a go ...

Watch Your Tongue

The strangled shout of 'Is it Me?' rises to a crescendo in the throats of those of a certain age, as the interference of the Nanny State, and the curse of Political Correctness threatens to overwhelm the age-old principles of Self-Help and Common Sense. 'Don't eat Salt!' 'Don't eat Sugar!' 'Don't get Fat!' 'Don't Drink!' 'Don't Smoke!' 'Don't just sit there! Do Something!' I could go on forever with the list of 'Dos' and 'Don'ts', none of which any sensible grown-up needs to be told. The warnings that are plastered over every product that you buy would be funny, if they weren't so pathetic. A packet of buns, labelled 'Plain, unless Filled', a bar of Fruit and Nut chocolate bearing the legend 'Contains Nuts' ... Recently in America, they had a contest to find the silliest labels: 'Do not use for personal hygiene' was the warning on a lavatory brush ...! A digital thermometer, with the words, 'Once used rectally, the thermometer should not be used orally.' A little bag of air used for packaging: 'Do not use this product as a pillow or flotation device ...'

It's our own fault, of course, or at least that of the ambulance-chasing lawyers whose ads overwhelm daytime television. We've become an excessively litigious society, ready to sue at the merest trip. Nuts can be fatal to those with an allergy, but doesn't every in-dividual have a duty of care to himself? We've reached a lamentable state when doctors, part of whose job used to be the placating and encouragement of the sick, now feel it incumbent on themselves to warn their patients of the worst-possible scenario, just in case the worst happens, and the patient's family sue, because of not being adequately prepared. Everybody's walking on egg-shells. How long is it since you said 'Boo!' to a goose? You have to be so careful these days; round every corner there's somebody waiting to take offence. They're out there, thousands of them: people whose job it is to take offence on behalf of others. Big ears pricked for the racial, ethnic, religious, sexist or feminist slur. Don't say 'black', don't say 'Red Indian', don't say 'woman', don't say 'coloured', don't say what Prince Philip said about the Chinese. You can't remember what he said? Well, if you think I'm going to repeat it without the railings of Buckingham Palace around me, you're mad. 'Red Indian' doesn't come up much around here as an ethnic slur, but try it in Canada, that most politically correct of nations, and they'll throw you in the slammer, and bury the key. Even 'Native American' doesn't cut the mustard in Canada. 'First Nation', is what the descendants of the original aboriginals are termed. And you upset them at your peril. The Canadians are burdened with guilt over the appalling behav-iour of their ancestors to the original natives, and they perform contortions to placate the 'First Nation'. While I was in British Columbia, the local council re-stocked a lake with fish, so that the First Nationals could indulge in a healthy pastime, and at the same time, provide food for their table. The boys got a couple of boats, with lights and dragnets, and cleared the lake of all living things overnight . . .

Nobody's advocating a return to the sad days of overt racial and religious prejudice; it's as well that we recognise that certain words are offensive to those of a different race or creed. Although it seems to be still acceptable to refer to the Irish as 'Paddies', or 'Thick

Micks', and the Scots as 'Jocks'. Didn't Anne Robinson cast several racial stones in the general direction of Wales, a little while ago? She's still got her job . . . and in case you think 'Paddy' is not offensive to the Irish, think again. Certain people have been calling Roman Catholics 'papists' for years. It's doubtful they'd try similar name-calling with, say, the Muslims. So what's the Politically Correct Stance here? If you're English, Irish, Scots or Welsh, people can say what they like, call you every name under the sun? Is there nobody to take offence on our behalf? We're the majority, I suppose. We're supposed to be able to look after ourselves . . . Oh look. We're back where we started.

Such Stuff As Dreams Are Made Of . . .

They say that the main problem with the British is that they don't beat their own drum hard enough. We value modesty above show; losing gracefully is more important than winning triumphantly; the bashful one is always preferable to the braggart. Our media don't even like success very much, at least not for any length of time. They build heroes and heroines to the skies, only to dash them to the ground at the first sign of a foot of clay. Our chums across the herring pond, on the other hand, revere success. Coming second is a disgrace; the winner takes all. In the United States, 'loser' is the most damning insult of all. Nobody can be a failure, or at least, admit to it. That's why there are no waiters in Los Angeles. Everyone who serves you at the table there, is either an actor, director or producer, currently awaiting a call from a big studio about something that's 'in development' . . . Sad . . . They must know in their hearts that only a lucky one in several million is going to make it, and that they haven't a hope in hell. Of course, we must all strive to achieve our own 'impossible dream', but in a society that admires only winners, what happens to the hopes and dreams of millions of also-rans? I think that they subsume their aspirations into adoration of the famous and successful. America is obsessed with celebrity. Watching Anne Robinson's stateside editions of *The Weakest Link*, it's striking to note the contestant's knowledge of movies, television and their stars. It reminds me of the old chestnut: how many actors does it take to change a light bulb? One. With twelve others at the foot of the ladder, shouting, 'That should be me up there, you know!' . . .

A society that puts such a premium on success and achievement is surely sowing dragon's teeth of frustration, envy and discontent. Since only the very, very few are lucky enough to be successful, where does this disappointment leave the vast majority? Leading lives of quiet desperation? Those privileged by wealth, education or intelligence, don't buy into it of course – they don't need to. It's always the underprivileged, the have-nots, the vulnerable in any society that are the victims of media manipulation. Recently, a spectacularly vulgar, glossy television series, *Footballers' Wives*, was received with enthusiasm by some reviewers, who praised its tacky glamour as 'great fun', and 'unmissable'. Delightfully ironic, my dear. Irony is wasted on most of the millions who watched it. They loved it, lived it, believed it, wished it were them. They did the same over *Pop Idol* . . . That could be me up there . . . I could be famous and rich, without training, hard work, study . . . I don't need to go to work, to earn a living. I'm gonna be like Will, and Gareth, and Posh and Becks, and Kylie . . .

You don't think we're losing that good old British phlegm, do you? We still believe that it's the taking part that counts, don't we? Rudyard Kipling said we should treat the two impostors, triumph and disaster, just the same. But that was before films and television, magazines and newspapers filled our heads with fantastical dreams. Without any irony at all, Manchester United's football ground at

Old Trafford is called 'The Theatre of Dreams'. Football is the dream, the escape into fantasy made by thousands every weekend. An escape from boredom, the dreary repetition of an everyday life. We should all love our dreams but never confuse then with reality. One of the most important things you learn as you grow up is that wishing doesn't make it so. It was always a fallacy that if you want something badly enough, you can get it. If you don't grasp the simple truth that there are some things, maybe most things, that you just can't have, you'll walk the world in pain.

It's only because most of us, even in these excessively aspirational days, accept that simple truth and adjust our lives as we go to the possible, the attainable, that life, and society, continues. Otherwise, we would be in a world of continual upheaval and revolution. Mobs would beat each other up at football matches, muggings and robberies would proliferate, rape and murder would be commonplace, there would be no respect for people's property, no civic pride, no shame. Thank heaven we don't live in a world like that . . . We can tell margarine from butter. Just because we read something in the paper we don't *believe* it. Spin doctors can't fool us. Who cares that Joanie Collins got married again? See if I care if Posh and Becks call their next child 'Essex' . . .

Don't Thank Me

Now, don't get me wrong, I like a bit of courtesy. As well brought up as your good self, I know when to say 'please' and 'thank you'. Just like you, I had it drummed into me when a lad, along with 'sorry', and 'I beg your pardon'. It was made clear to me that these were vital social tools, if I was to make my way in life. So, after a lifetime of sorrying, pleasing, thanking and pardoning, it may seem a little late for me to call a halt. And I'm not. These little courtesies enable us to circumvent the sleeping policemen of life, the trip wires and slippery slopes that threaten us, as we make our weary way through what an old poem calls 'the bludgeonings of chance'. Manners maketh man, as some old geezer in doublet and hose once said. On the other hand, I'm thinking lately that you can have too much of a good thing . . .

It's all the 'thanking' that I'm hearing and seeing on the radio and the television that's getting on my nerves: 'Now, over to our Political Correspondent, Andrew Marr, at the House of Commons.' 'Thank you, Sophie,' Andrew reports, all ears and easy charm. 'Back to you, Sophie.' 'Thank you very much indeed, Andrew.' Why the effusive thanks? It's only Andy's job, for Heaven's sake. Even the weatherman gets gushed over: 'Thank you very much, Michael.' A simple 'thanks' would do it, if you must. Personally I'd prefer if everybody just got on with it. The great and good John Humphrys drives me to drink in the early hours of the morning on *Today*, with his 'Many thanks' to every report, serious or half-baked. It's not a box of chocolates or a Christmas card, it's a report, dammit.

Superfluous verbiage has spread all over the language like a rash: 'At this moment in time', 'At the end of the day', are surely much more succinctly expressed by 'Now' and 'Finally'. A classic example of overkill was heard first hand, at least by me, from a TV weatherman: 'Hello to you', 'Good evening to you', 'Goodbye to you.' To who else for pity's sake? I don't think it's due to the frustrated performers trying to build up their part, to drag out their scant for seconds in the eye of the camera. It's just bad practice that slips into bad habits. Lately I received an incensed letter from a testy old geezer, who's being driven up the wall by the ever-increasing use of 'Let's not go there!' or 'You don't want to go there!' Where, in the name of all that's holy? It's a cop-out phrase, like the use of the aforementioned 'Talk to the hand', or 'whatever'. At best these mean you don't want to continue the conversation, but usually they're a tacit admission that either you can't think of anything to say, or you're losing the argument. Let's have more honesty:'Okay, you win, I give up . . .' Do you find yourself, when asked how you enjoyed something, such as a party, a wedding, a holiday, answering,'Oh we enjoyed ourselves thoroughly!' Or when asked if you agree with something, replying,'Oh, very much so!' No? Thank goodness for that, I sometimes feel I'm whistling into the wind here . . .

I don't know where this dressing-up of simple greetings and responses came from, but it always reminds me of the old saw: 'Brevity is the soul of wit.' Only great raconteurs can draw out a tale to impossible lengths, and keep it funny. Remember those endless monologues that Ronnie Corbett used to deliver on *The Two Ronnies*? Stephen Fry is another who can go on so long that you've forgotten how the story started, but the ending always leaves you laughing. The people who can do this are few and far between, but unfortunately there are far too many people out there who think that they can do it as well. And I must say here, and not just because this is a women's magazine, all these long-winded tale-tellers are men. Hand on heart, I have never heard a woman beat a funny story to death. Forgetting the punch-line, yes, but never turning what ought to be a laugh, into a dirge . . .

The worst thing you can accuse any man of is not being a hopeless lover, nor even a bad driver. If there's one thing every man thinks he's known for, it's his sense of humour. And his God-given ability to tell a joke. How many club dinners have I sat through, where some poor sap who has been encouraged by his family and friends into thinking that he's the new Bob Hope, goes into an endless routine involving funny faces, accents, eccentric walks, before bringing the tedium to a close with a line that we'd all seen coming half-an-hour ago? How many times have I stood at a bar, my good-natured smile turning into a rictus of death, as some eejit squeezes all the life out of a perfectly good joke? Finally, while I'm griping, is there anything worse than a party that turns into a joke-fest? All conversation killed stone dead, while everybody desperately tries to think of the good one they heard last week. And that terrible, embarrassing hiatus, when the half-hearted laughter stops . . . Still, we all thoroughly enjoyed ourselves, didn't we?

Mind you, I'm a fine one to talk, coming from Ireland, where it's a mortal sin to keep it brief. 'Top of the morning to you!', 'And the rest of the day to yourself!' Even in Gaelic, 'Hello' becomes 'God and Mary be with you'. To which the response is 'God and Mary and Saint Patrick be with you'. But in Ireland, when God made time, He made plenty of it, and it's not the same over here. Of course, we must make time for the little gentilities, but let's keep 'em 'little'. We've gone too far: how often do you hear yourself saying 'Sorry', for something that's not your fault? Someone, not looking where they're going, bumps into you in the street. 'Sorry'. That's you, not them. Same thing when an oaf takes the feet from under you with a shopping trolley. 'Sorry?' No, you're not, and you shouldn't be. It's good manners gone mad. Just count the number of 'thank-yous' you hear from people getting on and off a bus, or at the super market check-out.

American overkill puts us in the shade, of course, with 'Have a Nice Day', and 'Missing you already', but if you'd like some bracing relief from effusiveness, try France or Spain. No Spanish child ever said 'Gracias' for anything. It's their due, and if you hadn't wanted to give it, why did you bother? You never say 'thanks' to a Spanish waiter. He'll think you're taking the mickey. The French will never acknowledge it, when you give them the right of way on road or pavement. Why do you need to be thanked for something you chose to do? Bad manners? Well, have a look at how Spanish and French children behave in restaurants, next time you're over there, and tell me that it doesn't compare more than favourably with the behaviour of our own dear little ones . . . There's more to good manners and behaviour than mere lip-service.

I've had a couple of letters from my listeners on the topic that bear repetition:

Man to Little Woman: 'Would you like a cup of tea, dear?'
Woman to Man: 'Yes'
Man: 'What's the magic word?'
Woman: 'Now!'

My own particular favourite:

Granny to Little Boy: 'Would you like a chocolate?'
Little Boy: 'Yes'
Granny: 'And what's the magic word?'
Little Boy: 'Abracadabra?'

Oh, and thank you very much indeed, for reading this ...

Keep the Noise Down

Elitist running dog that I am, it's years since I lowered myself into the tube, and I have little cause, thank Heaven, to have recourse to the railways. So I haven't been subjected to what all and sundry tell me is the greatest malaise of modern living, the mobile phone. Or, to lay the blame where it truly lies, the mobile phoner. I occasionally pass them in the street, or listen to their bleatings in restaurants, or in airport lounges: 'Yes, I've just passed Liberty's, there's a sale on ...'; '... Oh, we're in the Ivy, I've just seen Dale Winton ....'; 'We're landing at five, so I should be home by seven ...'

Apparently, unbelievably, it's even more banal on the trains and the Underground ... 'Yes, I'm on the 6.30 from Paddington as usual, so I'll be home at the usual time . . . love you . . . ' For Heaven's sake, what happened to good old British reticence? Why do these people love to shout their business to the world? Time was, when you got into a railway carriage, a bus, or a lift, you kept yourself to yourself. No eye contact, no words, and keep the newspaper rustling down to a minimum. A friend tells me that he regularly, and for several years, shared a commuter train carriage with the same five people. They never in all those years, ever looked at each other, not to mind exchange a bright 'Good morning'. Year after year, they all took the same seats, read the same papers and, wordlessly, studiously ignored each other.

It was a 'Smoking' Carriage (this was a long time ago) and one morning, the man in the corner with the *Telegraph*, while stubbing out his fag in the ashtray, set fire to the bottom of his newspaper. Everyone else in the carriage spotted it immediately, as the flame took hold and then began to blaze merrily. The man in the corner with the *Telegraph* was the last to know and only copped on when the flames began to lick at his breast pocket. Leaping to his feet with a scream, he hurled the blazing newspaper to the floor of the carriage, and jumped up and down until all that was left were ashes. Then, wordlessly, he resumed his seat. Nobody in the carriage said a word. Everyone averted their eyes, or burrowed more deeply into their newspaper. But what struck my friend as the very epitome of the British reserve, was not that one man's embarrassment was decently ignored, but that the whole carriage saw the newspaper go up in flames, and nobody moved a muscle, said a word, or shifted a buttock to help. The man in the corner with the *Telegraph* could himself have gone up in a sheet of flame, and every one of the other occupants of the carriage would have sat there and looked on, rather than draw attention to themselves.

We must be grateful that people haven't started talking to each other in lifts. Yet. It's only a matter of time. The Irish have always spoken in lifts, and the country is the poorer for it. Can you imagine anything worse than a lift full of people stopping on the twelfth floor on its way down in a Dublin hotel, only for the lift door to open, and an eejit to enter with: 'Ah, here we all are! How's everybody today?' at the top of his voice?

It was better when people kept themselves to themselves. There's far too much communication, and most of it is a lot of old guff. Just listen to BBC Radio 2 in the morning between 7.30 and 9.30. Rubbish. Why can't he shut up and just play the music? I'll say one thing in his favour: he's got a mobile phone that he never uses. His children shout at him. But he never switches it on. 'It's for emergencies,' he says. 'For when I need the doctor. Or a priest . . .'

The Rocky Road

It was the Queen of the Algonquin Round Table, the matchless Dorothy Parker, who said: 'If you want to know what God thinks of money, just look at the people He gave it to . . .' It crossed my mind as I trudged through the endless trough of 'Rich Lists', to which we were all recently subjected by every magazine and newspaper in the country. Whatever happened to modesty? Wasn't it, isn't it, vulgar to talk of money, to boast of wealth? When the last sad, penniless drop-out is taken from our streets, and given a home and a life, even then, will it be acceptable to talk of billions made from Russian oil, cheap labour, and great tracts of land that somebody's forefathers grabbed? The compilers of these Lists will excuse themselves and their vulgarity by saying that the public love them, read them avidly, enviously. The public used to love executions, too. There's certainly a case to be made for not pandering to our baser instincts. Unfortunately, it's too late. The jury's been, and gone. Look at the recent flogging of the Beckhams; the shameless, demeaning 'reality' TV shows. Is there no decency left? Is there nobody in authority left in the media who will stand up and say: 'This far shalt thou go, and no further'?

We're hurtling to Hell on a downward spiral of depravity and degradation, but do you know anybody who wants to make the trip? I'm certain that not one of my eight million radio listeners approve of the voyeurism and soft porn that they see all about them on the television and in the newspapers. I don't, I don't know anybody of any intelligence who does, and I'll bet my last thin dime that you don't either. So who's leading the charge to Hades? It's not us. It must be them. And who are they, when they're at home? Is it the Yoof? Lager-louts who disgrace the name of England at every football match and every town in the land when the pubs close on a Saturday night? Hardly, they're consumers, not retailers; they go where they're led. Television producers, then? I can honestly say that I've never met a really debauched one. Drunken, yes. Self-important, yes. Badly-dressed, always. Determined to undermine the moral fibre of the nation, no . . .

It must be the print media's fault, then? Well, journalists as a breed are pretty pleased with themselves and their intelligence, mainly because they talk and socialise only with each other. They're drunk, too. On news. They can't get enough of it, and they can't wait to let us have it, or, more accurately, their spin on it. And the British Press goes further down the pan with every passing week . . . The papers will tell you that it's television that's eating away at the nation's vitals, but the hectoring, inflammatory words of the tabloids and broadsheets, with their daily revelatory scandals are doing nobody any favours, either. Still, as the old saw has it: 'You can lead a horse to water, but a pencil must be lead' . . . I know, I couldn't resist it.

I've met lots of newspaper editors, and while most of them would not make anybody's list of favourite dinner guests, I just can't see them as fifth-columnists, seeking to overthrow all that's best in British life. So who's dragging us down? It's not the Rich, is it? I wouldn't mind blaming them, particularly those who lie and wheedle to get into the List, even when they know that the books are cooked, and the bank owns everything. Maybe it is them. After all, who's running the country? Aha! I thought we'd get round to it, in the end. I knew it all along. It's the Government's fault. It has to be; they're in charge, aren't they? We voted for them, put them in power to watch over us. And that includes the moral health of the nation, doesn't it? Be fair, they're having enough trouble with the physical health. All that obesity everywhere ... And smoking, and speeding. And nobody wanting to pay tax. Least of all that crowd on the Rich List. Everyone of 'em in the Top Ten living over here, to avoid tax in their own country, or living in Monte Carlo to avoid tax here. Funny old world, and nobody's to blame for anything ...

I Don't Believe It ...

I know it's my age, but I have a hard time believing in anything these days. I don't mean politics or religion, or mankind in general. It's all the other stuff that stretches my credibility. Recently, on that gem in the diadem of daytime television, *The Terry and Gaby Show*, we had a Feng-Shui expert, guru, swami or master, whatever ... He wanted beds facing south, and work-areas in the north-east of your room. And he didn't want plants in the kitchen. As far as I could fathom, he didn't go a bundle on the kitchen anyway, as it was full of dead stuff. Apparently, the Chinese have been living according to Feng Shui principles for thousands of years, which, with the greatest respect to Confucius, may explain a lot ... It certainly doesn't seem to have advanced Chinese civilisation or culture, but then, neither do the slow-motion exercises that we see in every documentary on Chinese life. You know the ones I mean: parks full of old folk with inscrutable expressions, moving their arms and legs as if they were in a vat of treacle. What's that about, for Heaven's sake?

And it's not just Chinese exercises. I'm not a great believer in any form of exercise. I played a lot of sports in a wasted youth, particularly rugby, and it's done for my knees. Most of my contemporaries who played the great game are similarly afflicted. If it's not knees, it's backs, shoulders, necks or livers. Well, alright, the liver is more the result of the rugby-club bar, but surely that was part of the macho thing into which we innocent young men were lured. Nobody told us that a few short years chasing an oval ball would cripple us in mid-life. Excessive exercise is bad for you! The man who invented jogging died in his forties . . . Look at the number of athletes who pass away long before their couch-potato, beer-swilling friends. Only recently, a scientist made it clear that you could exercise until you were blue in the face, but the only thing that could reduce your cholesterol was medication. So much for those Scandinavian margarines . . .

With the greatest respect to Prince Charles, I don't believe in organic foods. They don't look better, every survey ever done shows that they don't taste any better, and any sensible scientist will tell you that they're not better for you. Natural chemicals are no better than synthetic ones, they're all molecules. And lots of 'natural' chemicals can do damage: arsenic, ricin . . . I don't believe in bad science. Which is why I don't believe in global warming. Man has become so full of himself that he ascribes every change in nature to himself. He is all-powerful, therefore everything is due to him, and subject to his control. Put away that underarm deodorant spray! Think of the hole in the ozone layer! Actually, it's the methane gas caused by animals breaking wind that's doing a lot more damage to the aforementioned hole; which anyway, is far more affected by natural causes – volcanoes, sunspot activity, than man's poor little efforts. In the seventies, one of the great supporters of the 'global warming' theory predicted confidently that by the nineties, London and Paris would be fried to a crisp. The real truth is that if it does get much, much warmer, the Polar ice caps will melt, push the Gulf Stream away from our shores, and we'll have the same temperature as Trondheim, or Montreal. They get snow there from November to March. How do you like that, for 'warming'?

I don't believe that Uri Geller can bend spoons by brain power; I don't believe in Ayurvedic Head Massage; I don't believe that any woman in her right mind ever wore anything designed by Vivienne Westwood or John Galliano; I don't believe that what Damien Hirst and Tracey Emin produce is 'art' – but I can't prove it. I don't believe in the privatisation of public utilities, such as water, and railways. I don't believe you can give directions to an address in London, from a call-centre in Jakarta, Indonesia. I don't believe that they gave an OBE to the fellow who designed the Bus Lane on the M4 – but they did . . .

You see, it doesn't matter a tinker's curse what I don't believe. It's only my opinion; my subjective, biased belief, or lack of it. If I or you forget that, then it's the Home for the Bewildered for all of us: you, me and Victor Meldrew . . .

Never Did Me Any Harm

Every so often, a news item bubbles up that seems to strike everyone over twenty-one directly in the mazzard. It brings the hidden curmudgeon that lies behind every one of us to the fore, causing ncreased blood pressure, hardening of the arteries, rising cholesterol, and probably exacerbates the hole in the ozone layer and global warming. A splendid example of the phenomenon was the directive issued recently, whether by the Department of Education or Health, I know not, in the matter of conkers. 'Play Conkers at your Peril!' was the order of the day, unless lads and lasses everywhere were prepared to wear gloves and goggles, and for all I know, a hard hat, Wellington boots and a gas mask. The Plain People of Britain rose like leaping salmon, and the Man on the Clapham Omnibus had a congestion fit. Rarely has a well-meaning, cautionary word had such a brisk reception. For most of the adult population, it was the last straw, the Camel's Back-Breaker. Unfortunate, perhaps, that this simple 'Mind How you Go' warning followed so closely on other strictures of our Nanny State, such as restrictions on School Sports Days, on the grounds that it was alright for the winner of the egg and spoon race, but what of the damaged psyches of the losers? The attempt to soften this draconian measure by announcing that it was okay to have competition, providing there were only three competitors in every event, so that every little chickabiddy got a medal (third, darling! Well done!) seemed to cut little ice with those dragged up in the Dotheboys Hall Educational gulags of the forties, fifties, sixties and seventies.

It's the kind of thing that encourages the 'They Don't Know They're Born' mentality. You know, the 'Kids Have It Too Easy These Days' mantra': 'Walked three miles to school every day, uphill both ways, beaten senseless by the teacher, and then the strap from father when I got home for not bringing the coal in. Never did me any harm . . . '

Someone calling themselves 'I. Speak-Frankly' (no one ever writes to me with their real name, I can't imagine why . . .) sent me a memoir of the good old days, 1979. Not 1879, you'll note: 'Marsden Junior School, high in the frozen Pennines. The boiler broke down for three days. Did they send us home? Did they shut the school? Pshaw! We huddled together for warmth in our coats and hats. Ten minutes before play-time, despite temperatures so cold that the paper snagged when I turned the pages of my exercise book, we were told to take our coats off. Otherwise, the teacher said, when we went outside to play we wouldn't feel the benefit. Happy days.' It's not an isolated example. Paul Walters, my distinguished, if barely human Radio Producer, gets quite worked up describing his sports-master taking the class to the open-air swimming pool in March, breaking the light covering of ice, before forcing his charges to strip off and dive in. 'Health-giving', the sports-master called it, as he watched the little fellows turn blue, from behind his duffel-coat and warming flask of coffee.

And the very mention of school dinners brings people out from behind the arras, foaming at the mouth. As he tucks in to his early-morning muffin, the aforementioned Walters is given to fulminating about some school-dinner lady, who used to ladle grey, lumpy mashed potato on to his tray. Whatever it did to his palate, it doesn't seem to have affected the old boy's appetite . . . I could fill an entire programme with the revolting contents of school dinners, from spam fritters to suet puddings. Nobody can recall the first thing about Algebra, Trigonometry nor Cosines, but everyone can remember the Macaroni Cheese with crystal clarity.

'The Great, The Good and The Nobody'

Recently, a loyal listener, wrote to me under an assumed name (in common with all of my listeners; it's not a ploy for anonymity nor even an indication of a hidden shame in listening to my rubbish, but usually an attempt to embarrass me with a double-entendre, such as a Miss Tickles, whose first name is Tess, or a Mr Peacock, whose first name is Drew. There's Mr Hucker, with a Christian name of Rudolph. There's treachery even in addresses: witness an imaginary town in Dorset, apparently called Far Corfe ...) But I see I have digressed from my loyal listener, who could have been the more innocently named Ma Mite, or Hellen Bach, Mick Sturbs, Edina Cloud, or Heidi Vodka. The listener, he, she or it, was keen to draw my attention to the latest mind-boggling out-pouring from their regional train service: 'Given that even they,' wrote my listener, 'recognise that their trains, apart from being late, dirty, inefficient and entirely dysfunctional, are also hideously and suffocatingly over-crowded, the train company are proposing three options, to ease the burden for their travel-weary customers. Option A) More frequent trains. Option B) Longer trains with more carriages. Or Option C) Take out the seats. Guess which option they are going to pursue?' asks my bemused listener. No need to ask. We all know the answer. All together now: a nationwide shriek of 'Is It Me?!?' Followed by a resigned 'Mustn't grumble' and a subdued chorus of 'Always Look on the Bright Side of Life'.

The sad thing is, we still have a trusting faith in those placed above us. There's still a strong under-tow of feeling that 'they' must know what they're doing. After all, we innocents cry, these people could never have achieved such positions of power, influence and wealth, without high intelligence, superior education, wise judgement and a level of knowledge far above that of you, me and the Man on the Clapham Omnibus. We little people pay our taxes, sit in our traffic jams, stand in our trains, without a murmur. The National Health Service, the education of our children, both of them, a disgrace. Yet, do we actually get up on our hind-legs and force the Government to do anything about them? Do we invade Parliament, as they have in Georgia? Do we even block the roads, like the French? No! We're law-abiding. We have respect. We still do what we're told by our betters. I daresay some of us would still charge the guns, if Lord Cardigan told us to ...

I'm no different, although the penny's beginning to drop. I've been fortunate enough, if 'fortunate' is the word I am looking for, to meet and socialise with Heads of State, Ministers of State, Members of Parliament, Lords, Ladies, Knights of the Realm, Captains of Industry, Chief Executives of Multinational Conglomerates, Billionaire Entrepreneurs, Chairmen of Banks, The Great and The Good. No more than yourself, I'm not naïve enough to think them all 'good', but again, like yourself, when I come across a Great Man, in my middle-class, naturally inferior way, I'm expecting Great Things. I don't expect him to snort fire through his nostrils, or even blind me with his brilliance in the first ten seconds, but I am anticipating something out of the ordinary. And, do you know, in all my years of scrambling for crumbs from the Rich Man's Table, it's never happened? I'll go further, at the risk of damaging the country's infrastructure – some of the biggest eejits I've ever met in my life are in charge of your country, your money, your life. I could count the politicians that I've met who are worthy of trust, not to mind respect, on the fingers of one hand. Captains of Industry turn out to be no more than lucky accountants, or crude hucksters who'd do you down for tuppence. One of the biggest names in the City, Chairman of this, Executive Director of that, is a social cripple, without the smallest notion of how to interact with anything other than a balance sheet.

There's a lot of talk these days about worthless 'celebrities', famous for being famous, no-talent nobodies who'll sell their grannies to get their pictures in the paper. Pathetic, but harmless. It's those with their feet of clay under The Big Table we should worry about . . .

The Working Man – Not!

When I tell them that I haven't done an honest day's work in forty years, people look at me strangely. Frankly people have looked at me strangely for much of my life, particularly those who pass me in the street and smile, thinking that they've met me at a party or in a bar, and then realise, to their chagrin, that they only know me from the television. They go on their way, hugely annoyed with themselves, wishing they could rush back to me and say: 'Look, I didn't mean to smile at you. I never listen to you, and I can't stand you on the television!' I know that it ruins their day, causing them to be rude to the tea-lady, and kick the cat, and I wish that I could run after them and apologise: 'Sorry! It's not my fault that you think you know me. I'll wear a paper bag over my head next time' . . . No, it's the old-fashioned look I'm talking about – the 'Oh, here he goes again with the false modesty' look. Believe it: I've never lived to work. The sanctity of labour, the philosophy of hard work being good for the soul, the whole idea that your life will be unfulfilled unless you put in a good forty hours a week at the coal-face, are for the birds, as far as I'm concerned. I should have been born with money. A dukedom would have suited me nicely, or being heir to a Greek shipping fortune. I was born too late. I subscribe to the good old British 18th/19th Century ideal: money earned in trade is ghastly. The only stuff worth having is that left to you by the old man. Incidentally, maybe that's not as old-fashioned as I thought. Was it in the late Alan Clark's *Diaries* that I read how he tended to look down on Michael Heseltine, because Heseltine had to buy his own furniture? Didn't inherit it, you see? Man's a bounder . . .

The 'a hard day's work never hurt anybody' thing was of course an enormous con-trick perpetrated on the working-class by their so-called masters, the mill and mine owners, and the landed gentry. 'You go out there, work yourself into an early grave, and I'll just tuck into another eight-course breakfast.' Encouraged by government, schools and the churches, it kept the people's noses to the grindstone, and the better streets free for the quality to walk in.

Now, in case you think I'm advocating anarchy, and everybody down tools while we march on Westminster, nothing could be further from the truth. I'm not one of those deluded media-folk who think that they have something important to contribute to the social and political life of the nation, just because they appear on the television. Anyway, the 'Jane Fonda effect' seems to be an American phenomenon. Over here, the support of a popular figure for a political party seems to act as a deterrent for voters. I'll mention no names, but a couple of big-hitters didn't help William Hague, last time around. Although only the intervention of the Archangel Gabriel could have helped there . . . The wheels of industry and commerce must be kept a-rolling on; just don't try and kid us that it's doing us good. We work to keep body and soul together, our children fed and our wives in the comfort to which they've become accustomed. Very few people, and I'm among them, get to do work that's fulfilling, that they really enjoy. Not many get to whistle while they work.

So what's brought all this on, I hear you murmur. Who's been rattling the old boy's cage? It's just that I've been looking at my diary. And it's empty. I've nothing to do. Yet, from November to last week it's been hell on wheels. Apart from the radio and television, it's been a never-ending cacophony of parties, dinners, presentations and hooleys. I don't know about you, but I was cream-crackered long before New Year's Eve. Why can't they spread it out a bit more? Whose bright idea was it to have the New Year a week after Christmas? Couldn't they give us a couple of months to pull ourselves together? February – as depressing a month as you'll find in any calender – what a great time to cheer up with a New Year's Eve party. Let's do it. Write to your MP. I commend the idea to the House – free beer for all the workers!

The Outro

The years I've been writing this deathless stuff have brought me great happiness – my luck has held; with my children's marriages, the births of my grandchildren, the good health and steadfast love of my wife and family, professional success. But into each life, some rain must fall. Actually, I've had more than my share of the wet stuff, having been born and brought up in the rain of Limerick (see *Angela's Ashes*), married in the rain, and been followed around by my personal black cloud ever since. Over the last three or four years, some of my dearest, closest friends and colleagues have thrown off this mortal coil and left me on my tod: Paul Walters, Pauly, my radio producer for many years; handsome, gentle, droll, an outrageous flirt, and a great putter. According to him, life would always be okay, 'as long as you can get a four up the first' of his beloved Mid-Herts Golf Club. He had 'good ears', too, espousing the hitherto hidden talents of Katie Melua and Eva Cassidy, among others. Although with typical modesty, Pauly always said *Wake Up To Wogan*'s music was 'only important when it was wrong', his theory was never really tested. He never did get it wrong.

Sir David Hatch was a boy producer in BBC Light Entertainment when an equally wet-behind-the-ears tyro arrived from Ireland to work for Radios 1 and 2, but we really didn't get to know each other well until he became Controller, Radio 2. He didn't stay long, but trailing clouds of glory, went on to the Controllership of Radio 4, and then Managing Director, BBC Radio. He was simply the best BBC executive ever. He cared about radio, his staff, the talent, and he let us know. He wrote notes. Boy, did he write notes. Complimentary, critical, always constructive, and always with wit. His lovely Ann died far too young, but he found love again with Mary, and I was proud to be his best man, second time around. We talked, ate, drank and went to rugby matches together. We saw each other's families grow up, and delighted in his idyllic happiness with Mary. He died in six weeks, and I still don't believe it.

In a country where nobody is really listening to anybody else, but only waiting to stick their own verbal oar in, my dear friend, Tom Lynch, was King. Amidst a population where every individual is convinced that they're a born storyteller, Tom could hold a group, a crowd, a hall, in the palm of his hand. Not just in Ireland, either. He was legend, from Hong Kong to Korea, and when I introduced him to my friends in Britain, they only invited me if I brought him along. I've seen him hold a table enthralled that included Clement Freud, Alan Coren and Peter Cook. Useless to try and repeat his stories, no one could tell 'em like he could. Although, as his brother Mick said, when we were saying our final goodbyes, Tom never actually finished a story in his life. He always burst into laughter on the punch-line. It was his secret weapon, laughter, and he entranced and enhanced our lives with it.

We said goodbye to a giant of Television Light Entertainment lately, Sir Bill Cotton. Bill thought that the most important ingredient was the 'talent', and he made friends of us all. Within ten minutes of meeting him, you knew everything there was to know about him. I remember a senior BBC mandarin telling me that Bill had unburdened himself of all his troubles to him, one afternoon. The mandarin had not got a wink of sleep that night, worrying about Bill, yet knowing in his heart that Bill was sleeping like a baby . . .

Sir Jack Page was my next-door neighbour, a former back-bencher, and a man who brightened the life of everybody with whom he came in contact. In typically English fashion, he masked his intellect with flippancy. His service of King and country in the desert and on the beaches of Normandy he turned into brilliantly funny stories. His champagne cocktails left you speechless. Another great storyteller's secret.

I've spoken at too many funerals and memorials of late – people are beginning to shy away, as if my friendship was lethal. I wish the old Grim Reaper would give it a rest.

Still, mustn't grumble, as some eejit one said . . .

INDEX